THE
IMPOSSIBLE
HERO

Gordon Pirie (1956). Jane Bown for *The Observer.*

THE
IMPOSSIBLE
HERO

A life of Gordon Pirie

Dick Booth

 CORSICA PRESS · LONDON

First published in the UK in 1999 by
Corsica Press
PO Box 29444
London NW1 7GW

A catalogue record for this book is available from the
British Library

ISBN 0 9536671 0 3

Designed by Merriton Sharp, London
Printed by Acorn Press Swindon Ltd

Contents

Author's note

During the 1950s Gordon Pirie captured the imagination of millions. He was a great athlete, who broke several world records. He was also someone who challenged tradition and helped a generation of people to change the way they thought about sport. Around the world he inspired others to run. He could be infuriating. But thousands remember him with affection and many have told me: he deserves a book.

Since no one knew him well throughout his life, the task over the past four years has been to try and fit together several hundred pieces, some large, some small, of one story. The account I give here brings together the many different truths that people have offered me. I have kept as closely as possible to facts, but used my imagination to try and bring those facts to life. Inevitably there are some parts untold; but this is a large part of the story and I hope it achieves a kind of completeness. It is a story which I think is well worth the telling.

I would like to thank particularly Peter Pirie, Shirley Pirie, Jing Guan Pirie, Sara Pirie and Debbie Lautenslager who have been generous in sharing their personal memories; Mick Firth and Ferdie Gilson of South London Harriers who have both spent many hours reading chapters, and have done much to help me identify sources of information; Jan Arild Larsen in Norway; and in New Zealand Rachel Brown, Perry Cunningham, Dave Harkness and Roy Williams. Hannah Griffiths, Ron Lawrence, John Pawsey and Ashley Stokes gave me important encouragement and advice at various stages. Special thanks must go to the designer of the book, Dorothy Sharp, who has used her technical skill and tireless attention to detail to help me bring the Gordon Pirie story to life. Many other people gave me time, were patient in replying to my enquiries and lent me photographs or letters. I have tried to include a complete list at the rear of the book. I alone am responsible for any errors.

My partner, Sandra Nicholls, has done more than help. She has welcomed Gordon Pirie into our home, imagined the story and its possibilities each step of the way, and laughed at its many ironies. Not only could I not have done this without her, I would never have wanted to.

Dick Booth
October 1999

1 Gone fishing

When you are 13 a school day can seem to last forever, especially if there is something special on in the evening. Jan Arild Larsen had been to the first half of the international meeting involving the Soviet team the previous night and he still had the programme in his pocket. There was a photo of Vladimir Kuts, "the master runner of the Soviets", on the cover. Kuts was down to run in the 5,000 metres at 8.00 p.m., against the Englishman, Gordon Pirie. Now and again, during lessons, Jan Arild checked the results of the races he had entered the night before, and when school ended for the day, he made sure he was first out of the classroom. Kuts against Pirie was a race to savour.

What Jan Arild did not know was that the race he was going to see had been planned in secret. Gordon Pirie had first run in Bergen in 1953, and he had made a great impression on his Norwegian hosts, who had adopted him as one of their favourites. In May 1956 they contacted Pirie and offered him the chance of a 5,000 metre race against Kuts on 19th June. Pirie was more than happy to agree.

The arrangements were kept under wraps. Kuts was to run 5,000 metres, the Soviet team had agreed, but no mention of Pirie was made to them at that stage. Pirie too wanted things done quietly. He had had enough of the big build-ups before races, of the press camping outside his mother's back door. A deal was struck. He would fly to Bergen on June 12th and the British newspapers would be told he had gone on a fishing holiday. There would be no interviews, no hassles, no predictions, just a week's preparation. His friends the Berentsens would put him up, they knew what he liked to eat and they knew his daily routine.

Pirie had carved out his own special place in the dazzling post-war revival of British athletics. He had been born into running. His father was one of the great stalwarts of club athletics in South London. But as a youngster he had never looked like the natural runner his older brother Peter was, and he had never been able to keep up with Peter in races. Then, at 17, something had switched him on, and he had taken on the task of making himself the best distance runner in the world. By the time he came to Bergen in June 1956, he was able to draw on nearly eight years of hard work.

The local paper, *Bergens Tidende*, built up an atmosphere day by day with reports of how Kuts was doing in other races on the Russian tour. Like many others in Bergen, the 13-year-old Jan Arild Larsen and his father discussed the prospects for the race for days beforehand. There was no television in Norway at that time and large crowds attended big sporting events. While the Soviet athletes inevitably were seen as the representatives of the Eastern bloc, Bergen had had a long association with England, strengthened by the war. And many local people had a soft spot for English athletes.

The man against whom Pirie was to be competing, Vladimir Kuts, had displaced Emil Zátopek as the toughest and most feared of distance runners.[1] He was born in 1927 in the Ukraine and during his teenage years he had been caught up in the campaign between Soviet and German forces and subjected to forced labour. He turned to running relatively late, while undertaking military service with the Balkan fleet, but once he established himself as a runner the Soviet authorities made sure he had plenty of time to train. In 1954 he won the 5,000 metres at the European Championships in Berne, not only beating Chataway and Zátopek but also edging inside Zátopek's world record. He had raced against Pirie only once – over 10,000 metres, in Moscow in the autumn of 1955 – and beaten him without difficulty.

Pirie was always spurred on by defeat. He had lost a number of big races as a young man, and he had not enjoyed the experience. But no one in the comfortable, amateur world of British athletics committed themselves to the grind of training quite like Pirie did.

Internasjonalt fri-idrettsstevne
RUSSERSTEVNET 1956

Programme for the
Bergen meeting.

---

[1] The words "Soviet" and "Russian" were used widely, and interchangeably, at the time to describe the team representing the USSR and also to describe Kuts. The same practice is followed here. In today's terms Kuts was a Ukrainian.

Pirie wins an interna-
tional race in 1955.
Ken Finding

On the tracks, on the roads, on the fields he ran, at first four or
five times a week, then daily, then, to the astonishment of most
of his contemporaries, twice a day. It paid off. In 1951, at the age
of 20, he broke his first British record, over six miles. He made himself the best cross-country runner in the land, and then, a little
controversially, he had begun to visit Freiburg to seek advice from a
German coach Woldemar Gerschler. Soon, Pirie began to show that
he had speed as well as stamina. In 1953 crowds flocked to the White
City stadium in London to see him run, as he broke record after
record.

3

He shared the spotlight of course with others, especially the great university athletes of the day, Roger Bannister and Chris Chataway. But Pirie had chosen his own route to success based on a strenuous training regime, much like that used by the best European runners. And he broke all the rules by running not only the day before, but sometimes on the morning of a race as well.

When he first broke through he was written up in no time as a world star. One English paper described him as "our own Zátopek." As his times improved and took him nearer to world class, he became more confident about what he could achieve. Whatever doubts Pirie had in his early days, his growing success made him more and more determined to stick by his own beliefs, whoever might be giving him advice to "go easy on the training". Already, at 26, he had something of a reputation as a rebel. He enjoyed the company of other runners, and they respected him, but he became increasingly irritated by officials and journalists who did not understand the demands on the modern athlete.

Pirie had watched in 1954 and 1955 as a remarkable group of runners had brought the world record for 5,000 metres down from 13:57.2 to 13:40.6 – first Kuts, then Chataway, then Kuts, then the Hungarian Sándor Iharos, Kuts again and finally Iharos for a second time. Pirie was not yet a member of this remarkable group but many thought his turn was going to come. Zátopek had said so, and so had Pirie himself.

Pirie stayed with his old Bergen friends, the Berentsen family, in their comfortable, relaxing home on the mountainside, just outside the city centre. Hjalmar Berentsen was a stalwart of the Norrøna Club and his son Bjorn had visited the Pirie household in London in 1955, and trained with Gordon on the Downs at Coulsdon. The Berentsens knew of Pirie's defeat by Kuts in Moscow the previous autumn, and how much it had mattered to him. "Gordon wanted to meet Kuts on neutral ground," Bjorn recalls. "He had a real hunger to beat him." This was to be a real race not a world record attempt.

The Soviet team management got to hear of what was planned at the last moment. Judging that Pirie was more vulnerable over a longer distance, they asked for a 10,000-metre race. But the organisers would not agree. They had their men, and they had their race.

Training at the Skanse-
myren track two or
three days before the
race.
Bergens Tidende

Pirie was in good shape. He was not a full-time athlete, as some
of his East European rivals seemed to be, but his job as a paint sales-
man gave him greater freedom to train. Alongside his running he
had developed his weight training, and become more and more
confident that this helped him to run fast. Once he got to Bergen he
settled into a daily routine. After breakfast he would walk up to the
old track at Skansemyren and train, then he would come back for a
little lunch and rest. Later in the afternoon, Pirie would go back for
more training, then have supper and, at nine o'clock, go to bed. Kuts
meanwhile was travelling with the Russian team and racing.

The Skansemyren track nestled high above the city, in a clearing
surrounded by trees. You could sit on the grass banks by the track
and see the harbour down below, and then you could put your running spikes on and step down onto the cinder track. Pirie would
arrive at mid morning in his tracksuit and his woollen hat, and anyone who cared to join in could do so. His training surprised even
his most ardent Norwegian admirers. Roy Jensen, of the Viking
Club, had seen nothing like it since the American, Mal Whitfield,
had visited some years earlier.

Pirie would begin his morning session by jogging for half an hour
to get loose. Then he would start the schedule that he had developed

under the guidance of his coach, monitoring his pulse between each run to ensure the maximum benefit from the session. The local press kept an eye on what he was doing. One day, they reported, he ran 1200 metres four times with five minutes jogging between each run. Three of these runs were done in 3 minutes 9 seconds and the last in 3 minutes 13. This was followed by a four-mile jog to warm down, maybe 15 miles running in all. But the afternoon session was even tougher. He reeled off twenty 400-metre runs, each in around 62 seconds, with two minutes jogging between each.

Pirie was doing a lot of work at a pace of around 62–3 seconds per lap. Iharos had run his 12½ lap world 5,000 metres record at just under 66 seconds per lap. On the Monday Pirie ran for only 45 minutes and on the Tuesday, the day of the race, he worked out fairly gently for an hour or so in the morning. Although he coveted a world record over 5,000 metres, his focus was chiefly on winning.

Kuts was coming into the race not off some sustained training but some excellent racing. Only four days earlier he had broken the Soviet record for 3,000 metres at the Bislett stadium in Oslo. Like Pirie, Kuts had several years of hard work behind him, though he had less natural speed. He had prepared for his record runs over 5,000 metres by repeating high quality 400 metre and 800 metre runs in training close to maximum effort. In most of his 5,000 metre races his approach, up until then, had been simple: to run a uniform pace at the highest possible speed for the entire distance. This was the way Kuts chose to beat other athletes who had a faster finish than he did and who might beat him in a slower race. Kuts had also shown in his longer race against Pirie in Moscow the ability to use pace variation to disturb the rhythm of his opponents. It was a tactic Pirie had to be ready for.

Just before six o'clock Pirie travelled across town with the Berentsens to Krohnsminde, where the match was taking place. At about the same time Jan Arild Larsen finished his tea and got ready to make his way to the meeting.

The stadium was constructed in the 1930s on a piece of wasteland not far from the centre of Bergen and was now hidden away by a cluster of industrial buildings and blocks of flats. Looming over runners as they came into one bend was a gasholder. That night, instead of the languid summer evening Pirie might have hoped for, it was cool and grey.

On the back straight was a piece of football terracing and here Jan Arild Larsen pushed against the crash barriers in his raincoat. His programme had become somewhat crumpled but he studied again the welcoming messages to visiting athletes in Russian and German. He favoured Pirie to win rather than Kuts and read aloud to himself the special message to the London athlete: "To our English guest, *Gordon Pirie*, we extend our very best wishes. We are always happy to have you among us, Gordon. Your fine running impresses us, your personality charms us. Good luck to you!" Rather ominously it seemed to the young schoolboy, Kuts had been given number 1, and Pirie number 20.

In the home straight was a concrete stand, which held about 1,000 people. There were some modest changing rooms on the ground floor, and above them terraced concrete steps with wooden slats to sit on, and some cover from the rain. Spectators filtered in from about 6.30 p.m. By the middle of the evening, there were 4,000 or so in the crowd. Small boys who could not afford to pay leant their bicycles against the railings and stood on their saddles to watch.

As always there was some anxiety in the crowd as to whether the top names would turn up; Jerzy Chromik from Poland had already dropped out of the 5,000 metres. So Jan Arild began to look for Pirie and Kuts. He soon spotted the Russian runner, with his distinctive blond hair. He was jogging round the outskirts of the track, still feeling the effects of the Bislett run in his legs. But where was the Englishman?

Pirie did little warming up outside. He kept out of the rain, and did some jogging and exercises in the dressing room. He felt relaxed from his gentle run that morning. But he needed to race. When he saw from the window that the 800 metre competitors, who were running just before him, had been called to the start of their race, he went outside. As he sat on the grass putting on his spikes, Bjorn Berentsen came over to give him a word of encouragement.

There were two other runners in the race: Gerhard Hönicke of the German Democratic Republic and Leif Egge of Norway. It was a big night for Egge, a railwayman who had to fit in his training every night after work. After making the national cross-country and skiing teams in 1955 he had broken a leg and missed a whole season. This was one of his first races returning after the injury.

Neither Egge or Hönicke had a realistic chance of keeping in touch with the leaders, but both nursed hopes of being pulled to personal best times.

As the 800 metre runners finished their race, the four competitors for the 5,000 began their final warm up strides on the back straight. When the runners took off their tracksuits Jan Arild could see their numbers and pick out more easily who was who. Bjorn Berentsen had got into the inner field, where his father was acting as an official, to get a better view.

All eyes were on Pirie and Kuts. Pirie in his English vest with red and blue stripes, white shorts and white Adidas track shoes with the distinctive red stripes. Kuts of course was in the red vest of the USSR. Pirie was the taller, by some five inches, but about a stone lighter. Kuts' hair blonde and thick, Pirie dark and close cropped. Kuts the sturdy locomotive, Pirie angular and thin but with a powerful muscularity in his legs. Both all engine and heart.

Pirie knew there was no room for error. If Kuts got away it would be hard to get back, just five or ten yards would be enough. Pirie knew that Kuts might try to vary the tempo of the race, before taking a longer run for home. But he knew that it was he, Pirie, who had the faster finishing speed, with good mile and 1,500 metres times to his credit.

Promptly at eight o'clock the four men were called forward. As they assembled on the curved line that marks the 5,000 metres start point, the marksman conducted his elaborate ritual, making sure no toe was over the line. There had been the usual chatter in the crowd but, as the starter raised his gun, 4,000 spectators waited in silence with the runners.

Pirie lent forward on the line, feeling his spikes on the damp cinder track.

Pirie felt Kuts push to the front. He was content to let him lead the field round the first bend. Quickly they came into the home straight and saw the marker telling them there were 12 laps to go. Kuts was into his rhythm, with Pirie comfortably placed behind. Kuts stocky, with his arms driving steadily, Pirie with that powerful stride, blowing out his cheeks a little, and leaning slightly into each bend. The other runners were already a few yards back. The air was damp, but still.

Vladimir Kuts.

8

Kuts pressed on around the second bend, his running urgent and powerful. Pirie stayed back a fraction, giving himself room to reach out in his rangy stride, to let the tension out of his body. Both knew, before they heard the call of 60 seconds at 400 metres, that they could not sustain this early pace. Now Pirie felt the Russian let the track come back to him a little, eased up to training pace, perhaps just above. Twice in the third lap, Pirie, feeling a fractional slackening in the pace, came up to Kuts' shoulder to maintain the steady tempo he wanted.

When Kuts had set his own world record, a year or so earlier in Belgrade, he had gone through the 1000 metre point in 2 minutes 42 seconds. Now as he approached the finishing post with ten laps to go he heard a teammate counting off the seconds "two minutes, 34, 35, 36…". Kuts had never run this fast in any of his record races over 5,000 metres.

They moved into the second and third kilometres of the race, Kuts driving on in steady laps of 66 and 67 seconds, Pirie a metre or so behind. Only once again, in the fourth lap, did Pirie have to press Kuts forward to stop his rival gathering energy for some later burst. On the back straight Jan Arild watched as Kuts went on, with Pirie striding behind blowing out his cheeks. Then they went away from him and there would be a strange lull before he heard the crowd begin to cheer as they went past on the far side.

Lap times were given to the crowd in Norwegian and aficionados waited for the 3,000 metre time. Pirie's best for that distance was 8:09.4, Kuts had just run 8:01.3 in Oslo. The announcer gave Kuts 8:09 with Pirie just behind. They were, unbeknown to Gordon, who was getting no times in English, running close to Pirie's best time for 3,000 metres. Egge and Hönicke were nearly 100 metres down.

There were five laps left, and the leaders were seven seconds inside Iharos' time in his record run in Budapest. Could anything stop them? Young Jan Arild Larsen was in two minds – he wanted to savour the speed and rhythm of the runners, but he wanted the finish to come. A world record? Was it possible, here in Bergen? But who would want a world record if the Russian won? Why did the English runner stay behind?

Bjorn Berentsen ran from side to side on the inside of the track urging his man on, trying to shout something, anything, that would help his friend keep in the race. Some spectators began to wave programmes and shout Pirie's name, surprised by their own excitement. "Heia, Pirie, heia," came the cry. Now, as Kuts and Pirie took the back straight the cheers of those standing on the terrace swelled and lifted them. And, before that noise had died away, the crowds sitting in the stand began to stamp and cheer.

Pirie could sense that Kuts was strong. Perhaps he could not be beaten. But although Pirie was running much faster than he had ever run before, he knew that he still had one reservoir of energy left, that secret source of power he could turn to, when most needed. Two final laps in the race's even rhythm of 66 or 67 seconds would not be enough for Kuts to win.

But Kuts knew this too. Pirie sensed the Russian begin to gather himself as they went down the back straight for the penultimate time. The spring of tension, which the runners had released a little during the race, began to tighten again.

With one lap to go Kuts was still in front, and Pirie knew that the Russian was now striving to take the race away. If Pirie had been anxious he would have gone at the bell, snatching at the race before it left him. But he waited, feeling the speed left in his legs. Then, with 270 metres to go he moved out, lifted his arms a little and quickened his stride.

It was easier than he expected. He was soon up with Kuts, and almost before he knew it, he was past. Within seconds he was five metres ahead, and then ten. Pirie came to the final bend, back on the very inside of the track, accelerating away with his long stride. The crowd in the home straight began to rise to their feet to greet him – at first in ones and twos, but then in a united roar, urging him on. On the infield, Bjorn Berentsen watched Pirie half turn to look back. They could both see that Kuts was beaten.

Into the straight Pirie came. As sometimes happens, on the best nights, the faster he went, the easier it felt. He came to the finish, blowing out his cheeks, and as he reached the tape raised both hands in a kind of salute. He was almost 20 metres ahead. The last lap had taken just 55 seconds.

Around the stadium now, everyone stood. Pirie turned to greet Kuts and they shook hands. They nodded to each other in acknowledgement and then moved away to let the other runners finish. Egge and Honnicke still had over 200 metres to run. Jan Arild

waited, half wanting to run home at 5,000 metre record pace to tell his parents what had happened.

Pirie stood, hands on hips to help himself recover, only now the sweat breaking out on him. He walked this way and that, waiting for the time. There were three watches to be examined. If it was a record of any sort, all had to be checked not once but twice and the official time agreed. Knots of officials and journalists clustered round the timekeepers. Pirie put his tracksuit back on, and his woollen hat. For the moment, there was nothing much in his mind at all.

On these occasions announcers like to have their moment. After some delay, and to much cheering, the record time was given, but not without a little teasing. "The entire world press is waiting for the result of this fantastic race…" Not only had Pirie beaten the old record, but Kuts had too. The watches read: 13:36.8, 13:36.4 and

Pirie and Kuts photographed a few minutes after Pirie broke the world record for 5,000 metres.
Bergens Tidende

11

One of the three
stopwatches used to time
Pirie's world record run.
Bergens Tidende

13:36.8, so the official time was 13:36.8. The two runners began a
lap of honour together, running past the football terracing and waving at the crowd just where Jan Arild stood. On the home straight
they embraced for the cameras. Through the public address system,
Pirie paid tribute to the part Kuts had played in the race.

Eventually, after all the autographs had been signed, the
Berentsens took their guest home. Bjorn was beaming at everyone,
unable to contain his pleasure. But Pirie was beyond excitement,
sitting quietly in a kind of stunned calm. He had been training for
this for a long time. He had been certain he could do it. But actually doing it, that was something different.

He gave an interview to an Oslo radio station. "I knew Kuts would
run fast, but I felt in good form. I stayed in the dressing room to
warm up out of the rain. I felt really comfortable – I can't believe
the time. I wanted 68 second laps, to keep a good speed going but
not allow Kuts to go 'fast and slow'. I didn't run as fast as I could over
the last 80 metres – I relaxed because he was way down. Kuts is a
very great sportsman – if he hadn't run strongly there wouldn't have
been a world record."

A few English tourists sought out the house to offer congratulations. Phone calls began to come in from English newspapers – none
of them had had a reporter at the meeting. Pirie spoke to the Bergen
press and inevitably they asked him how fast 5,000 metres could be
run. Pirie had no hesitation. He felt he could run it faster himself
and he saw no reason why someone could not manage 64 seconds

a lap, a time of 13:20. The press soon got to Iharos and his coach Mihály Iglói. They hoped for a meeting with Pirie at Budapest in August and they were sure they could get the record back.

And Kuts? He had run faster than ever before, and had beaten the old world record. But like Pirie, Kuts was not someone who enjoyed second place. As he looked out of his window that night in his Bergen hotel he thought of the Olympics in November and his will hardened again.

On Wednesday Jan Arild Larsen found it even harder to cope with lessons than he had the day before. At lunchtime he slipped out of school and went down to the newspaper offices in the town to see how *Bergens Tidende* was handling the story. There, in the office window, was a photograph of the stopwatch at 13:36.8.

That morning *The Times* in London had an agency report but its athletics correspondent added a special comment: "Quite simply this performance of Pirie's is the best by a British athlete since RG Bannister accomplished the first four minute mile. Perhaps it is even better since Pirie has gained this amazing record in the heat of fierce competition."

Pirie went on racing that summer, in Trondheim, in Amsterdam, in Copenhagen and then in Malmö, where he met the great Hungarian runners and beat them all. He and Kuts raced again in Australia in November, at the Olympics. Pirie's travelling went on over the years, alongside his running, orienteering and coaching. He was in Bergen again in 1979 with two young Norwegian athletes he was coaching. Still bronzed and fit, but with his collar-length hair slightly grey, he was interviewed for *Bergens Tidende* by their sports editor, Jan Arild Larsen.

2 A very early age

On a summer afternoon in the early 1940s a middle-aged man was running through the Surrey lanes on the edge of London. With him was a young boy on a bicycle. The man was tall and upright, a little severe looking with a military moustache. Although he was already some miles from home, his running was sure and steady. The boy would sometimes fall behind, investigating something in a hedge and then, when they came to a hill, he would pedal furiously ahead.

The man was Alexander Sutherland Pirie, "Alick" to all his running friends, but "Sandy" at home. He was born in 1901 in Bermuda where his father was serving in the army, so the family was often on the move and Alick attended schools in India, Aden, England and Wales. On leaving school, he got a job with the Eastern Telegraph Company, a forerunner of Cable and Wireless, and in 1920 was assigned to work in London.

Athletics was growing in popularity in those post-war years and Alick Pirie would have been able to join the crowds flocking to the Stamford Bridge stadium in west London for the AAA championships where the great Finnish runner Paavo Nurmi and other stars ran. Alick had a strong interest in running and through the good offices of a work colleague, Francis Knott, who had run for Britain in the 1908 Olympics, he soon joined South London Harriers. The club was always known in the athletics world as SLH – and Alick Pirie remained a member all his life.

In 1922 Alick's work took him to Leeds and for the next 12 years, although he occasionally travelled south to run for SLH, he was active in Yorkshire athletics, organising and managing races and often competing in them himself. He met and married a Yorkshire

Facing page: Pirie (back to camera) greets Frank Salvat after a muddy race at the White City, London in July 1961. *Gerry Cranham*

15

Alick (533) running
in the Southern
Cross-Country Champi-
onships in 1926.
SLH

woman, Martha Stead, known affectionately as Marnie. By 1931 there were four children, all born in Yorkshire: Ian (1925), Pamela (1927), Peter (1929) and Douglas Alistair Gordon, always known by his third name, born on February 10th 1931.

Both the houses in which the Piries lived in Yorkshire were near to open countryside and Alick developed a liking for long runs and walks, sometimes covering a circuit of over 20 miles from the house at Bramley on the outskirts of Leeds to Fewston reservoir and back. In 1926 he was picked to run for Scotland in the International Cross-Country championships at the De Stockel racecourse near Brussels, and finished 30th. In later years he became a keen road runner and he was still running regularly in his sixties.

In 1934 Alick was moved back to London with Cable and Wireless and he chose to put down roots near to South London Harriers. He and Marnie moved into a comfortable three bedroomed semi-detached house with a long, narrow garden at the rear: No. 7, Meadway in Coulsdon, at that stage facing open countryside on the southern edge of the London conurbation. The house was a 15 minute walk from Coulsdon South station or, as Alick put it, "a five minute walk if I run like hell." Alick could jog down to the SLH headquarters just off the Brighton Road in five minutes and even closer, just across the road and up a hill, lay Farthing Downs and the wider expanse of the North Downs.

He was a man of some independence. A few weeks after the outbreak of war in 1939 two plain-clothes policemen called at the house to make enquiries about Franz Stampfl, an athlete and coach of Austrian origin who had been mentioned in the *SLH Gazette*. Stampfl was the official club coach at the time. Much later he had a hand in Roger Bannister's preparation for the first four minute mile. Alick Pirie courteously showed the detectives into his front room and listened to their enquiries. It was his duty to help them he said, but they had no business reading the club's private documents. Thereafter the gazette always carried an imprint on the front cover: "For private circulation only".

Alick could sometimes seem severe to youngsters, but he was always ready with a word of advice and enjoyed a good rapport with his sons. Above all he loved to talk running. John Jewell, a veteran road runner from those days, remembers: "If we came back to tea at Meadway after a run Alick would soon have his scrapbook of cuttings out. Sometimes it was difficult to get him to talk about anything but athletics." Gordon Pirie much later referred, affectionately, to his father's love affair with distance running as "an affliction".

Only occasionally could Alick and Marnie get to London to watch the big meetings but in 1936 they went with their great friends from Yorkshire days, the Whitakers, to the prestigious post-Olympic meeting between the British Empire and the USA at the White City. When they got home the children, including Gordon who was only five, listened from their bedrooms to the excited talk below about the great athletes their parents had seen.

Alick Pirie had no truck with those who advised runners to go cautiously. For much of the war he was on a night shift which

Programme for the British Games at Stamford Bridge, 1926.
Ken Finding

Alick Pirie running in a
club event on Farthing
Downs in his sixties.
Susan Prout

involved leaving home at four o'clock in the afternoon and travelling up to the city for a 16 hour stint at work. He would then get two
days off. This allowed him the pleasure of long daylight runs and it
was not unknown for him to run three laps of his favourite seven
mile circuit in the morning, retire to bed for the afternoon and then,
vaulting the gate as he left the house, do another lap in the evening.
At a time when running on the road was not common, he was a
familiar sight on the pavements of Coulsdon and the nearby Surrey
lanes, occasionally with one of the children alongside on their bike.

Gordon Pirie timing his
father while training on
the downs.
SLH

In July 1942 he decided to organise a 20 mile open road race, starting and finishing at a school close to the Pirie home. He came
almost straight to the race from a night shift, and had to content
himself with running just the first ten miles. At these and other
events the Pirie children often acted as cyclist guides to make sure
no runners went off course or took short cuts.

When Gordon Pirie recalled in later life his memories of those
days he was in no doubt that they provided a kind of informal
initiation into running, and runners: "Chief among the lessons I
learned from these accomplished (and slightly eccentric) athletes
was something of the habits of top class distance runners. At times
they seemed crazy. They were extremely aggressive and often at
war with the world... I would cycle off ahead of the runners I was
guiding in order to avoid finding myself in the middle of an
uncomfortable confrontation with an angry motorist, cyclist or
pedestrian... the runners truly believed that the roads belonged to
them while they were on a run." (*Running Fast and Injury Free* by
Gordon Pirie, pub. John S Gilbody, 1996)

But while Alick Pirie loved to see his children involved in these
activities he never badgered them to take part. Derek Nicholls, a
professional tennis coach and fitness expert, who was a friend of
Gordon Pirie over many years, was in no doubt that Alick put no
pressure on Gordon to run, but that his approach to running had
been an important influence. "What Gordon got from Alick was his
discipline and determination, and that counted for a lot."

The Pirie family base was a firm one, which had survived some hard times and in which Alick and Marnie provided, in their different ways, a strong centre. Marnie was a Yorkshire woman, warm with people but always getting straight to the point in conversation. She shared Alick's dry, sometimes laconic sense of humour, something that Gordon himself later displayed. She was spare in build but hard working, coping unflaggingly with the comings and going of four adolescents. She stood on the Downs in her tweed skirts and woollen stockings to cheer the runners on and, then, often supported by Pamela, made the teas. The children inevitably jockeyed for attention but she stayed serene most of the time and worked hard for them, urging them to success in whatever they tackled, and never discouraged them from any venture or expedition they proposed. The door was open to the children's school friends and club colleagues, as they were in later years to visiting athletes from around the world.

Peter Pirie, just 18 months older than Gordon, recalls: "For as long as I can remember we always had a constant stream of visitors, many of whom would go out for a run. We sometimes had to have as many as four sittings for one meal." Mrs Pirie made sure the hospitality worked and Alick enjoyed playing the host. Marnie had her own hobbies too, taking golf quite seriously from middle age, so much so that she would sometimes be off to play before the family left for school. No doubt she would have been a successful sportswoman, given the chance.

Much of the children's time in those first years at Meadway in the 1930s was spent on the North Downs, walking and rambling. "Our lives involved activity at a very early age," recalls Peter. "We would often walk to the Harrow Pub at Whitehill, which now overlooks the M25 motorway, and then walk into Caterham or Godstone for a bus back to Old Coulsdon. I don't think we found it difficult or unusual and the total distance walked, including playing, must have exceeded ten miles. Much of this took place because we enjoyed the countryside, not realizing that it would give us a natural ability to cover a lot of ground in a short time."

Once the Battle of Britain started in the summer of 1940 (the family sighted the first German plane in daylight in June) the children stayed closer to home. But later in the war years the family walks and cycle rides continued. Gordon, as the youngest, had the freedom to pursue his own activities, and he was the most adventurous in outdoor pursuits. Roaming the woods with friends he was keen to take each expedition a little further. Bob Jones, who was in Gordon's form at school, remembers him at 13 or 14 climbing an elm tree and then edging along the branches to get birds' eggs while his friends waited anxiously below. It was Gordon who stayed out longest hunting butterflies, long after he knew lunch would be on the table.

Some family vacations were spent on the Isle of Wight staying with Alick's father who, on his retirement from the army, had become the warden on a firing range at Porchfield. Gordon and his younger cousin Keith formed an affinity during these holidays. "I remember various pranks we got up to," Keith recalls, "including one occasion when we helped ourselves to Grandad's shotgun and tried to shoot the blackbirds on the strawberry patch. We didn't get any birds but we smashed a few strawberry plants. Gordon and I would sometimes have races up a cliff. He'd wait until I was half way up before he started and still beat me to the top. Then we'd go home and eat bread and honey."

Only when they began to run in races did the young Piries find how much fitter they were than other boys, and how much this owed to all those childhood hours spent cycling, walking and exploring. Gordon often reflected on this in later years. "I walked miles and miles in the Surrey hills, even at the age of five or six," he recalled in a radio programme recorded in 1961. Much later, in a letter to a friend, he wrote: "One could say that I started to run at about five years old as play activity and I spent my life tripping round the countryside."

Keith Whitaker, born in the same month as Gordon, remembers travelling down from Yorkshire for family holidays with the Piries in Coulsdon.[2] "The house in Meadway was on the edge of country with the Downs only a hundred yards away, woods further up where we kids could roam, climbing trees, birds nesting, chasing and catching butterflies, always active. Up a long garden at the back of the house was a substantial vegetable patch." Once Ian, the oldest

---

[2] Keith Whitaker was an active athlete and remained so into his sixties. He became chairman of the British Veterans Athletics Federation and helped to organise the World Veterans Championships in Gateshead in 1999.

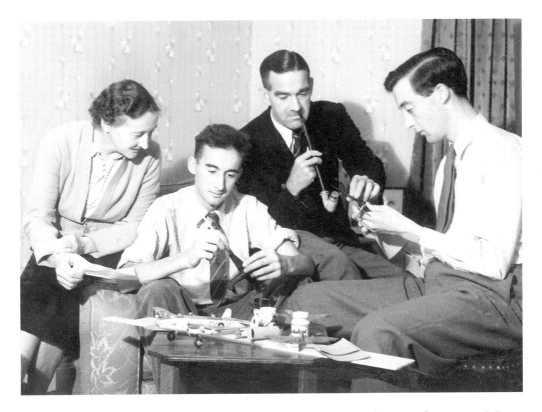

Gordon (left) at home with Peter Pirie and their parents.
SLH

brother, had been called up (in 1943, when Gordon was 12) Peter assumed some of the duties of an elder son, taking on the lion's share of the gardening work. There was a phase when train sets were all the rage. They were set up outside the house if it was fine and there were occasional expeditions by the boys to a specialist model railway shop in central London to buy supplies. Don Spinks, who lived next door, recalls long hours playing with Peter and Gordon's Hornby "O" gauge railway. "We even started making a railway round the air raid shelter. And when Gordon and I got to making balsa wood aircraft we fitted a metal vice to the outside coal box so we could work on our model Spitfire."

Gordon Pirie was eight years old when war broke out, and 14 when it ended, but his childhood life was largely protected from its worst effects. Alick was in a "reserved occupation", working with signals and cables, and lived at home throughout the war. "It wasn't normal on the street – most of the men were in the Middle East or somewhere," recalls Peter.

School was nearby. Ian, Peter and Gordon (once he had finished at Bradmore Green Primary) all attended Purley County School for Boys, while Pam went to Purley School for Girls. Once, and sometimes twice, a day from the age of five to 17 Gordon walked, or ran, the steep hill from 7 Meadway to school, and back down. The County school managed as well as it could in the war years, endeavouring to provide a grammar school education during a period of real difficulty, but it could not offer the variety of activities and subjects that developed later. Mr Mitchell the head was remembered in a school history as a strict disciplinarian. "Every form had its own conduct book; any misbehaviour was duly noted and Saturday morning detention awarded for serious offences. The cane of course was also used. This was administered by the Headmaster in his study after school. Many pupils regarded the worst part of the ordeal the friendly handshake afterwards to show there was no ill feeling." (*History of Purley County Grammar School* 1914–88). Peter Pirie's recollection is that in the time that he and Gordon were at the school any discipline that was administered was "fair and prompt".

There was no great encouragement for runners at school. Peter and Gordon played both rugby and cricket there, but although there were occasional cross-country races with other schools there was no real training for athletics. If the rugby pitch was flooded, some boys would go for a run instead. This, Gordon later recalled, is more or less how he started, and it provided good experience.

"Our school course started with a three-quarter mile descent then rose sharply up another hill to the top of the Downs, levelling off for about half a mile along the summit, before descending again into the valley. These races finished with another steep climb back to the school. We became very skilled at streaking down and smashing up any hill with enough energy left to sprint away at the top." (*Running Fast and Injury Free.*)

The Pirie boys also taught themselves to swim at the local pool, played badminton in the SLH clubhouse and, later, squash on the courts at Kenley aerodrome. A new head of Purley County, Dr Birchall, appointed in 1946, was particularly keen to have prefects who were successful sports players. Birchall, an ex-squadron leader, also encouraged the development of a branch of the Air Training Corps. The ATC offered its members smart uniforms, elementary classes in navigation and aircraft recognition, and some flying opportunities. It also had a comprehensive sports programme, including athletics competitions, which culminated in finals at the White City. When the school group was formed, Peter soon joined and became an NCO, and Gordon was also a member.

There were some interruptions to school life. On the day Peter began at Purley County School in September 1939 the pupils were sent home on the first day so the authorities could try and find a full complement of staff. By the time Gordon started in 1942 most young teachers had been replaced by older men who had delayed, or been called back from, retirement. There were interruptions to take refuge in the shelters. The lights down there were poor, and the seats were damp, but you could work.

Peter remembers: "One week-end a Spitfire came down and wiped out the school tennis courts next to the gym and this was only 50 yards or so from the nearest air raid shelter where Gordon and others were sheltering. Quite a lot of bombs were dropped in the fields – the planes may have turned round before they got to the city and gone home early. Sometimes the alarm would interrupt meal times. At first we used to go down to the shelter but after a while we didn't bother, we just stayed at the table." When planes crashed nearby guards were quickly stationed at the scene but to local boys it was a great prize to get hold of ammunition or other trophies, smuggle them home and hide them in the garden hedge. Towards the end of the war the fearsome V1 Doodlebugs and V2 rockets were the main menace. One hit a house just down the road from the Piries and killed a family of four.

Only once was the pattern of life for all the family seriously disrupted. During the Battle of Britain, and when the German forces were making invasion preparations, Alick and Marnie decided that life overhead was getting, as Peter puts it, "just a bit too busy", and that it was best to go up to Yorkshire to stay with their friends the Whitakers. Marnie and the children left at home at four o'clock that afternoon, each carrying a suitcase on the walk down to Coulsdon South station. Before they reached the station an air raid took place and they had to take refuge in the nearest shelter. Eventually they were able to press on with their journey and during the evening the Whitakers received a phone call from Doncaster station announcing their arrival. They stayed in Yorkshire for six weeks but found it difficult to get the children into local schools and decided to return.

South London Harriers had been formed in 1871, at a time when a new generation of amateur runners, many of them from the emerging middle class, was beginning to establish a presence in athletics. Like other clubs, SLH used local hotels or pubs as bases, moving south from Peckham Rye, where it began, in search of continuing access to open running territory as the London sprawl grew. The move to Coulsdon took place in 1913, and in 1919, just before Alick Pirie joined, the club obtained the use of a hall which has continued as its headquarters to the present day.

The hall was close to the Brighton road, which runs down through Coulsdon from central London, and just a few minutes from Farthing Downs. This area of countryside was – and still is – administered by the City of London, and protected from housing development. There were stretches of grassland, woodland of various types and cultivated farmland, all traversed by public footpaths. This was an ideal venue for cross-country running and, since 1913, the SLH "home course". Runners could change in the hall, trot over to the start, race, and then return to the tin baths, later showers, to wash off the mud. However, from the outbreak of war in 1939 until 1946 the club headquarters in Coulsdon was commandeered for use as an emergency shelter and gas decontamination unit, so SLH used temporary facilities on Banstead Downs and, later, a scout hut close to Coulsdon South station.

On many Saturdays during autumn and spring, especially in the pre-war years, there were matches for the Pirie boys to watch including SLH races and the annual sports meetings organised by their father's firm. During the war there were fewer events, and much less participation though Ian Pirie ran in some races.SLH joined with other London clubs to put on some track meetings. After the war the big summer meetings at the White City stadium in London began again. Peter and Gordon were there in the summer of 1946 for the AAA championships, the first since 1939. The organisers had a few teething problems, not least that the leaders in the marathon came into the stadium to run the required lap of the track while the steeplechase was still in progress. But there were some wonderful races. In the three miles Sydney Wooderson overtook the Dutch runner Slykhuis just before the finish and broke the British record. Wooderson's final sprint, in the home straight, made a lasting impact on the 15-year-old Gordon Pirie.

Sydney Wooderson.

25

Over the years South London Harriers used a variety of running tracks including that at Stamford Bridge. From 1937 when the London County Council opened a new cinder track at Tooting Bec, some seven or eight miles away, SLH began to use it as a base and it was here that Gordon Pirie ran a number of his first track races. When he first came to train regularly he used Tooting Bec, or the makeshift track in the grounds of the Netherne Hospital which lay just over the other side of Farthing Downs from his home.

SLH had for many years a reputation as a club for "city gents" and some of its most prominent members worked in banking or insurance, usually at middle or managerial level. In the 1930s a man who was keen to join the club but who worked as a messenger in a bank deliberately concealed his actual occupation on his application form, describing himself simply as "Midland Bank". But by the late 1940s the club was certainly on the look out for young athletes of ability whatever their social origins. Martin Crickmore recalls: "At that point, it was all bankers and insurance people, but there was no side. No one would feel out of place." The club recruited across a wide catchment area, and its annual meetings and club suppers – to which celebrities from the sport were often invited – were sometimes held in central London.[3]

Alick was club secretary from 1936, throughout the war, and Gordon's schooldays, to 1947. The club gazette which started appearing regularly in 1885 was produced two or three times a year during the war and all the Pirie family helped address and stamp over 400 envelopes. In 1942 the gazette published the records Gunder Hägg was setting in Scandinavia. Alick was proud of what the club meant to people and helped SLH to keep in touch with those overseas, sending parcels to some who were prisoners of war.

Those who had been dispersed by the war came together in December 1946 for one of the club's great occasions, the 75th anniversary dinner. Peter and Gordon, who were 17 and 15 at the time, went up with their father to the Bedford Hotel in Balham, chosen because it has been the club's headquarters for a period in the 1880s. In all 90 people crowded into an upper room – old

---

[3] Women's athletics were generally organised through separate clubs at that time. SLH became a mixed club in 1982.

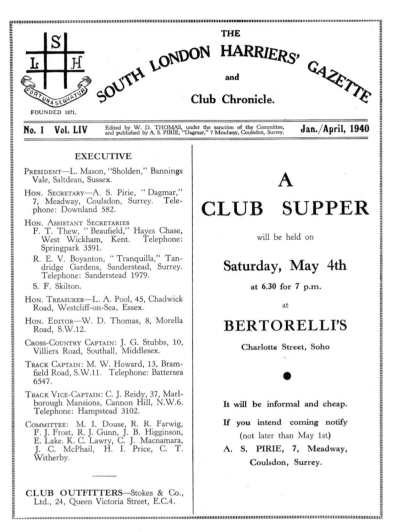

THE
SOUTH LONDON HARRIERS' GAZETTE
and
Club Chronicle.

FOUNDED 1871.

No. 1   Vol. LIV   Edited by W. D. THOMAS, under the sanction of the Committee, and published by A. S. PIRIE, "Dagmar," 7 Meadway, Coulsdon, Surrey.   Jan./April, 1940

EXECUTIVE

PRESIDENT—L. Mason, "Sholden," Bannings Vale, Saltdean, Sussex.

HON. SECRETARY—A. S. Pirie, "Dagmar," 7, Meadway, Coulsdon, Surrey. Telephone: Downland 582.

HON. ASSISTANT SECRETARIES
F. T. Thew, " Beaufield," Hayes Chase, West Wickham, Kent. Telephone: Springpark 3591.
R. E. V. Boyanton, " Tranquilla," Tandridge Gardens, Sanderstead, Surrey. Telephone: Sanderstead 1979.
S. F. Skilton.

HON. TREASURER—L. A. Pool, 45, Chadwick Road, Westcliff-on-Sea, Essex.

HON. EDITOR—W. D. Thomas, 8, Morella Road, S.W.12.

CROSS-COUNTRY CAPTAIN: J. G. Stubbs, 10, Villiers Road, Southall, Middlesex.

TRACK CAPTAIN: M. W. Howard, 13, Bramfield Road, S.W.11. Telephone: Battersea 6547.

TRACK VICE-CAPTAIN: C. J. Reidy, 37, Marlborough Mansions, Cannon Hill, N.W.6. Telephone: Hampstead 3102.

COMMITTEE: M. I. Douse, R. R. Farwig, F. J. Frost, R. J. Gunn, J. B. Higginson, E. Lake. K. C. Lawry, C. J. Macnamara, J. C. McPhail, H. I. Price, C. T. Witherby.

CLUB OUTFITTERS—Stokes & Co., Ltd., 24, Queen Victoria Street, E.C.4.

A
CLUB SUPPER

will be held on

Saturday, May 4th

at 6.30 for 7 p.m.

at

BERTORELLI'S

Charlotte Street, Soho

●

It will be informal and cheap.

If you intend coming notify
(not later than May 1st)

A. S. PIRIE, 7, Meadway, Coulsdon, Surrey.

Alick Pirie helped to keep club traditions alive during the war years.
SLH

stalwarts, including many of the men who had dominated British athletics for half a century, club members and one or two youngsters. The talk all night was of running. Of the European championships held that summer in Oslo, of the London Olympics, barely 18 months away, and of the four minute mile, and what Wooderson, but for the war, might have done.

The Pirie boys listened as Lord Burghley, the aristocrat of British athletics, made the toast to the club. Replying for the guests was Harold Abrahams, like Burghley a former Olympic gold medallist, and a man who had become the radio voice of the sport. The President of the club also had to speak and this brought Billy Holt to his feet. Holt was a spry, confident figure, a bank manager and a man of considerable importance in the sport. He had just become honorary secretary of the International Amateur Athletic Federation (IAAF), the governing body of the sport worldwide. He was in charge of preparations for the track and field programme at the London Olympics to be held 18 months later and subsequently he went to Australia to help in preparations for the Melbourne Olympics of 1956. But Holt was also very much an SLH man and an experienced coach. Gordon Pirie recalled in later life that Holt was one of the people who taught him how to run, beginning with simple prancing and bounding exercises. Billy Holt spoke that evening about the difficult discussions going on at international level with those who wanted to relax the rules on payment to athletes. He did not want "circus" meetings, managed by private promoters, and built around races designed for the stars.

The main guest at the dinner was the best-loved runner in Britain: Sidney Wooderson, President of SLH's greatest rivals, Blackheath Harriers, and the man whom Peter and Gordon has seen at the White City stadium that summer. They knew how close he had come to Hägg's world record for 5,000 metres a few weeks later, when he won the European championship race at the Bislett stadium in Oslo. Bert Liffen, an SLH member, had run for the British team at those championships and made friends with Norwegian athletes from the Norrøna club in Bergen.

John Jewell kept a diary of those days, and attended the dinner. "A first class evening. First class speeches. Dinner itself a bit skimpy," he recorded. It was indeed a grand occasion, although no one could guess that Burghley and Abrahams were to be the heroes years later of a film which became a box office success world wide, *Chariots of Fire*.

What mattered most to Alick Pirie and, later, to his sons, was the everyday life of the club: the training runs over the downs when you could chat to friends, races against old rivals, seeing new youngsters come through and make the team.

3 Like a machine

I t was the winter of 1945–6. Gordon Pirie was a lively, quick-witted 14-year-old, with boundless energy. In the mornings he would sometimes chase the local bus as it pulled its load of schoolboys and teachers up the hill to the school, often getting got there first. Peter Pirie, who was 16 and had just entered the sixth form at school, was beginning to race fairly regularly. He did not do a lot of training but he had begun to find out that, with all the cycling and walking he had done, he had a good level of basic fitness. In November 1945 both boys travelled down to Sussex and ran for SLH in an annual fixture, first held in 1913, against Lancing College, over the school grounds and neighbouring fields and across ditches deep with water. Peter was fourth, and Gordon, some 600 yards down on his brother, 13th.

The rules governing age groups were complicated and slightly different for cross-country and track, but there were "Youths" races for boys aged 16 and 17 and then, before you joined the senior ranks at 21, three years as "Juniors". In early January Peter won the Surrey county Youths' race and progressed on for the first time to the national cross-country championships, held that year over farmland on the edge of Leamington Spa. Gordon travelled up with the family and watched his father, Alick, now 45, make one of his last appearances in the SLH team as a senior. Peter who was competing in the Youths' race against runners most of whom were a year older, ran himself almost to exhaustion and finished fourth.

In the following winter, 1946–7, came more success. Gordon had his first victory, in a race organised for novices by SLH over Farthing Downs. A deviation had to be made to avoid a military camp at Alderstead Heath, as part of the Downs had been cordoned off during the war. This increased the length of the course to over five miles.

Gordon Pirie at 14
(1945) before one of
his first competitive
races.
SLH

For the first mile the runners ran easily together but, on one of the climbs at Netherne, Gordon, still only 15, began to attack. He moved swiftly ahead and won by almost a minute. A few weeks later Peter won a club five mile race over a similar course, and then won the Lancing race, with Gordon second, and also retained his county title.

The two boys were getting better and better and gaining a local reputation. They were both tall with a good stride, Peter the more strongly built, Gordon more obviously lanky. Richard Bray, a pupil at Purley County, remembers a telling incident which suggests that Gordon was well aware of his own ability: "For some reason I was unable to play rugby which was my first love and was sent running instead and I found myself leaving the school grounds with Gordon. We ran quite comfortably for a couple of miles and then, suddenly, he said something about 'starting to work now' and simply left me standing. Despite my best efforts and I really was quite fit, he disappeared from sight in about three minutes flat and I never saw him again that day…"

All the walking and cycling was paying off. Peter had done a lot of cycling round southern England in the summer of 1947. And Keith Whitaker remembers when Gordon came to stay in Yorkshire about that time. "We borrowed a tandem, a great big heavy pre-war thing, and we had regular trips of between 40 and 100 miles and would delight in passing any slow moving cars on downhill stretches with a blast from a bulb horn which we had fitted on the rear handlebars." At home there would be a school run during the week perhaps, a race occasionally at weekends and maybe one evening run on another day.

The Pirie boys rarely ran together or with their father. They all fitted in their runs as best they could amidst the busy routine of work, travel and study. Being on shift work, Alick Pirie was often at the office in the evening. Peter did his occasional evening run before bed – it saved changing twice – and by the time he got ready to go out Gordon might well be asleep. For all the boys the running was little more than an extension of their other regular exercise but they enjoyed the social aspect of club races, the chance to meet and talk to people. In those early days they had no great ambitions: "We had no expectations or hopes, we just fell into it" Peter recalls.

In the cold winter of 1947 however came a sign of things to come. Peter won the national Youths' race in Hertfordshire. Britain was in the middle of one of the worst spells of weather for many years and shortage of fuel led to a wide range of economy measures. Due to heavy snowfalls in early March some runners planning to compete in the national cross-country championships failed to arrive at the venue, near Hemel Hempstead, or got there only just in time. The Piries made the difficult journey by train from Euston to Apsley and the Dickenson paper works where the runners were to change. Some competitors from the north had reached London in the middle of the night, and then caught the milk train out to Hertfordshire, arriving at 5 a.m. The caretaker opened the dressing rooms and the runners spent a couple of hours hugging the hot water pipes to keep warm.

When the race got under way Peter was helped by the inexperience of some runners over plough. Instead of following the edge of the field where they could run along the furrows, many competitors ran across the furrows, which were concealed under the snow and found themselves in great difficulty. In other parts of the course overtaking was extremely difficult because the snow on either side of the narrow path made by the runners was so deep. Gordon watched his brother come through well clear at the finish and a photo of Peter breaking the tape featured prominently in the athletics press.

In the following summer Gordon was 16 and due to take his School Certificate examinations. He had not found study difficult but preferred other teenage pursuits, at the local youth club or out on the Downs. "We were always playing the fool and laughing about crazy things," he wrote later. He failed the mock examinations but, put on his mettle by the headmaster, and goaded by a taunt from his chemistry teacher, he set himself the task of working hard for several months so he could catch up.

That summer he and his brother tried their hand in various track races at Tooting Bec. Gordon competed over 1,000 yards, a mile, three miles and six miles, and also showed talent as a high jumper. Then at the end of July, came a special opportunity. He went with Peter to the annual ATC camp at Syerston airfield in Nottinghamshire. The cadets were allowed to take part in a camp athletics meeting and Gordon, somewhat to the disgust of the older competitors, won the half-mile. As the national ATC championships fell during the same week, the RAF flew the brothers down to Kenley so they could travel up from home to the White City. The flight from the East Midlands made a lasting impact. It was a fine summer's day but when the boys stood up behind the pilot and looked out, large parts of London were shrouded in industrial smog.

So now the young schoolboy found himself in the very stadium where he had seen Wooderson race. The reputation of the place, and the huge stands around him, were not inhibiting. Gordon had been entered in the junior mile. He ran freely and easily, winning in 4 minutes 42 seconds, a fine time for a boy of 16. This performance confirmed Peter in his view that his brother was well suited to the mile.

Gordon's application to study paid off. He found that he had the capacity, if the will was there, to apply himself seriously to a task. He passed his School Certificate examinations that summer and returned to school in the autumn of 1947 and entered the sixth form. Peter, who had the qualifications to enter university, had to go into the RAF and start his National Service. He had time only for a ten day cycling holiday and six weeks work on a farm before enlisting. The boys met again for the Lancing race in November, when Peter was home on leave. He had done little running and was out of condition. But the two brothers led the field, breaking the ice on the frozen dykes for the runners behind them. As they came to the last half mile of the race and climbed the hill to the school the water froze again on their legs. They stood in the hot showers in full kit to recover, Gordon the winner for the first time.

Gordon was already tall for his age, a little angular, and thin. "There seemed to be nothing to him," remembers one school friend. In the little running he had done, for the club and at school, he had performed fairly well but he had not won any major races and he had not yet competed against the best young runners from clubs in other parts of the country. This was to happen during the winter of 1947–8 when he competed in the cycle of county, regional and national races that made up the English cross-country season.

The cycle began with the county event in December 1947, when Gordon was still 16. The Surrey county race was at Cheam Park, only a few miles from home, and there were hopes in the club that he might win. He had the measure of all 60 runners in the field bar one. "Stumpy" Green from Reading (who was born in Surrey) pulled away at the half way point and won easily, with Pirie about 200 yards down in second place. At this level, he was to discover, winning was not easy.

Up to this point Gordon had not taken his running too seriously. It was something he seemed to be quite good at without having to try particularly hard. But it did not come to him as easily as it did to Peter and at the beginning of 1948, still not quite 17, he started to train a little harder. Once or twice teachers saw him running in boots. One of them, George Love who taught woodwork at the school, remonstrated with him: "It all helps to strengthen my legs," Gordon said, and turned away to get on with his running. Pirie, returning to the school a few years later, found George Love, and asked if he could build him a running machine so he could exercise more effectively indoors, during bad weather. This was before the days of multi-gyms.

Now Pirie moved on to the next big race of the winter, the Southern championships, held that year on the Aylesford Paper Mills course, near Maidstone in Kent. Another youngster taking part there was a local boy, Frank Sando, who had won a number of races at Maidstone Grammar School as a 15- and 16-year-old. Frank's father met an official of Maidstone Harriers by chance at a social event, Sando joined the club and ran for them for a couple of years. He

Aylesford, Kent, 1948. The SLH Youths' team in the Southern Cross-Country Championships. Gordon Pirie, second from right, back row.
SLH

trained and raced with a small band of enthusiasts who changed in a local pub. They came back afterwards to wash down in the garage next door, one tub to get the mud off and another to rinse in. But the big club in Maidstone was the one attached to Aylesford Paper Mills and Frank reckoned that if he made an impression with them it might lead to a job at the works, and so it did.

Sando was shorter than Pirie, and to Gordon's leanness was added a touch of frailty. Even when he was young people talked with some awe about Sando's lightness over the ground. His mentors knew he had to be protected from too much running as a young man and they did quite a good job, because he became one of the most respected runners in the country and won the international cross-country championships twice in the 1950s.

The Pirie family went over Maidstone for the race, Alick, Marnie and Pam as usual in support. This was Gordon's biggest event to date and he faced the prospect of racing against the best young runners in the south. There had been a foot of snow in Kent a week before and although much of it had gone by the Saturday, conditions were still difficult. When Pirie and Sando lined up, shivering in their singlets, there were another 160 runners beside them, the largest field either had known. Some runners were jogging up and down on the frozen ground, shouting cockily to their friends. For the first time, Pirie was nervous.

He managed to stay quite close to the front throughout the race but he was never on terms with the leaders. The Surrey winner Green was first again. Gordon finished behind the leading pack in sixth place, with Sando just a yard or two behind him. Pirie was disappointed, yet pleased that he had more or less held his own. There was one round of championship races left, the national event a fortnight later in Sheffield. It was here that Pirie and Sando were to meet the best young runner in England.

Walter Hesketh came from a different pedigree. He left elementary school in Manchester at 14 and had a patch cleaning shoes on the pavement in St Ann's Square, near to a Red Cross centre frequented by American soldiers. Until then his only running had been chasing the trams from the city centre to home in Chorlton. But once he got into Manchester Athletic Club there were plenty of people to run with and plenty of races. Walter was stronger than many of his contemporaries and he soon began to win races, at first locally and then all over the North, beating senior runners into the bargain. At 16 he got a pair of spikes from Fosters of Bolton (later to become Reeboks), and at 17 his first tracksuit. Walter was the favourite for the National Youths' title that year – he was only three months older than Pirie but his running career was well ahead and his victories in the North had given him considerable confidence. "We've always thought of ourselves in the North as the best distance runners," he said many years later.

Sheffield was packed with sporting traffic on that March day. Over 200 coaches arrived for the cross-country, and 50,000 fans were converging on the city for the football semi-final between Manchester United and Derby County. In Graves Park where the cross-country races were held there were 20,000 spectators, many keen to see Sidney Wooderson make his last attempt to win the senior title.

If Maidstone had seemed a big race, this was enormous. There were 450 starters in the Youths' race and for the first time Pirie found himself almost overwhelmed by the numbers. He was a confident boy in his own circles but now he found runners around him who were not only a year older, but tougher and more ruthless as they fought for places. Even Hesketh seems to have been slightly over-whelmed by the size of the field. At half way he was 120 yards adrift. But his coach, Walter Parrott, pushed his way out of the lines of spectators and shouted at him furiously. Hesketh came to life and moved up, eventually catching the leaders and finishing several seconds in front. Pirie ran strongly and almost established himself in the leading group but he finally finished eighth. Frank Sando, who always seemed to get better as the winter went on, was fourth.

It was a long journey for the SLH party back to St Pancras and then across London and down to Coulsdon. Peter had been ninth in the Juniors' race so it had not been a bad day for the family. The general verdict was that Gordon had run well but that his lightish frame was against him in the heavy conditions. But Hesketh was a class above him, and most other runners, at this stage. A week or two later they looked in the monthly magazine *Athletics* to see what it had to say. Its editor Jimmy Green had too experienced an eye to be taken in by youthful prodigies but he had no doubt who was a star in the making. He saw in Hesketh "… an exceptional boy who, with reasonable development, should have a great future."

When Gordon turned out in an inter-school race a few days later he was second, much to the disappointment of his teachers. "He has obviously run too much during the season," said the report in the school magazine. But the cycle of cross-country races had come to an end and Gordon had reason to be content with what he had achieved. In March of 1948 he had not yet decided that he would beat Walter Hesketh and Frank Sando and all the others, or how he would do it. At that stage, still, there was more to life than running.

That summer, at 17, Gordon Pirie was thrust into the adult world. He had not done well enough at school to stay on for a final year. Peter, who had preceded him through Purley County, had stayed on until 18 and taken Higher School Certificate, the equivalent of today's "A" levels. Gordon always regretted that he had not studied harder. Now, young, active and energetic, he had to find work. But first, there were the Olympics.

The Games opened in London in July of 1948, a few days after Pirie left school. London had been allocated the Olympics at fairly short notice and there was no time to build a new arena, or do much about accommodation for visitors. "Enjoy such hospitality as our

Young SLH athletes,
watched by Alick Pirie
(seated), try out model
Olympic torches on
Farthing Downs, 1948.
SLH

circumstances will allow," wrote Ernest Bevin, the Foreign Secretary, in the Official Souvenir. Adaptations were made to the Empire stadium at Wembley and for the first time in Britain a 400 metre track, rather than 440 yards, was laid. South London Harriers was much involved in the preparation for the Olympics. Three club members were selected for the British track and field team and a club official, Billy Holt, was Director of Athletics for the Games. Alick Pirie, Gordon's father, was among dozens of volunteers who acted as a marshal during the marathon.

In the lead up to the Games one other moment involved Gordon's family. In 1947 some SLH members, including the Piries, had been involved in trials of prototype Olympic torches, of various designs, on Farthing Downs. Now, in the summer of 1948, the real Olympic torch, which had been brought across Europe from Greece by a relay of runners, was carried through Kent and Surrey by leading local athletes nominated by their clubs. Alick Pirie was chosen to take one leg, and he invited Gordon to run with him. At 7.35 on the morning of July 28th they took over the torch at Priory Motors in Reigate and began their stretch of just under two miles. Alick carried the torch, with Gordon alongside him, father and son in the compulsory club vest, white shorts and white shoes. Crowds of people stood and applauded as the two went by.

The Games began on July 30th. SLH had organised a block of seats for their members in the stands near the end of the back straight, where they could sit together, watch the events and compare notes about the performances. The Pirie family travelled into central London and then out to the north-western suburbs to the great stadium. Gordon and his parents went up into their seats with their programmes and took in the vast scene. There was the brand new track. It was immaculately marked out and glistening slightly in the sun.

The programme got off to a slightly delayed start, but by late afternoon, when the first big track final of the Games, the 10,000 metres, came on, all was well. The favourite for this event was Viljo Heino of Finland. He was the world record holder and European champion. A huge crowd had seen him break the British all comers record for six miles at the White City Stadium the previous summer, running at such a pace that both Jim Peters and Jack Holden retired. Another Finn, Evert Heinstrom, and Alain Mimoun, an Algerian representing France, were also expected to do well.

Pirie, however, had spotted a new name – Emil Zátopek of Czechoslovakia. Zátopek did not come from one of the great homes of distance running like Sweden or Finland, nor did he have the fluent running style of the champions. But he was a good height (5 ft 8 in) and weight (10st 7lb) for a distance runner, and although not widely known to the general public he had run the best times in the world that year over 10,000 metres.

Zátopek was born in 1923 in Moravia, and first came to prominence in Czechoslovakia as a runner while serving in the forces towards the end of the war. When the war ended he stayed in the army because it gave him good opportunities to train. And train he did. The talk in running circles was that his sessions were not only harder than anyone else's, but also harder than anyone had thought of doing. Repeat 400 metre runs, with a short break between each, were a feature of distance training among the top men on the continent. The hard men might do 20 in a session or even more. The word was that Zátopek did 60. The aficionados who went to the Olympic training track at Uxbridge and saw him train confirmed that he worked very hard indeed.

But measured against the reputation of Heino and Heinstrom, Zátopek was an outsider. He had won cross-country races in Britain

An unofficial programme and visitors' guide for the 1948 Olympics.

in 1946 and 1947 but they were not big events. His victory over Heino in a 5,000 metre race in Finland in 1947 had gone largely unnoticed in the British press. But he perhaps had one thing in his favour: Heino had missed six weeks of training in May through injury and, then, two days before the Olympic final he got a stomach bug.

At six o'clock the runners assembled near the start line and jogged up and down. Across the stadium Gordon Pirie and the other SLH members tried to pick out the individual runners. Was that Stan Cox, against whom Alick had run so often? Where was Jim Peters? Gordon searched for the red vest of Czechoslovakia. At last he spotted Zátopek and leaned across to his mother to point him out. At that moment the starter's pistol fired, and the runners were away.

Heino and Heinstrom were soon in the lead. After an early burst they slowed the pace a little but then began to move steadily on, circling at 72 seconds a lap. It had been a hot day and it was still warm in the stadium. One by one other runners in the field fell back until, with barely half the race gone, only Mimoun and Zátopek were in touch with the two Finns: four runners who seemed to have the race in their hands. But then, just at the mid point of the race, Heino faltered, and almost stopped. Immediately Zátopek saw the weakness, and moved up. Gordon watched as, instead of relaxing comfortably in front, Zátopek picked up the pace for three laps, gradually opening a gap. Then, a minute or so later Heino, who was suffering from a stomach upset and had been reduced almost to running on the spot, was helped off the track by a teammate.

Zátopek now began to run as no one in the stadium had seen a 10,000 metres run before. He put in little bursts of speed, then slowed down, confusing those behind him, and destroying the even tempo of the race. Pirie watched. As his lead got bigger Zátopek's head rolled more and more, the tongue reaching out, the arms twisted. He went further and further ahead, occasionally looking round to relish the damage he had done, the cheering growing in volume and filling the stands with noise. Zátopek finished almost a lap ahead of Mimoun, a small group of Czech supporters chanting his name. According to *The Times* the crowd's response was "one of the greatest ovations in the history of athletics."

The 1948 Olympics. Zátopek approaches the finish of the 10,000 metres race.
British Olympic Association

39

The Piries' family friends, the Whitakers, had come down from Yorkshire for the Olympics but missed the first day. Keith Whitaker remembers clearly the impression that the 10,000 metre race had made: "When we got to Coulsdon that evening everyone was full of Zátopek's performance. Gordon in particular couldn't stop talking about the surges and the way Zátopek had finally broken all the opposition."

Later that week Zátopek won the silver medal in the 5,000 metres. Thousands of people who saw him run wanted to go out and do what he did. Most of them got up and went to work the next morning, still hearing the cheers but putting that ambition to one side.

But Gordon Pirie was ready for what happened and peculiarly well prepared to respond to it. His life lay open before him. If the truth were known, he had left school feeling somewhat disappointed with what he had achieved. Perhaps now he had the chance to prove himself. He told a radio interviewer a few years later: "Zátopek inspired me to do something different. From that moment I wanted to run like Zátopek, like a machine. I wanted to run every day." (*Frankly Speaking*, BBC Radio 1962)

Everything Pirie saw and heard of Zátopek in the months and years after the 1948 Olympics confirmed him in his belief that this was someone to admire and emulate. Sometime soon, he knew, there would be other Zátopeks. Why not him?

But all this was some years off. Because it would take three more years, and quite unusual determination, before he would have the beating of his young rival, Walter Hesketh.

40

4 Breakthrough

Now, in the autumn of 1948, Gordon Pirie knew what he wanted to do, he knew perhaps who he wanted to be. But he can hardly have imagined quite what was involved. To match the best British runners and, more than that, to challenge the great European athletes he had to learn a new way of doing things, a way no one in Britain really knew about. Outside his family, there wasn't much help available. He had to do it more or less on his own.

He had no problem finding work. All the big banks maintained excellent sporting facilities and there were good links between Lloyds and South London Harriers. Someone in the bank quite likely thought that it would be a good idea if the young Pirie could be found a position, if only to strengthen the bank's athletics team. Gordon went into the Eastern department in the City and travelled up to London every day on the train. It was largely routine clerical work, mostly at a desk but occasionally taking documents to other branches. He left home at about 8 o'clock and got back around six in the evening. They liked him in the office. The young Pirie, who enjoyed larking about with friends and loved good stories, knew what was expected at work. To the older staff, he was the quiet, slim lad in the corner.

Lloyds Bank had an active sports association with flourishing clubs based on its spacious ground at New Beckenham on the southern outskirts of London. The bank had purchased 28 acres here in the 1920s to provide recreational facilities for their staff and encourage corporate feeling. The grounds were kept in excellent condition by a group of full-time staff and the pavilion, which had eleven dressing rooms, a dance hall, and two bars, was one of the best in the country. By arrangement with the railway company, staff

Pavilion at the Lloyds
Bank Sports Ground,
Beckenham, opened
1925.
Lloyds TSB Group

travelling out to Beckenham, and to other sports clubs, could obtain reduced price tickets from central London.

These facilities, and those of other banks and companies, were an important part of the social and recreational life of many Londoners in the post-war years. People took their sports bags or racquets to the office on Saturday mornings – and you worked on Saturday mornings in those days – before going on to the sports club. The big banks had got together and employed a professional athletics coach, JB Robertson, who spent one evening a week with Lloyds; the bank also had seven unpaid honorary coaches, as many as some of the strongest athletic clubs. The inter-banks athletics championship held each summer was a prestigious meeting, and generally took place at Motspur Park seen by many as the best track in the country. At Lloyds sports day in 1948, competition in varied sports was followed by a concert and dancing in the evening. A report in the bank's magazine caught the flavour of a showery day:

"Beneath the plastic capes and flowered umbrellas were flowing dresses and New Look coats, but there were no picture hats; and the few tweed costumes and brogues reminded one of an English summer. Men flung aside their raincoats to display semi-hacking jackets, and green snap-brim pattern hats were peppered amongst the crowd. Over 3,000 people turned up; tea (an excellent tea) was served in three sittings and the service was first class. The whole organisation of the sports was excellent, and the committee must be congratulated on interlocking activities so that from three in the afternoon until 11 o'clock at night there was something to see or something to do. The only criticism I have to make is – was not the cloakroom accommodation too modestly advertised?" (*The Dark Horse* magazine)

But some things were still being put straight after the war. That autumn the Piries were out on the club cross-country course helping to replace the barbed wire with wooden fences. The bank's cross-country race was held there in November and Gordon, still only 17, won. On the same day older brother Ian went to Cambridge to run for SLH against the University. In that race a young Chris Brasher was second.

Gordon was soon involved in the next cycle of cross-country championships. In the Surrey event he was second, as he had been the year before, but by the time the National Championships came round again in March of 1949 he was 18 and had to run with the Juniors. This time the championships were held on the Bromford Bridge racecourse at Birmingham. Pirie was 12th, some way behind the leading group. Walter Hesketh, also in his first year as a junior, was third, almost two minutes ahead of Pirie.

Hesketh was maturing fast. He had begun his National Service – in the army – in February and before long was winning army championships over the country and on the track. Walter was physically stronger than many of his contemporaries and he soon found out that he had the beating of many established runners. He was probably the best all round distance runner of his age in England. But for an incident during a six mile race at the White City in June, when he was pushed off the track, he might well have been selected for the Empire Games the following year. And, despite some initial difficulties, army service was not getting in the way of his running. He was undoubtedly the up and coming star.

If Hesketh's achievements were something of a spur to Pirie, so were those of Chris Chataway. Born within a few days of Pirie and, like Gordon, a youthful spectator at Wembley, Chataway had been a good all round sportsman as a boy. Although his school, Sherborne, did not have a strong tradition in athletics he had come third in the mile at the Public Schools meeting in London at the age of 17 and his path crossed with Gordon's at a number of sporting events during National Service years. But Pirie was also battling with someone else. "My greatest enemy was never the athletes I raced against. My battle was constantly with myself. I was much more interested in overcoming my own limitations than in smashing my opponents." (*Running Fast and Injury Free*)

When it came to choosing where to do his military service Pirie quickly opted for the Royal Air Force. Peter had been in the RAF for over a year already and it was a natural choice for those who had been in the Air Training Corps (ATC) at school. The RAF could be choosy about those it took and in general it treated its recruits well. Those who compared notes with friends in the army found that their experience was somewhat more leisurely and, as Peter Wiles recalled in a book of reminiscences, "the officers were friendly and fairly apologetic".

Towards the end of May, Pirie got his brown envelope with joining instructions, railway warrant and 4 shillings (20 pence) advance pay. On June 9th he reported to Padgate, near Warrington in Lancashire and, along with the other new recruits, packed his clothes into a brown paper parcel and sent them home. It was an abrupt interruption to life for many young men. But Pirie had the advantage that he had seen the inside of RAF stations before with the ATC, and Peter had been able to give him some idea what to expect.

It helped to be an athlete. All the services wanted to recruit the best sportsmen into their ranks, even to the extent of spotting who was coming up for enlistment. The Air Force was perhaps best at this. Roger Dunkley remembers ringing up the appropriate senior officer with news of another runner, and discussing the best possible posting. Within the RAF there was considerable rivalry between individual commands, and trophies were displayed on "dining-in nights" because they brought prestige to the camp. Runners, boxers and other sportsmen who were competing regularly, were given privileges: lighter duties, time off to prepare, better food sometimes. It was much the same in the army. "If you were any good, you were given every support," recalls Chris Chataway.

Peter Pirie won two races after he got to his station, Cranwell, and quickly found out that there were benefits in being a good runner. "One morning the Sergeant came bursting into the room because there was extra guard duty to be done and we all moved to get out of bed. 'Not you' he said, pointing at me. I was needed for running." This generation of runners made an impact on service life, however brief their stay. "At Oswestry," says Chataway "the Commanding

Surrey championships, 1952.
David Thurlow

Officer became passionately interested in athletics as a result of my success. He decided to build a track and had scores of conscripts digging earth and moving hundreds of tons of soil in the rain. It didn't do much for my popularity."

Pirie was at Padgate from June to September for his initial training: the form filling, inoculations, the standard RAF haircut and some square bashing. He learned how to march, how to shoot, whom to salute and when, and how to look after his kit. The first eight weeks were quite hard: route marches, some runs, and physical training five days a week. But running in boots was no novelty to Pirie. He soon began to attract attention and to be picked for races – it meant turning out for the station of course, and for the command. The club, the bank, and now the RAF, both Peter and Gordon could run with any of them if they wanted to. At the inter-services championships that summer, held just after he joined the Air Force, Pirie was a reserve for the RAF team. In the mile, a young army recruit, John Disley, was second and Chris Chataway fourth.

In September Gordon went to Cranwell in Lincolnshire for five months training as a ground wireless mechanic. Peter was an instructor in the radio school there and he remembers a particular incident a few weeks later: "I suggested we go for a run, but he said it was too wet." It must have been the last time that Gordon let the weather come between him and his training. But Gordon had chosen the Cranwell course for the same reason as Peter. "I opted for a radio course," recalls Peter, "because there was a good running track at Cranwell, and tracks were not very numerous then. Also, Derek Burfitt, who was a good runner from the Belgrave club in London, was there." If you were good at sport, you were released from duties when needed.

So Gordon settled into life at Cranwell for the winter of 1949–50. He did his technical training in a small wooden hutted classroom, passing without difficulty, coming out as Aircraftman First Class. He did his training runs around the old aerodrome and through the country lanes nearby. And in Warrant Officer Ernie Harrison, who was attached to RAF Swinderby nearby, there was an experienced runner who kept an eye on him to make sure he did not do too many long races. Then in February Pirie made his final move, to the RAF station at Watchett, on the coast near Minehead in Somerset.

Watchett was the base for the RAF Regiment, but also a gunnery school. There were four or five hundred men there, living in wooden huts, with a gym, a camp cinema and a NAAFI. Pirie was there until his discharge in June 1951. He lived in a hut with 15 others, a lino floor, a row of beds, each with its locker, a coke fire and a few pin-ups. Pirie had a photo of Zátopek by his bed. Pirie and the other radio men had to help train the gunners. An old Anson plane would pull a huge drogue across the bay, so the trainee gunners could try and hit it. Pirie's job was to get signals to the pilot. There were few drills or parades. It was an unexacting, low-key life.

Pirie was able to settle into some serious training. Peter Allis, who became one of Britain's best golfers and then a leading golf commentator, was in the next hut. "Gordon was always good company, but totally devoted to his running," he remembers. Allis has told the story of how occasionally he would run out of the camp with Pirie, take a rest in a field nearby while Gordon clocked up a few miles, and then run back in with him. The people on the gate never did understand why he was so fresh.

By the spring of 1950 Pirie was into a regular training routine. Most days he would train at around five o'clock in the afternoon, usually going out from the camp for a five or six mile run on the hills nearby. He would come back, do some stretching and shower. Then it would be over to the NAAFI to collect the pint of milk he had on order every day. He topped up the meals served in the camp with extra food he bought himself.

His hut mates remember him as approachable and friendly but someone who was focused on his running, and kept himself to himself. "He was perfectly friendly," remembers Bob Chapman, who was in charge of Pirie's signals group, "but when we went to a race he generally sat by himself on the bus, with his jar of glucose". Occasionally, when he went to bed early, his hut mates would come back from the pub and tip him out of his sheets. Ken Wilson, who knew something about running because he had been coached by Wooderson at the Lewisham track in London, got back from a weekend once without having his pass stamped. He passed it on to Pirie to use again. Gordon went up to London for a race – and brought Wilson 20 Churchmans' cigarettes on his return.

Pirie's family and club background had given him an excellent induction into the world of running. But had now begun to strike out on his own. "The athlete does not embark upon a sport but upon a way of life," wrote WR Loader. "That way of life is solitary and self-oriented." (*Testament of a Runner*, published by Heinemann, 1960). At Watchett Pirie adopted the disciplines that stayed with him for much of his life. He did not have to think much about work, food, clothes, because most of those decisions were taken for him. He had already decided to become a great runner. What he needed was a couple of years to put down the foundations. That is what National Service provided.

But it took time for Pirie to get the measure of what he wanted to do, and how best to do it. He was tall, by now over six feet, with a good stride but he was still relatively light, almost frail, compared to some young men of his age. He found he had the determination to train hard, but that he needed lots of rest. Peter Allis remembers Pirie saying that after a night's guard duty it took his body three weeks to recover. And success did not come easily. Just as he saw signs of progress, there would be a defeat.

The Southern Championships at Eastbourne in February 1950, was the first breakthrough. Two months earlier, in the Surrey Juniors, Peter had won a fine race, with Chataway third and Pirie fifth. But now Gordon turned the tables. Buoyed perhaps by his success on the Cranwell radio course, which he had just finished, Pirie produced what was, to that point, the best race of his life.

The course was flat and badly waterlogged in places. Harry Hicks, who won the senior race that day, remembers the water almost up to his calves in places. "Even the bridges over the ditches were under water – they had to mark them with posts so the runners could see where to cross." In the junior race Gordon and Peter went in front early on and they ran together for some time. Peter as always was the more relaxed and more stylish runner, Gordon working hard. Then, for the first time in a big race Gordon, only just 19, began to pull away from his brother and he held onto his lead, finishing 15 seconds ahead. Alick Pirie confided to friends that perhaps Peter was holding off the rest of the field to let Gordon win. But it did not feel like that to Eddie Ellis who was third. "I just couldn't get to either of them and I don't think Peter could get back to Gordon." What Peter remembers is that when Gordon went ahead he called to him to be cautious and then, finding himself

Surrey road relays 1952. Gordon hands over to Peter.
SLH

Alick and Gordon, 1950.
SLH

comfortably placed in second position saw no point, from a club point of view, in contesting first place.

But then, at the National Championships at Aylesbury a few weeks later, things went wrong. There was some expectation in SLH that this might be Pirie's year, that this time his increased stamina would give him the edge, even over Hesketh. But he looked stale, dropping back after the first mile and finishing 20th, a place lower than the previous year. Perhaps he was tired from the effort of running in both RAF and other races, often competing twice a week. The winner, of course, was Hesketh. He had had his own fill of service races, but had never looked stronger.

Pirie went back to the camp at Watchett. In their spare time the men he lived and worked with were doing ordinary things, going to the camp cinema, or to a dance in Minehead, organising passes to get home to see families and girl friends. But the social life had few attractions for him, he was barely tempted. Pirie had the option of easing back on his training, especially as some people were beginning to hint that he was over-doing it. Instead he decided that, if he was to have the beating of Hesketh, he had to work still harder at his running. All runners are spurred on by the deeds of their rivals and Walter Hesketh reflected later in life that "I was the stone on which Pirie sharpened his sword".

There were few practical obstacles in Pirie's way as he increased his training load. His working duties were light, he had few chores and drills, and his senior officers largely supported him in his running efforts. During the summer of 1950 he was able to combine his regular training with races for the RAF, and also for the club in South London and still, occasionally, for the bank. But there were more setbacks to come.

He raced mostly over the mile and won the RAF championship at that distance. But in the AAA championships, running for the first time on the track against the best seniors in the country, he could place only seventh in his heat. In the inter-services meeting, Chataway scored a decisive win, with Pirie third.

In the light of all this, and with nearly a year left in the RAF, what was he to do? He wanted to bring to an end the series of defeats that Hesketh, Chataway and others were inflicting on him. Chataway, he wrote later, was "haunting his thoughts." More than that, he wanted to get up to true international standard. That August, in Brussels, Zátopek won both the 5,000 and 10,000 metres at the European championships, and in the longer race lapped Frank Aaron, the best British runner of his generation. The gap in standards seemed to be growing. And Pirie, of course, wanted to succeed both over the longer distance and, if he could, at the mile.

Pirie had no coach. He respected coaches but he had found no one who really knew about distance running. He had begun at an early stage to read a lot about running but much of what he found seemed out of date. The classic "textbook", *Athletics*, written by members of the Achilles club in 1938 was still popular after the war. The chapter on distance running by E A Montague dealt first and foremost with style. It acknowledged that "long, gentle trots of up to six or seven miles across country are healthy." There was nothing gentle about what Pirie was doing.

But Pirie was also surrounded by talk of running in SLH and at home. Jimmy Green reported in *Athletics Weekly* on a discussion he had held with Gordon. "He thinks that only experienced distance runners are competent to advise on distance running; points out that there are in his club runners who, though not officially coaches

49

Inter-Bank champion-
ships, 1952 or 1953.
From left: Peter Pirie, Ian
Brodie, Gordon Pirie.
Ian Brodie

have 20 or 30 years experience behind them; and adds that he actually lives with a man, his father, who has been running for nearly 30
years. Men such as these, he says, are always worth listening to… but
he gives every piece of advice a lot of thought before adopting it…"

Reflecting on Pirie's defeats – by Hesketh in the winter, and by
Chataway in the summer – some people suggested that Gordon had
not got the balance right between training and racing.

Pirie reached a different conclusion. It was not that he was doing
too much training. He was still not doing enough. In the autumn of
1950 he stepped it up still further, running himself some days to
exhaustion on the hills and lanes around the camp. If he needed any
extra impetus it came at the Surrey road relays in September when
Chris Chataway ran ten seconds faster than Gordon and beat Peter
Pirie's lap record in the process.

Pirie described later in his own book *Running Wild* what he now
did to himself.

"I gradually with great effort increased the severity of my training. I ran longer and harder until my legs actually gave way. Many were the times when I had to lie down in the hedgerows to recover and then walk back to the camp because I was so exhausted. The winter was extremely wet, and the paths I used often turned to quagmires of mud, ankle and sometimes knee deep. I wore out a pair of shoes every week or so and had to tie them on with cords round the ankles, for many times I lost them in the mud. This cord kept them on but it cut weals in my ankles. There was terrible conflict between me and my body's exhaustion and the pain in my ankles." (*Running Wild*, Gordon Pirie, W.H. Allen, 1961)

Later in life he came to acknowledge that as a young man he had occasionally punished himself in training for losing a race. He knew that, about this time, in 1950–51, people were beginning to query the amount of training he was doing, what he referred to, in *Running Wild* again, as: "… my inflexible will to train to the physical limit, far in excess of what was considered safe." But in 1951 he began to find that the punishment paid off.

It began in the Surrey Juniors at Petersham. Pirie went ahead at the start and never let anyone near him, beating the second placed runner by nearly a minute over a five mile course. As a result he was picked to run as a senior for Surrey in the inter-counties race at Aylesford a week later. Hesketh had flu but Pirie beat a whole clutch of good senior runners, apart from Frank Aaron who won the race. Then at the Southern Championships, run over a six mile course heavy with rain, he finished two minutes ahead of the field. On the same day, Walter Hesketh won the northern event.

Pirie was growing in confidence. People now knew he would go out in front to win. The real target each winter of course was "The National", held that year at Richmond in Yorkshire on a dry and fast course that would normally suit Pirie well. But Pirie too went down with flu and barely had time to recover.

If Pirie was below par, Hesketh was at his very best. Walter remembers the occasion well. "Everyone was going on about how wonderful Pirie was. But the Sunday before the race at Richmond I ran a time trial on the track in appalling weather. I gave David Coleman half a lap start and my time was inside the British record for six miles. So I knew I was going to win on the Saturday." Although

Pirie took an early lead, Hesketh caught him on the first hill and raced on to take a lead he was to hold throughout the race, beating Pirie by almost a minute. A young runner from Longwood Harriers in Huddersfield, Derek Ibbotson, was 18th.

So, well as Pirie had run, it was again something of a setback. He may have taken some comfort from the commentary in *Athletics Weekly*. Hesketh, it said "… was in devastating form, which has come at just the right moment. That he will follow in Frank Aaron's footsteps there is little doubt. Gordon Pirie no doubt feels a little disappointed but it is no disgrace to be beaten by such a good runner and Gordon will give his rival a lot more trouble in the future…"

But the winter was over, and so, nearly, was National Service. Pirie had one important victory at the end of the cross-country season. He was chosen for a combined services team to run in an international event at Freiburg in southern Germany. Pirie won the race, beating a number of internationals. The start and finish of the race were at the university running track, close to the house where the coach, Woldemar Gerschler, lived.

In running terms Pirie had put his time in the RAF to good use. He did discuss with Bill McMinnis, a fellow runner and Physical Training Instructor (PTI) whether to stay in the RAF as a PTI but Bill felt Pirie did not have the all-round sporting skills to succeed in the job. At Easter Pirie wrote to the secretary of SLH saying there were "87 days to my demobilisation," suggesting his mind was turning to life at the bank again.

He was also thinking about the track, and whether he could carry his winter form through to the summer. There was much attention on the mile and particularly on Roger Bannister. In May of 1951 Bannister ran a three-quarter mile time trial, paced by Chris Chataway, in 2 minutes 56.8, suggesting a mile inside four minutes was within reach. Peter, who had seen Gordon's speed over the half mile as a boy, thought the mile was the distance where his brother could excel.

In fact Pirie tried a range of distances on the track that summer. He won the RAF mile and three mile championships and then he got an invitation to compete at the big early season meeting at the White City in May (The British Games). This brought him into contact with a different kind of company, the track stars. Among the

winners were all the post-war favourites: McDonald Bailey, Arthur Wint, Mal Whitfield and Bannister too. Pirie was in the two miles. Characteristically he led for the first six of the eight laps before Chataway and three others went past him. But *Athletics Weekly* was impressed. Pirie, it said, looked as though he could make an even bigger impression on the track than he had done already on the country.

But somehow all the work he had done had still not quite come to fruition. By June he was on demobilisation leave and back home in Coulsdon. It was nearly three years since he had seen Zátopek run and he was more convinced than ever that this was the man he wanted to emulate. Everything suggested that Zátopek was operating at a far more serious level than anyone in Britain. A report in *Athletics Weekly* revealed that the Czech runner was supported by a personal physician who was on the staff of the Department of Sports Medicine at Charles University in Prague. The university held

Chataway leading Bannister and Pirie in the mile at the Kinnaird meeting, 1951. Athletics Weekly/HW Neale

53

records of various tests Zátopek had undergone and monitored his physical well being. In his training programme sessions of forty 400 metre runs were standard. This was an approach to training unknown in Britain. Gordon was putting in a lot of work but, at this stage, he was still working the whole thing out for himself.

In an inter-club meeting at Chiswick Pirie ran in a mile race with Bannister and Chataway. It was huge field, and a slow race, which Bannister won in 4:16.2, with Pirie second, the only time the two of them met on the track. But the AAA championships were a more serious target and that summer Gordon decided to forego the mile and go for the two longer events, the three miles and the six. By chance, the six miles was run first.

This race was almost always the main track final on the Friday evening of the championships. Hesketh was also down to run. It would be the first meeting on the track of the great cross-country rivals from north and south. The really big crowds did not come till the Saturday but there was a good turn out of athletics supporters at the White City that Friday evening, most arriving straight from work. When the gun went for the six miles at seven o'clock, many of the other runners were clustered in their usual place opposite the steeplechaser barrier to watch. There was talk, *Athletics Weekly* reported, that Pirie was looking for a time of 29:20, well inside Frank Aaron's British record of 29:33.

Pirie did not adopt his cross-country tactics. He held back and let Bill Gray the Midland champion take the lead. He kept an eye on Hesketh and then, just before half way, moved to the front. At three miles the time was 14:40, spot on for 29:20. For three laps there was a struggle between Pirie and Gray but Gordon gradually established himself and then went further ahead. Hesketh made a brave attempt to catch him but Pirie stayed relaxed and finished strongly. His time, 29:32.00, just beat Frank Aaron's record and was less than ten seconds outside the fastest time for the distance ever run in Britain.

The next day, when there were 40,000 in the stadium, attracted in part by the prospect of seeing Bannister run, Pirie ran the three miles. It was a great race between Bill Beckett and Chataway (won by Beckett) and Pirie was fourth. He was the only one in the leading group to have run the six miles the night before. He had had a good weekend.

In the winter of 1950–51 he had become well known in the running fraternity because of his good runs over the country. But the six mile record was rather different. He got headlines in a number of papers because his was the star turn on the Friday night. Journalists tracked him down. His mother and father began to get phone calls. Three years earlier he had been a promising schoolboy runner. Now, still only 20, he held a British record. He had stuck to his guns and it seemed to be working. Doug Wilson in the *News of the World* was ecstatic. Britain, he thought, had found "its own Emil Zátopek".

Pirie was pleased with such praise, if wary of it. But the "quiet slim lad in the corner" was becoming much more confident about his running. Unlike many of his rivals he not only had ambitions but was willing to state openly what they were. For him, you could not get to be the best by pretending otherwise.

5 Helsinki

A week or two after Gordon Pirie's win at the AAA championships in July 1951 a bulky brown envelope arrived at his home in Coulsdon. Inside was his first international vest. The selectors had chosen him to run for Britain against France at the White City in August. Walter Hesketh received a similar envelope at his home in Manchester, and he, like Pirie, was to be in the six mile event. So the two rivals, or so they were seen by many, were to race together against the French in their first international.

Pirie was still only 20, back living at home with his parents after National Service. He was proud of his selection but could hardly believe it. And he was wary about showing off. He recalled later how he closed the bathroom door in the morning so he could try the vest on without being observed. Hesketh remembers putting his vest away in a drawer, lest it fade.

Pirie was excited. He had proved himself. But he knew where the real challenge lay – at the Olympics, which were still a year away. That was where the world-class runners would meet. That is where he wanted to be.

Nonetheless the match against France was a big event for both Pirie and Hesketh, running for their country for the first time. Some people believed Pirie was better suited to the three miles or even the mile, a view shared by Hesketh himself. But Pirie had made his mark more obviously over six miles and that was where the selectors felt they needed him most. Hesketh had a national reputation as a cross-country runner but his track performances had been largely in the north and had not registered so much with the London papers. In the *News of the World* Doug Wilson, himself a former international athlete, had suggested that Hesketh would be spurred on by Pirie's

Facing page: The young international athlete.
Ken Finding

57

recent victory over him: "He won't rest," wrote Wilson "until he has avenged this defeat." So Walter had a lot to run for, and he was always someone who could "turn it on" when he was psychologically prepared. In the event, he did so decisively.

The race took place at the White City on a wet Bank Holiday Monday. There were already puddles on the track at the start and conditions worsened as the runners cut it up with their spikes. The two Englishmen were soon in front and the lead alternated between them for lap after lap. The two French runners were all the time falling further and further behind, gradually losing sight of the leaders in the unrelenting rain. By mid race all four competitors were covered in mud, thrown up from the waterlogged track.

For the spectators, huddled in the stands, trying to keep dry, it was a question of whether Hesketh would get his revenge. Although the weather dampened the excitement of the occasion there was still great anticipation of a head to head between the two British runners over the last few laps. And indeed Hesketh and Pirie remained within a stride or two of each other until well past four miles. Then, on the 18th lap, the organisers announced over the public address system that they were within reach of Shrubb's long standing best time for five miles. Who would get there first? Groups of supporters were urging their men on.

Although Pirie was just in front at that point it was Hesketh who immediately increased his pace, and pushed ahead to reach the 20 lap marker as quickly as possible. Pirie made no immediate response and Hesketh forged on to win by about 150 yards, in a new British record of 29:13.8. Pirie, who had realised with a lap to go that he could not win, was over 100 yards behind. It was a decisive victory. The northerner had shown that he could beat Pirie, on the track as well as the country.

Pirie invited his rival back to Coulsdon for the night and Hesketh recalls a wry comment from Pirie on the way home: "My Dad might be a bit annoyed with me, Walter, for losing my record." But Hesketh found Alick and Marnie very welcoming and relaxed. Away from the track, Pirie and Hesketh were friendly enough but their athletic rivalry became more intense with each succeeding race.

Signing autographs.
Hildegard Gerschler

Pirie's period of National Service had come to an end in June, and in August 1951 he returned to a job with Lloyd's Bank. He had set his mind against working in the city again, finding it polluted. This time, instead of travelling to London every day, he got a post near to home in Croydon, in the Executor and Trustee Department. His brother Peter worked in the same building, but in a separate department. Gordon had a clerical job, dealing with paperwork at a desk, with occasional errands to other banks. He had reached his full height – 6 feet 1 inch – but was as thin as ever, only 10 st 8 lb. Life in the bank allowed him to train twice a day. At lunchtimes his long-legged gangly figure could sometimes be seen striding round the playing fields of the Whitfield school in the centre of Croydon, where a shopping centre now stands.

The bank was generous to him in providing time off for racing. Indeed, Pirie had only been back at work for two or three weeks when he was chosen (along with Hesketh again) for a British team that was to tour the Balkans, and Lloyds gave him a few days leave. So, all in all, he was quite well looked after. He may have felt that the University runners had a privileged position but Bill Gray remembers that to an ordinary club runner in Birmingham like him, "Gordon Pirie moved in the right circles."

In the team for the trip to Yugoslavia, Greece and Turkey, the selectors included Pirie with an eye on both the 5,000 and 10,000 metres. He now found himself alongside McDonald Bailey, Bannister and Chataway and the other internationals. It was an arduous tour, with three matches over seven days in hot conditions. The British Athletics Board took the unusual initiative of chartering a special aircraft to take the team to Belgrade and then on to Athens and Istanbul. There was little coverage of the events in the British press but it gave Pirie his first taste of the pressures of back to back racing, and his first experience of travelling with an international team. His performances gave some indication of his reserves of stamina:

August 26th	*first in the 10,000 metres in Belgrade (ahead of Hesketh)*
August 30th	*first in the 5,000 metres in Athens (where Beckett retired)*
September 1st	*second (to Chataway) in the 5,000 metres in Istanbul*
September 2nd	*first in the 10,000 metres in Istanbul (beating Hesketh again)*

The times were relatively modest. They included personal best times at both distances but he had rarely run the metric races before. However, he had performed well. A number of the team, including Bannister, picked up a stomach bug in Athens and suffered badly. Pirie had managed four long-distance races on the track in eight days.

Back home a week later he went out to watch the SLH 30 mile road race in Coulsdon. Another spectator was a promising young runner who had not long been in SLH, Michael Firth. Pirie suggested they go for a run on the Downs. Mick had no kit, but Pirie would never let that stop someone going for a run. "Gordon went indoors and found me a pair of cut-down RAF shorts and off we went. He went on ahead at one point and did a bit extra but he waited and joined up with me and then we went back to the house. He had a log in the garden which he used for weight lifting, so we finished off with a bit of that." Throughout his life, Pirie loved to encourage young runners.

The international races strengthened further his growing self-confidence. In September he got a further boost when he was included in the list of Olympic "possibles", athletes who were told by the British Board they were shortlisted for selection the following summer. It was little more than three years since he had been to the Wembley Olympics, but his determination to run every day, "like a machine", had paid off.

He was one of five listed for the 10,000 metres and one of 11 for the 5,000. It was generally assumed that three would be taken for each event, so there was still a lot to play for. But he knew he was among the most serious contenders. He began to tell people at work that he was preparing for Helsinki.

That autumn, as had become the custom, the athletics statisticians published the "ranking" for each event in Britain, showing the relative position of leading athletes on the basis of their performances during the previous summer. Pirie was showing well at a range of distances:

One mile	*9th (4:14.4 behind Bannister's 4:07.8)*
Two miles	*6th (9:15.4 behind Chataway's 9:03.8)*
Three miles	*3rd (14:03.0 behind Beckett and Chataway's 14: 02.6)*
Six miles	*2nd (29:32.0 behind Hesketh's 29:13.8)*

The longer the distance, the better Pirie's ranking. This reflected not so much his own abilities as the strength in depth in different events, and the amount of racing he had done at each distance. Pirie had little doubt that had he had the chance to run as much over the shorter distances he would have moved up the list there too. But it was hard to keep all the options open, since in preparing for different distances athletes needed to adopt a different balance of speed and stamina work in their training. It was a dilemma he was to continue to face throughout his career. In the meantime the published rankings reinforced the selectors' view that he was the man for the longer distances.

Pirie could reflect well on his progress but he knew what international standards were. Neither his three mile or six mile times, adjusted to their equivalent for the metric distances, would have put him in the top ten in Europe. That very month, September 1951, Zátopek produced two memorable runs in Czechoslovakia within a fortnight, twice beating world-best times for 20 kilometres and for the distance run in one hour. During the second of these two runs he passed the six mile point over 20 seconds ahead of Hesketh's British record, and then ran a further six miles at the same pace. British distance running, Pirie knew, was still in the second division.

Against this background he settled down to the hard graft of winter training, the long months of unrelenting work that he hoped might lead to Olympic selection. Tooting Bec had become his main venue for track work. Stan Allen was a promising schoolboy athlete at the time and had just joined Herne Hill Harriers. He remembers Pirie doing repetition runs on a very congested track, blowing out his cheeks in the way that earned him the nickname "Puff-puff Pirie":

"There were hundreds of us there and you had to arrive early to get a peg in the changing rooms. There were three or four arc lights, each giving about 80 yards of light to run by, but the rest of the track was pretty dark. We all used to stand about waiting for a gap to get onto the track, and in the middle of all this was Gordon churning out 440 yard runs. He was as thin as ever, with those scissor legs, and puffing away as he ran. He'd started wearing a woolly hat and before long half of us were doing the same."

The track at Tooting was open only on Tuesday and Thursday evenings in winter. Pirie began a habit, which he retained almost all his life, of doing hard training on those two evenings. Sunday mornings were reserved for the really long runs, often up to 30 miles out onto the Surrey hills and often with David Smith, Martin Crickmore and others. Sometimes there would be a long walk later the same day. "At times we covered as many as 40 miles in the day, just for the hell of it," Pirie would recall. In the autumn of 1951 he also began to run every morning for 30 minutes on the Downs before going to work, as well as training each evening. By the end of the year he had covered 2,700 miles in racing and training, 1,000 more than in 1950.

During the winter cross-country season the papers again began to talk of Pirie as an Olympic prospect. He had some good wins in minor races in the autumn and by the time of the inter-counties event in January, Pirie felt he could hold his own against anyone. Indeed, writing in the *Daily Telegraph*, the British team manager, Jack Crump, described him as "abnormally confident". It was a significant choice of phrase.

    If anyone was at the centre of British athletics it was Crump. His own sporting ambitions had been terminated by injury at the age of 20 in 1925. He got involved in athletics administration by arranging some races during a flower show organised by the local Ratepayers' Association. Before long he was acting as an athletics official for Surrey, and, steadily climbing the ladder, be became British and AAA team manager in 1937. As a Surrey man who knew SLH well, Crump was well acquainted with Pirie. Crump also had one foot in journalism. This dated back to the time when, as a young man, he had grown a moustache, added four years to his age and obtained a post with a new motor-trade paper.

    As Crump's position in athletics became more influential he began to write for national papers and magazines, often commenting on the performance of the very athletes he had helped to select and manage. Unlike some of the others involved at the top of British athletics, Crump's social origins were quite humble. But his position was a powerful one. He and Pirie often helped each other out, but they were to have a number of clashes over the years. Crump greatly respected Pirie's ability, not least in delivering the goods when running for an international team. But he had begun to register that the Surrey runner had an unfamiliar degree of self-confidence and assertiveness. Pirie was not someone you could boss around.

Jack Crump

The inter-counties race was held on the Rowntree sports ground in York and Pirie demonstrated decisively why he had such self-belief. He was clear of the field after 200 yards and no one came close to him. the *Daily Telegraph* provided an evocative picture of his performance: "There is now an ease and grace about Pirie's running suggestive of enormous reserves and infinite staying power. His breathing at the finish could barely have blown out a match."

There was already some discussion about the amount of training Pirie was doing, but the paper gave him encouragement: "He is so much a better runner for it that he should be allowed to go his own way." He dominated the southern counties race in similar fashion and he was ready now for the National Championships, where Hesketh would be running again. Surely, this time, Pirie would win.

Walter of course had won almost all the big cross-country events which he and Pirie had entered, and beaten Gordon every time:

1948 National Youths   *Hesketh 1st; Pirie 8th*
1949 National Juniors   *Hesketh 3rd; Pirie 12th*
1950 National Juniors   *Hesketh 1st; Pirie 20th*
1951 National Juniors   *Hesketh 1st; Pirie 2nd*

Now they were to meet for the first time in the senior event. Most of the predictions, in the London-based papers at least, went for Pirie: Jimmy Green in *Athletics Weekly*, Roy Moor in the *News Chronicle* and the McWhirter twins in their new monthly journal *Athletics World*. Travelling up to the Midlands with the SLH party, Gordon must have felt confident.

But Walter Hesketh was confident too. Pirie had beaten him over some of the shorter continental courses before Christmas but Walter's plan had been to build himself up fairly slowly over the winter with a view to being at his best in March. As usual he had been doing time trials on the track and these had been producing increasingly good results. He believed he could beat Pirie on the big day.

The course at Perry Barr in Birmingham was a hilly one, but dry. There was a good turn out of supporters from around the country, all with their favourites to cheer on but many excited most of all by the prospect of the duel between Hesketh and Pirie. In the senior race there were over 400 competitors and, as usual, Pirie did not hang about at the start. He pushed into an early lead taking the first half mile at a speed very close to Hesketh's own best for that

Hesketh leads Pirie in the National Cross-Country Championships at Great Barr, Birmingham, 1952. *Kevin Kelly*

distance. But Walter never let him get far away. There were varying reports as to who was leading after the first mile but they were undoubtedly close together and both inside 4 minutes 20 seconds, a quite reasonable time for a track mile at the time. And they still had over eight miles of undulating country to come. They ran on together for nearly six miles almost stride for stride. For the spectators clustered at key points round the course, it was a dramatic spectacle, watching at each turn to see who would appear first and trying to judge which of them, if either, was flagging. It was just before the seven mile point, on a large climb, that Hesketh edged ahead and then, sensing that Pirie could not respond, pulled away decisively. Pirie began to feel a tendon that he had injured in training and he never got back in touch, losing a lot of ground, nearly a minute in all during the last mile. At the finish, his foot was so sore he needed assistance to get away from the course. It was a great triumph for

Hesketh and he savoured it at the top of the final hill, where he paused and turned and looked at the rest of the field struggling after him in the distance. Among them, finishing well up the field in 85th place was his training partner, David Coleman.

So Hesketh had beaten Pirie again: five out of five in national cross-country championships. Walter's admirers pointed out that he could do it when it mattered. At the International Championships two weeks later, which Pirie missed because of his injury, Hesketh, in fourth place, was the first English runner home.

The cross-country season may have ended with a defeat but the winter's performances generally had been Pirie's best yet. He had every reason to think he would gain Olympic selection but there were doubts over which distance he would run. He was just 21, young for the 10,000 metres, (the six mile equivalent), but his cross-country form over even longer distances marked him out to the selectors as a tempting choice. As their long list of possibles for the 5,000 metres showed there was a much wider choice for the shorter race.

To complicate the issue Pirie produced two great runs at the White City in the first half of the summer, one over three miles and one over six. In the shorter race, at the end of May, he and Frank Sando had a thrilling tussle and both beat Sidney Wooderson's British record of 13:53.2. This was the record, remember, that Gordon, then a 15-year-old schoolboy, had seen Wooderson set in 1946. Pirie's time was 13:44.8, and Sando, who fell back only during the last lap, 13:48.0.

Wooderson's record was an honoured one, and for Pirie (and Sando) to break it marked some kind of watershed. It was a day on which many felt a new era in British distance running had begun. There was a wave of affectionate applause and cheering for both athletes. They were young runners who had come up through the ranks of cross-country and club athletics and the crowd was proud of them. And Pirie knew he was no longer just the best of the young stars, he was the new champion.

In no time the press were predicting that Pirie would do well in the Olympics. "There seems no question," said the *News of the World* "that Pirie is number 2 to Zátopek in the world over 5,000 and 10,000 metres." But Pirie knew what ground he, and Sando, had to make up. Zátopek's best time for the metric equivalent would have put him some 100 yards ahead.

All this increased anticipation of the six mile race at the AAA championships at the end of June, and raised the expectations upon Pirie. The final selections for the Olympic Games had not yet been made and Hesketh, Sando and Fred Norris of Bolton were all entered. Pirie had fine-tuned his training carefully and spectators were relishing a fine race between the top runners. Little did they know that two of them would almost come to blows.

Hesketh had lost some form through illness and was not at his best. He needed to prevent a fast race developing if he was to have any chance of finishing in the first three. But he had a problem.

"I realised within the first two miles that Pirie was going so fast that he was going to break the British record, and he was taking Frank Sando and Fred Norris with him. If I could slow it down there was still some chance of them putting me in the team. I got on the inside of the track and pushed Gordon with my elbows towards the middle. He was giving it back and we ended up in the third or fourth lane."

To cheers from the crowd, someone called for the track referee, Walter Jewell, who was in charge of ensuring that all races were fairly conducted. He had to make a snap decision as to how, if at all, to intervene. Jewell was in no doubt that he had to stop what was happening. Hesketh again: "He stepped right onto the track and warned us – 'Any more of that and you're both off…'"

Walter Hesketh's tactic did not work. Pirie got away, increased the pace, and although Norris came back to him for a while, Gordon established a lead of 30 yards during the last mile and finished in 28:55.6. He had reclaimed the British record from Hesketh. There was little doubt now that the selectors would want him – first and foremost – for the 10,000 metres at the Olympics.

Pirie was greatly encouraged by these races. He began to feel more and more confident that he had the beating of any of the English runners. He knew that he was drawing not only on his preparation that summer but on two to three years of sustained, demanding training. He must have reflected that his three mile time that summer was some 150 yards better than his previous best and his six mile time over half a lap better. He had been right not to heed the advice of those who told him he was over-doing it.

The races between Pirie and Sando and between Pirie, Hesketh and Fred Norris were also important to Gordon's wider reputation. They were classic duels and helped to cement the growing enthusiasm for athletics. And they set a pattern for the next ten years in which thousands of spectators would ask as they discussed whether to travel to the stadium: "Is Pirie running today?"

The AAA Six Mile Championship, 1952. Pirie leads Gray, Hesketh, JF Green and Sando.
David Thurlow

Helsinki had been waiting a long time for the Olympics. It had been awarded the 1940 Games and built a stadium, lost them because of the war and then lost them in 1948 because London was deemed a special case. So Finland was well prepared and one of the greatest distance runners of them all, Paavo Nurmi, was chosen to bring the Olympic torch into the stadium.

The selections for the British team were made amid the usual controversy. A young woman sprinter was omitted because (*Athletics Weekly* said) she was "rather young for what is a rather exacting distance for a girl." The distance was the 200 metres and the young woman was Shirley Hampton, later Shirley Pirie.

Pirie never felt part of the athletics establishment but to some in the north he was the beneficiary of a pro-Southern attitude by the selectors. Walter Hesketh, looking back over 40 years later, saw this as a part of a selection bias that had several layers: "A northerner will have to run themselves into the team, because they will always pick a southerner in preference. And we believed that they would always choose a university man over a non-university man, and of the university people Oxford and Cambridge over the rest."

The men the selectors chose for the two long distance events were quite a mix. For the 5,000 metres they selected Pirie, Chris Chataway and Alan Parker, who was from Barrow. For the 10,000 metres they went for Pirie again, Fred Norris and Frank Sando. So there were two northern clubmen, including a miner, and three, including an Oxbridge man, from the south-east. Interviewed by the local paper in Coulsdon Alick Pirie reminded the press that during the war all his sons had been rejected for evacuation to Canada because they were not considered to be strong enough.

Four years, earlier, just out of school Pirie had watched Zátopek at Wembley. Now he was likely to race against him twice within a week. Chataway had been at the 1948 Olympics too, taking himself off on his own to the first athletics meeting anyone in his family had ever attended.

In the Pirie household, the family was excited and hopeful, but realistic. Gordon's record over the previous 18 months had been a fine one but he was still only 21 and had little experience of international competition. He told anyone who asked him that he planned to win. He saw no point in approaching races in any other way. He knew the races were, as he put it later "the supreme test". But Peter Pirie could see the difficulties his brother was in.

Helsinki Olympic stadium.

"For some time before the Games people were on the receiving end of a great deal of expectation. It put them under a great deal of pressure. They not only have the competition to contend with but the other pressure too." From Peter's perspective, Gordon had been given far too much to do. "I threw up my hands in horror that he was expected to run the 5,000 and the 10,000. Why not Hesketh?" Peter's view was strengthened when he saw the schedules: the 10,000 metres final was on day 1, the heats of the 5,000 metres on day 3, and the final on day 5. Three big races in five days.

The press had certainly been pushing Pirie's chances for some time. As early as the inter-counties race in January the *Daily Telegraph* headline was: "Pirie raises Olympic hopes." Roy Moor thought

Pirie had the ability "to force Zátopek to the limit in both races," and that he would be in the first two in the 10,000 metres and fighting for a place with Chataway in the 5,000. The *Daily Express* saw Pirie as "the brightest of our many young stars". But those closer to the international scene were more cautious. The McWhirters invited four overseas "experts" to make predictions for both races and Pirie got few mentions. The favourites were Zátopek, Schade of Germany and Mimoun.

The British team had had an uncomfortable journey to Helsinki in an old Avro York aircraft but once they got to Finland they were impressed by all the arrangements. Pirie was struck by the clear and healthy feel of the air, and the excellent warm up facilities. There were friends around because a party of SLH members had travelled over to give support, not to only to Pirie but to another club member, Jack Parker, who was competing in the 110 metre hurdles event. Tommy Thomas, the club secretary, and John Jewell put their tent up on the island of Seurasaari, a mile or so from the stadium and within sight of the Olympic flame. They were there in their seats on Sunday July 30th, the first day of track competition, to see Pirie run, and they waited patiently through a total of 26 heats in other events before the time came for the 10,000 metres race.

At six o'clock, the runners assembled for the longest track race of the Games. Pirie had prepared himself well. He was in a clean, new British vest and shorts. His shoes were much used favourites, made for him by Laws of London several years earlier, the spikes worn down by all the racing he had done in them. But nothing can quite prepare a 21-year-old for a race against the most experienced runners in the world, in an Olympic Stadium.

There were 30 others in the race and they lined up three deep at the start. There was Zátopek of course who had quickly made friends with Pirie on the training ground and who wickedly wished everyone well as they waited; there was Mimoun, winner of the international cross-country in 1949 and 1952 and respected by everyone as a great runner; there was Alexander Anufriév of whom the Russians expected so much; and from England there were also Fred Norris, who had given Pirie a good race a month earlier in London and Frank Sando, who had first raced against Gordon in Kent when they were just 17 and still at school.

Helsinki Olympics. In the early stages of the 10,000 metres Zátopek leads from Mimoun and Pirie.
British Olympic Association

Pirie settled at the back of the pack, intending to keep an eye on Zátopek. An initial burst by Les Perry of Australia had helped to string the runners out in a line but Pirie was tall enough to see that Anufriév was leading. Then, as Zátopek began to move through the field, Pirie and Mimoun went with him and in the sixth lap Zátopek took the lead. The three of them were out in front and then Pirie went ahead and for half a lap he led the runners round. But it did not last. Zátopek quickly took control of the race, and began to reel out a succession of 70 to 71 second laps.

At first Pirie hung on. At the halfway point he was up with Zátopek and Mimoun and some 50 yards ahead of Anufriév, thinking he might just get a bronze. But the pace was telling. He began to lose contact with the other two, then on the 17th lap Fred Norris went past him, followed soon afterwards by Anufriév, Hannu Posti of Finland, Frank Sando and Valter Nystrom the Swede. Pirie struggled on gamely but he was very tired. He just got past Norris at the end and finished seventh. Ahead of him, Zátopek had pushed on from Mimoun and, helped by a last lap of 64 seconds, won by 100 metres in 29:17.0. Sando, running most of the race in one shoe, had judged the pace well and come through to finish fifth in 29:51.8, a

British record and faster, en route, than Pirie's six mile record.

There was some dispute about Pirie's final time but he was given 30:4.2 in the official records. Judged by his six mile time earlier in the summer he might have hoped for something 25 seconds or so faster. He had shown courage in trying to stay with the leaders but he had over-reached himself. He might have got a bronze medal had he run a different race, but that was not the race he was ever going to run. "I made up my mind to go and I had to stick with it," he told *Track and Field News*. Some of the press began to regret that they had mentioned him in the same breath as Zátopek. "What ever made us think," said the *Daily Telegraph*, "that Pirie would beat this superb distance runner?"

Two days later, on the Tuesday, Pirie had a good run in his 5,000 metres heat, leading all the way but qualifying without too much exhaustion. Alan Parker and Chris Chataway also got through to the final.

The prospect for the 5,000 metres final on the Thursday afternoon was all you could hope for. Not only were there Zátopek and Mimoun (gold and silver on the Sunday) but a clutch of fine runners who had not run the 10,000, including Reiff, Schade and Chataway. Pirie had gone to Helsinki thinking the 10,000 his best bet but he desperately wanted to salvage something from the 5,000. He decided he would try and take the field on about three laps from home. But he knew this was a really big race for a whole cluster of major runners. By the time the runners were called out on the track, he badly needed the race to start. It was easier to run than to wait.

The race began at 4.40 p.m. and it was much hotter than earlier in the week. There were over 60,000 in the stadium and large pockets of supporters chanting the names of their favourites, especially Schade and Zátopek. Schade was soon in the lead, with Reiff, Mimoun and Chataway not far off the pace. Pirie held back, at the tail of the field, watching Zátopek again and then moving through with him. When Zátopek took the lead during the second kilometre Pirie was in touch with the leading group and seemed comfortable. He maintained this position during the middle part of the race. Ahead of him Zátopek and Schade were sharing the lead, with Chataway and Reiff not far behind. Then in the tenth lap Pirie followed his plan and went in front. But it was a nominal effort. Zátopek and

Helsinki Olympics. Soon after the start of the 5,000 metres Schade leads from Chataway and Reiff. Pirie is tracking Zátopek at the rear of the field.
British Olympic Association

the others in the leading group soon passed him and bit by bit, Pirie began to fall away. By the bell, he was ten yards down on them and knew he was out of contention for a medal.

So there came that famous last lap, in which Pirie had only the most minor role. From the bell, first Schade, and then Zátopek, went in front but on the back straight Chataway swept past them and into the lead. He began to accelerate away from the field as British supporters had seen him do so often in races at home. It looked like a winning strike. But on the top bend he began to tire and in a few moments Zátopek, Schade and Mimoun were up to him and then Chataway caught his foot on the kerb and fell as they brushed past. Seizing his chance, and determined above all to beat the German, Zátopek found one more sprint and, grimacing more than ever, won the gold medal (14:06.6).

Pirie was some way behind all this, and concentrating only on finishing. "I can't remember the last two laps – I was in a little world of oblivion," he said later. In fact Pirie passed the injured Chataway, who had picked himself up and struggled on, just before the tape. This may have seemed ungentlemanly to some but he had only done what any runner would have done. The home straight of an Olympic final is no place for favours. Chataway and Pirie were given the same time, but Pirie was placed fourth and Chataway fifth.

If there was any doubt about Zátopek's position in the world of distance running his two gold medals settled it; and, just to underline the point, he won the marathon three days later. No one else has ever matched that feat.

There was the usual post-Olympics depression in the British press. But in fact the distance runners had done well: three in the first eight in the 10,000 metres and two in the first five in the 5,000. John Disley's performance in the steeplechase, where he took the bronze medal, was the best of the lot. He too had been at Wembley in 1948, and there he had seen all three British steeplechasers fail to finish in the first six in their heats. Sando's run in the 10,000 metres was the best ever by a Briton at that distance or its imperial equivalent. Chataway's performance in the 5,000 metres suggested he was a future star at the event. He, like Pirie, was only 21. "If anyone had told me at Wembley that in four years time I would be leading Zátopek on the final bend of the final, I'd have thought they were mad," he recalls. *Track and Field News* said that "the boyish looking student who trains as hard as any but likes to give the impression he doesn't," was the heir apparent of those who beat him. Pirie, they thought had run "with more guts than brains".

Pirie put it differently when he was asked about the Olympics some ten years later: "I was a young, skinny lad and I killed myself." (*Frankly Speaking*, BBC Radio, 1962). To get there was an achievement, and he had run, as he put it, until he was "utterly spent." But he remembered Helsinki for one particular reason. A surprise victor in the Games had been Joseph Barthel in the 1,500 metres, and there was soon talk about his training programme. At the airport, Pirie had the chance to meet Barthel's coach – Woldemar Gerschler – and they exchanged addresses.

Jimmy Green had perhaps got it right before the Games when he wrote that Pirie's youth and inexperience in this class of competition would work against him. When Pirie got home he told his local paper in Croydon that the national press had written "ridiculous tripe – they forecast medals and then blame the athletes".

He stepped up his training. It was what he had done before when things had not worked out, and he must do it again. He was young and his chance would come again. Other runners were older and were perhaps past their best. But there would be other young runners somewhere – in Hungary, or the Soviet Union, or Australia –

who would be training now for the Melbourne Olympics. Perhaps no one knew their names, but Pirie felt sure they were there.

And he needed to avoid distractions. He loved to socialise a little with other runners around the club scene. But he was determined not to get sucked into anything which would distract him from his mission. If he was to be at his best at the next Olympics, four years later, he had to start now, digging deeper. When he was invited to a presentation at a local cinema for Croydon sportsmen and women who had been to Helsinki he was the only one to decline. He had increased his evening run to two hours, he explained, and afterwards wanted nothing more than to go to bed.

6 Recognition

The summer of 1953 changed Gordon Pirie's life. In April he was a young man making a name in his sport; by September he was a household name. He did not turn down all the invitations he received in the autumn of 1952 after the Helsinki games. He gave a talk about the Olympics to the bank sports club at Beckenham, "keeping us enthralled for hours", remembers David Wykes. But his main concern was to step up his training again, responding to what happened at the Olympics as he had to earlier disappointments. That autumn he was running nearly 100 miles a week and it was a time when he did some of his training in what he called "ammunition boots", in an attempt to strengthen his legs.

He still lived at home and had the support an athlete values so much: kit washed, meals provided on a regular basis, sleep when he needed it. And the rest was important. His routine of early nights was not a fetish but simply something his body required. Peter Pirie again: "Gordon was an early to bed man from 1951. He had to get more rest because there was a lot of stress. He didn't decide to do it, he did it because he had to."[4]

His form was so consistently good in the winter of 1953 that it began to set him apart. He seemed able to run close to or at his best

---

[4] Pirie's approach has something in common with a rather different sporting figure, the great cricketer W G Grace. "Temperance in food and drink, regular sleep and exercise, I have laid down as the golden rule from my earliest cricketing days… The capacity for making long scores is not a thing of a day's growth… great scores at cricket, like great work of any kind, are, as a rule, the results of years of careful and judicious training and not accidental occurrences." (Quoted in *W.G.* by Robert Low, Richard Cohen Books, London 1977.) It is often forgotten that Grace – usually remembered as the great old man of English cricket – was a youthful prodigy, scoring a double century at the Oval just after his 18th birthday. He was also a keen athlete who, in the course of that Oval match, was allowed time off to travel to Crystal Palace to compete in a 440 yards hurdles race. He won.

at almost any time. Just after his 22nd birthday in February, he was back at Aylesford for the Southern Championships over the very course where he and Frank Sando had first met in 1948. Soon after the start they raced out ahead of the field and they matched each other stride for stride for almost ten miles before Pirie pulled ahead to win by six seconds.

There was no re-match with Hesketh in the national championships at Reading because Walter sadly was ill, and never really at his best again. Pirie ran most of that race on his own. By the half way point he was 200 yards ahead of the other 450 runners and he was so far in front at the finish that spectators waited in a strange silence for over a minute before the second man came in. A feature of Pirie's commitment at this time was that he not only trained hard when he lost, but when he won too. Victories in England were not enough, he wanted more. Next day he went for a 15 mile run and told Roy Moor of the *News Chronicle*: "You can't afford to rest in top class athletics, especially if you're after Zátopek's records as I am."

Two weeks later at the International race near Paris, he could not stay with the leaders, had trouble with his shoes and finished 19th. Pirie said later that he had been misinformed about the course and had worn spiked shoes expecting it all to be over soft ground. He then found there was a section over cobbled streets, so he took his shoes off and left them on someone's doorstep. The race was won by Mihalic of Yugoslavia, with Frank Sando second. Sando was always well prepared for this event. His placings between 1953 and 59 were: 2nd, 4th, 1st, 2nd, 1st, 3rd, 2nd.

Training with Laurie Reed (right) at Withdean Stadium, Brighton.
Laurie Reed

For two to three years Pirie had been steadily establishing himself. Now the picture was changing. People were accepting he had enormous potential and there were growing expectations every time he entered a race. The only debate was about how soon he would break this or that record. Jack Crump did a major profile of Pirie for *World Sports* at this time, assessing what he might achieve.

Pirie, said Crump, had "a mixture of the dourness of his Scottish ancestors and the grit and obstinacy of his native Yorkshire," and "an unusual degree" of confidence. He believed Pirie had the ability to become one of the world's great runners. But he thought he lacked the pace judgement or tactical sense of more experienced runners, with the result that he had lost races he might have won. He had yet to reach either physical or athletic maturity.

"Confidence", "grit", "obstinacy", even the suggestion of immaturity: this was a picture which was drawn again and again over the years. It owed something to the single-minded commitment which Pirie brought to his sport, shutting out of his life a host of everyday things which form an ordinary part of most people's lives. He had channeled all his reserves of fight and determination into his running and, whether training or competing, the inner resolve was there for all to see: someone never backing down, and never diverted from the task he had set himself, to "run like a machine".

There were those of course who noticed not Pirie's victories but his defeats. The string of races against Hesketh, the relative "failure" in the International cross-country. Some of these were reserving judgement on his long-term ability until they had seen more of him. Others simply disliked the attention he was getting.

He received more attention partly because he ran more races. In the summer of 1953 he seemed to appear everywhere. Pirie now had rather more say over when and where he would run and over what distance. Sometimes a little persuasion was needed to get officials to include him in particular races, but as the weeks went by and he made more and more headlines they began to need him more than he needed them.

Pirie was still experimenting across a range of distances. He was almost the only British runner that summer who was moving up and down between the half mile and the six miles, the 800 and the 10,000 metres. He was able to draw now on a great well of stamina, and speed, that he had built up through more than four years intensive training. But he was not just feeding off his training in races; he was learning how to race and getting better at it all the time. And, most of all, he had acquired a tremendous appetite for running.

Pirie had his first big chance to test his track form at the Southern Counties Championships in April. His cross-country form had been so good that there was talk of him going for the world record at six miles. That was not to be, but he took eight seconds off his own British record, so dominating a huge field of 38 runners that only Jim Peters could stay with him. "I was most surprised my run was so easy. I'm much more confident of the world record after that," he told the press. It was comments like these that made Roger Bannister refer later to Pirie's "startling frankness."

At the Whitsun Bank Holiday meeting in May, Pirie won the three miles inter-counties event on the Saturday, had a training session on the Sunday and then turned up for the international two mile race on the Monday, an event won by Chris Chataway. But in June Pirie was back at the stadium to beat his own British record for three miles. He now had a three week build up before the AAA championships.

He wanted one more crack that summer at the six miles, and there was even some speculation that Zátopek might be invited over for the race. Certainly many believed that someone, perhaps Pirie himself, had asked for a timekeeper to take his time should he run the extra lap or so to take him up to 10,000 metres. But the officials would not countenance this.

The world record for six miles, held by Heino, was 28:30.8. Over the previous two years Pirie had brought the British record down first to 29:32.00, then 28:55.6 and finally 28:47.4. He still had to find 18 seconds from somewhere.

It was not a problem. He was helped in the second and third miles by the young Scots runner Ian Binnie. Both went through half way in 14:02.6 seconds. This was the time of Chataway and Beckett's great three mile race in 1951, and even Pirie's greatest admirers could hardly believe it. Binnie inevitably fell back but Frank Sando, who as always had been running an even-paced race, joined Pirie for a while. In the last mile Pirie pulled right away and, as was the custom, runners who had been lapped moved aside as he passed them. He could not sustain the early pace but finished to great applause in 28:19:4. Hesketh improved on his own previous best time, but was almost lapped.

So Alick and Marnie welcomed a world-record holder home to Coulsdon that evening. There was much congratulation, but little celebration. Pirie had not finished his weekend's work. He was back at the White City by midday on the Saturday and in the afternoon he won the three mile event. Joe Binks, former world-record holder for the mile, was one of the most experienced athletics writers reporting for the Sunday press: "Such running in a boisterous wind so soon after his six miles is something I can barely understand."

As the summer went on, the expectancy grew, an expectancy fuelled by the headlines he was getting in the press. These had begun

Pirie's first world
record: Six Miles, White
City, 10 July 1953.
Kevin Kelly

with the 1951 British record over six miles, the race which had led
Doug Wilson to comment that "Britain had found its own Zátopek."
In the summer of 1953 Pirie seemed to be in the headlines every
week. He was, at first, "the 22-year-old bank clerk". Then the alliter-
ative phrases were wheeled out to try and capture him for readers.
"Shy, sensitive and sharp-featured," said one paper. "Lean and lanky,"
said another. As he became better known, the language became more
familiar: "Galloping Gordon" was a common one. But "Puff-puff
Pirie" was probably the nickname he was most often given in the
press.

There was little TV coverage but the big races were featured by Pathé and British Movietone news in the weekly newscasts shown in cinemas up and down the country. It was the large cinema audience of the early 1950s that first got to know the distinctive Pirie running style, and the puffing cheeks. He was quickly adopted as a popular figure, someone who, it seemed, could do no wrong. Now, for the first time, he began to be stopped in the street by well-meaning strangers who wanted to chat.

Performances need a stage of some kind and Pirie's arena was the White City stadium in west London.

The stadium was built in 1908 on a large site at Shepherd's Bush. It was part of a huge development of exotic, white exhibition halls – hence "White City"– constructed for an Anglo-French exhibition, but with that year's Olympics also in mind. After the Olympics it fell into disrepair, though Harold Abrahams would occasionally slip in there and train with his coach Sam Mussabini before the 1924 Olympics. The arena was taken over by the Greyhound Racing Association (GRA) in 1927 as a centre for dog racing in London.

In 1932 the AAA did a deal with the GRA and athletics was moved from its old home at Stamford Bridge to the White City. A new 440 yard track was built, inside the greyhound track, and athletics stayed there until 1971, when it moved to Crystal Palace. It was the success of greyhound racing, and the fact that until the early 1970s you could bet only "on course", not at shops in the high street, that made the White City such a going proposition and enabled it to host not just track and field, but equestrian events and big boxing matches too.[5]

In 1947 the London Transport authorities moved the local underground railway station, then known as Wood Lane, about 300 yards nearer the stadium and renamed it White City. Athletes and spectators could travel easily to the doors of the arena, in only a few minutes from central London and in a half an hour or so from the suburbs. All this helped competitors, many of whom travelled to White City on Saturday lunch times straight from work, and

---

[5] The GRA last used the stadium in 1984. They sold the land to the BBC, who subsequently sold it for development, and a big dairy firm now has a factory on the site.

especially those in the north, who sometimes left work at lunchtimes on Fridays and took the train down to London for a Friday evening race.

There was tiered and covered seating all the way round. There were good sight lines from the stands and a restaurant from which you could look out on the finishing straight. One drawback was that spectators were some way back from the track. Between them and the athletes was a level forecourt where some additional spectators could stand, then the greyhound track and then a fence. The arc lights that normally illuminated the greyhound track at night were wound down to almost ground level when an athletics meeting took place.

Athletes grew fond of the White City because it was the home of so many good meetings, and because it became a great place to meet friends in the sport. By the standards of the day the track was good, though it cut up badly in wet weather. Before competition athletes had to go down underneath the stadium and then, just prior to their events, they were led up a staircase to emerge into the main arena near the long jump pit. On one occasion in 1952 Freddie Green was kept waiting in the tunnel because of a cloudburst above only to find

County teams parade their standards before a large White City crowd, May 1954.
Ken Finding

when he finally emerged that his race, in which Pirie was one of the competitors, had already started. There were no real warm up facilities. Many athletes jogged round under the stands, a circuit of some 600 yards, dodging the spectators or greeting friends. Pirie astounded some of the old timers by sometimes leaving the stadium and taking a 30 to 40 minute run in local streets to get himself warmed up before his races.

The *News of the World*, which sponsored many of the meetings, would pay athletes' expenses, accommodate them where necessary and, for international meetings, arrange a formal dinner at the Dorchester Hotel. Gate money would go to the AAA or, in the case of floodlit meetings, usually put on by the *Evening News*, to a group of London athletic clubs who helped to organise meetings.

People poured into the bank holiday and floodlit meetings and for the really big events there was a cup final atmosphere. "Before the 1954 match between London and Moscow," recalls Chris Chataway, "not only was the stadium full but it was extremely difficult to approach it. There were mounted police on the streets and traffic jams out in Park Royal." That night, the stadium had to be closed, as it had been for the great race between Wooderson and Andersson in 1945, when the young Roger Bannister and his father found themselves pushing their way in.

Pirie and his contemporaries entertained huge crowds at the White City. And in the summer of 1953 it was the scene of his most unexpected triumph.

White City programme, 1938.
Ken Finding

Sir William Emsley Carr, owner of the *News of the World*, and a keen patron of athletics, decided to make his own contribution to ensure that the first four minute mile was run in Britain. He donated a trophy to be competed for annually by the world's best runners: "The Emsley Carr Mile". For the first running of this race, on August 6th 1953, attempts were made to secure the world's top names. For Landy it was out of season, and Bannister had made his great efforts in May. But the American Wes Santee, who had run 4:02.4, was recruited, as were Ingvar Eriksson of Sweden, Olaf Lawrenz of Germany and, from Britain, both Bill Nankeville and Chris Chataway.

There was talk of Barthel coming from Luxembourg but he dropped out, leaving a place at the last moment for someone not best known as a miler, but who was keen to run. Only the *Daily Tele-graph* took a lot of notice. "Pirie might just spring the surprise of the meeting," it thought. Chataway and Pirie were running so well that summer that, as someone put it, "they could draw a crowd for a wheelbarrow race."

This was the August Bank Holiday meeting and there were over 30,000 people at the White City. Before the race four record holders from the past – Joe Binks, Paavo Nurmi, Sydney Wooderson and Gunder Hägg – were paraded round the stadium in an open top car. With some ceremony the competitors were asked to sign their names in a special book, with a space left opposite for the winner to enter his name after the race.

There was great excitement in the crowd. Any of the six could win and there was every prospect of a thrilling last lap. Santee had not yet run in Britain but the fans knew something of his form because he had come close to four minutes in June, and was also fast over the half-mile. Chataway and Nankeville were both inside 4 minutes 10 seconds that summer. Pirie had a few weeks earlier improved his best time for the mile to 4:11.00 at a banks' meeting. On paper he looked to be slightly out of his depth. But he never entered a race for fun. In the week before the Emsley Carr Mile he went down to the Withdean stadium near Brighton with SLH friends to sharpen his speed. He wanted to get his name on the other page in the book.

So there he was lined up with the other five runners on the Monday afternoon. It was Lawrenz who took the group out, through one lap in 61 seconds, and through the half mile in 2:04.4, with the small field in file behind. On the third lap Pirie moved to the front and held his position until the bell, taken at 3:08.4. He was close to his best time but all the real running in the race was still to come.

Santee was just behind Pirie at the three-quarter mile mark and, as many expected, he soon moved past Pirie and led the field down the back straight. He came to the top bend, with about 150 yards to go still in the lead, but Pirie had stayed in touch. Many spectators had already seen Pirie win five or six races at the stadium that summer and sensed that he was not beaten. "Would you believe it?" his fans were saying in the crowd. "He's been winning races from the front all summer. Now he's going to try and nick this from behind."

Pirie gathered himself as they came to the finishing straight and Santee began to tire. As the American tightened up, and struggled harder to maintain his pace, Pirie started to gain on him. With 60 yards left he was drawing level, and all around people began to stand to urge him on. As they did so others did too, and within a few seconds the whole stadium seemed to be on its feet. At 50 yards, Pirie was past Santee and sprinting to the tape, looking more and more relaxed the nearer he got to the finish. His last quarter was run in 58.4 seconds, to finish in 4:06.8, with Santee some three yards down. Nankeville was third, some 25 yards adrift.

Pirie jogged in front of the stands, as the large crowd rose again to applaud him. It was a far cry from those National Service days, when he never seemed able to win, and drove himself over the muddy fields again and again. His supremacy was sealed. For now, at least, he was King of the White City

Santee of course had just completed a very tiring European tour – 26 races in 44 days said one report – and he had not beaten 4:06 seconds for a mile during that period. Looking back today he feels that the great demands the American college system placed on him to keep running races early in the summer had put him at a disadvantage.

But Pirie had run a beautifully judged race and in the process taken over four seconds off his best time for a mile. According to Sydney Wooderson, Pirie had proved that "long distance work – if done properly – does not impair one's speed." Joe Binks went over the top in the *News of the World*: "Hail Pirie – the British Zátopek." Pirie was "the most extraordinary runner the world has known."

Congratulations from Gundar Hägg.
SLH

Comments of this kind reflected the astonishment amongst an older generation at the amount of training Pirie was doing and the range of distances he was racing. Some, like Binks, implied that Pirie might be on the brink of breaking every record. Others thought he would burn himself out. Gunder Hägg who presented the Emsley Carr trophy to Pirie after the race said soon afterwards that Pirie's training would finish him off in two years. Peter Pirie's response to this was interesting. "Yes," he said, when a journalist put Hägg's remarks to him a few weeks later, "Gordon's training is too hard – for anyone except Gordon."

After the Emsley Carr race Gordon Pirie was known to almost everyone who followed sport in Britain and many who did not. The race also sharpened debate about his best distance. Peter never had

August 1953. Pirie wins
the first Emsley Carr
title. Behind him Santee
(obscured), Eriksson,
Nankeville and
Chataway.
SLH

any doubt that his brother had great potential as a miler. He had
thought this ever since he seen him run as a teenager. And he began
to think now that the four minute mile might be within Gordon's
grasp. "He knew this, because I told him so," recalls Peter. Gordon
himself was reported as saying: "This win has decided me to have a
go at everything in the future. if somebody took me round (he meant
in laps more or less of even 60 seconds) I think I could do a four
minute mile. All the same I prefer the three miles – you can run them
into the ground."

But British officials saw things differently. "It is as a three miler
and six miler that Britain needs Pirie most," said Jack Crump. Pirie
was never really to find out how good he could be at the mile.

White City, London,
September 1953. Pirie
hands over to Bill
Nankeville during a
successful attack on
the world 4 × 1,500
metre record.
Kevin Kelly

In August Gordon went with his SLH club mates on a visit to the
Norrøna club in Bergen. There began his love affair with Scandinavia, where he was to run such great races. And the town of Bergen
began their love affair with Pirie. The Norwegians resolved to get
him back in later years for one of the international meetings in the
town.

But in the autumn of 1953 there were still two internationals to
run for the British team, against West Germany in Berlin and against
Sweden in Stockholm. Pirie thought that, if conditions were right,
world records might be on. He began with the 5,000 metres in the
German match, on a track made sodden by rain during the day.
A slow second lap put him some way behind Hägg's world record
schedule and although he made up some of the ground he finished
4.4 seconds outside Hägg's time. It was a new British record: 14:02.6.

In Stockholm a few days later Pirie and Sando teamed up for the 10,000 metres. At half way Pirie was eight seconds ahead of world record pace but by eight kilometres he was tiring and he finally finished 14.6 seconds outside Zátopek's time, in 29:17.2. Pirie was very disappointed. In *World Sports* Harold Abrahams berated Pirie for not running his races at a more even pace.

Pirie had not quite completed this remarkable year. During the next month he broke the British 3,000 metres record in Oslo (8:11.0), the two mile record (8:47.8) and, in a team with David Law, Bill Nankeville and Ralph Dunkley, helped to break the world record for a 4 × 1,500 metres relay (15:27.2), improving a time the Hungarians had set earlier the same day. He finished his track season in Birmingham. Birchfield Harriers had started floodlit meetings before anyone else and they got Pirie to run a four mile race there on October 3rd. It was a little-run distance and inevitably Pirie produced a world best time (18:35.6).

In 31 races that summer, calculated *Athletics World*, Pirie had broken 36 records, counting those he had broken twice and including what are termed "world's best times" for unofficial distances. At one point he set, in the space of 12 days, new British records for two miles, three miles, 5,000 metres and 10,000 metres, an achievement no one else has approached.

Pirie was now getting on terms with the world's best. But he was assiduous in keeping in touch with the world of athletics. New rivals were coming on the scene all the time, and Pirie would have spotted the names as they emerged. One such was at the World Youth Games in August where second place in both the 5,000 and 10,000 metres was taken by a little known runner from the Ukraine – Vladimir Kuts.

Best Wishes to Woldemar
from Gordon Pirie

7 The coach

Pirie's achievements in the summer of 1953 owed almost everything to his own efforts. But he had some help, from someone he had met in Helsinki in July 1952, just after the Olympic Games had finished. The British team had arrived at the airport that day for the flight home at the same time as officials and competitors from other countries. There was a little time to spare and, in the spirit of friendship that the Games evoked, rival runners and coaches took the chance to exchange ideas. Among those mini conferences taking place was a small circle of middle and long distance athletes clustered around the man who coached the new Olympic 1,500 metres champion.

Woldemar Gerschler was the man who had coached Rudolph Harbig and in 1939 Harbig had set a remarkable new world record over 800 metres. Harbig was killed during the second world war. But at Helsinki Gerschler emerged into the spotlight again when his new protégé, Joseph Barthel of Luxembourg, won that 1,500 metres gold medal. In the airport lounge Chris Brasher, who had met Gerschler at the world student games in Luxembourg in 1951, introduced Roger Bannister and others to the German coach. The English athletes were particularly interested in how Gerschler had helped Barthel develop the capacity to handle a number of races in a short period of time.

Standing at the edge of this group, Pirie's interest was soon aroused. The German coach spoke quietly and with calm assurance, he used the vocabulary of scientific research and he spoke of people's potential. Just before his flight left, Pirie managed to get a few minutes with him on his own. They made an interesting contrast, the "young skinny lad", only 21, and the shortish, rather thick set, slightly professorial man, nearing 50. Yes, Gerschler could assist

Facing page: The young Gordon Pirie prepares for a training session on the Downs at Coulsdon. *Hildegard Gerschler*

him, but it could not be on a regular face to face basis, it would have to be through the post with periodic visits by the athlete to Germany. And Pirie would have to go to the University of Freiburg in southern Germany, where Gerschler worked, and take a series of tests, so that a programme could be devised that matched his potential.

The correspondence between the two men began in the autumn of 1952. As their exchange of letters developed, Gerschler pressed the Englishman for more information about his training and his programme of competitive races. By the early autumn of 1953, after Pirie's great season of races that year, Gerschler was getting impatient to see him. "I should like to see you in Freiburg," he wrote. "You know we have the modernst clinique [sic] for sportsmen, and it would be easier for you and myself to find the best schedule for you."

Pirie had put money aside to go to Germany and in October 1953, with £15 in his pocket, he made the long train journey from London, through France to Mulhouse in Alsace, and thus to Freiburg. It was not his first visit, because he had won the inter-services cross-country there in 1951. The thought of returning to the scene of that victory, and to an area he found attractive, may have been an additional impetus. But it was in 1953 that the friendship and collaboration between coach and athlete, which had begun at the airport in Helsinki, and continued through correspondence, was put on a new and lasting footing. If Zátopek was Pirie's greatest inspiration, Gerschler was probably, in the years after 1952, his greatest influence. The fact that he, the athlete, went to Gerschler, that he sought him out was important because Gerschler did not go looking for runners. The athlete had to take that first step. And Pirie made the commitment, referring to himself at that stage as Gerschler's "pupil". As he wrote later: "I put myself unreservedly in his care."

During that first visit to Freiburg, Pirie was asked to sit at a desk and take intelligence tests; he did work outs on a cycling machine and a treadmill to assess the capacity of his heart and lungs; and he ran on the track. Gerschler and his colleagues observed, measured and recorded everything.

The feedback they gave Pirie helped him make sense of the experiences he was having in training, to understand the physiological basis of what he was doing. In a radio interview at the end of the 1953 season, when he had just made his first visit, Pirie explained why he felt he had to go to Germany. "The main reason is that

Welcomed at Freiburg
after the train journey
from London.
Hildegard Gerschler

Gerschler is very scientific and he needs to know an athlete's physique
and mind personally. We had corresponded… but at the university
clinic he was able to give me a rigorous physical examination." (BBC
Sports Report, November 1953). Looking back at that period Sir
Roger Bannister comments: "There was nothing like that in England
at that time. Gordon would have got a better physiological check at
Freiburg than anywhere in England." And Pirie found out one thing
quite quickly. When most people take strenuous exercise it takes
their heart over ten minutes to recover fully. In his case it took three.

Woldemar Gerschler was Director of Physical Education at the University of Freiburg and had oversight of the sports programme there.
He was born in Meissen near Dresden in 1904 and after completing
his studies he worked as a secondary school teacher for several years.

91

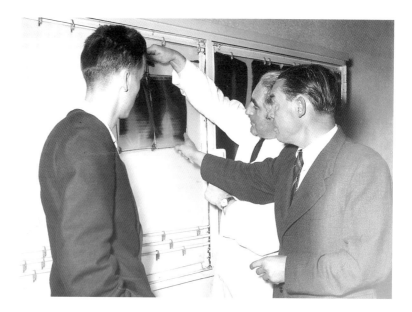

Woldemar Gerschler (right) and Professor Reindell look at X-rays of Pirie's heart with the athlete.
Hildegard Gerschler

He then became Director of an Institute for Physical Education at Braunschweig near Hannover. Gerschler conducted research about human performance with athletes and other sportsmen and women over a long period, beginning in pre-war days, before moving to Freiburg in 1949.

Gerschler and his family lived near the university running track and playing fields on the edge of the Black Forest. Gerschler's specialist expertise was in physiology but the strength of the set-up at Freiburg was the partnership he had built up over many years with Professor Herbert Reindell a heart specialist and radiologist, whose clinic was a couple of miles away. They collaborated in some of their work with psychologists from the university who were interested in the mental attributes of successful sportsmen and women. This multi-disciplinary approach was unknown in Britain at the time. The expertise developed was used not only with athletes but also in health work with the general population, for instance in researching ways of preventing heart disease.

But Gerschler's name is most often associated with interval training. This form of training had been practised, in different ways by different athletes, over many years. It has a number of distinct features: the athlete runs a specific distance, for example 200 metres; the distance is run at a pre-determined speed; the athlete then rests or jogs for a specific period of time; and the athlete repeats the fast run a pre-determined number of times. The distinct interest of Gerschler and Reindell was in how best to maximise the benefits of this kind of work out.

The research they undertook convinced them that the effects of interval training could be maximised by careful attention to the pulse rate of the athlete. Reindell's contribution to this was his work on the stroke volume of the heart, which indicated that it increases with the work load placed on it but reaches its maximum at around 120 beats per minute (bpm). He concluded that the heart adapted to increased effort by enlarging its own capacity, so that it could deal with increased supply at peak effort. It followed, he believed, that during the recovery period of an interval training session the heart not only recovered but developed. The distances selected, and the speed at which they were run, might vary from athlete to athlete or from day to day but the formula was constant. The warm up should raise the pulse to 120; the fast runs should be at such a speed as to take the rate up to about 180; the rest or jogging periods should allow the pulse to return to 120 within 90 seconds, at which point the next fast run should begin. It was this recovery period, the period during which the pulse rate was returning to 120, that really mattered.

From the autumn of 1953 onwards Pirie visited Freiburg two or three times a year, sometimes more often. Between visits Gerschler wrote to him with guidelines for his training, and with schedules that he could use. The schedules specified the "intervals" he should attempt, the repeat distances varying from 300 to 1,600 metres. On the day before, and after, race days he recommended no hard training, only jogging – but the training programmes themselves were tough.

The timing of Pirie's visits to Freiburg varied but they were often between athletic "seasons" or in the run up to major championships. Sometimes Pirie would have a competitive race in a meeting nearby to help assess general fitness; there would always be some sustained work outs on the track, often with Gerschler holding the watch and monitoring Pirie's pulse before and after each run, or taking an electrocardiograph after every fifth run; and sometimes more tests with Professor Reindell to check on general conditioning. George Reuschel, who worked at the Institute from 1952, recalls: "I remember Gordon Pirie training with the Director, Woldemar Gerschler. My job was to note the pulse rate, the distances run (for example ten

In the Gerschler's garden.
Hildegard Gerschler

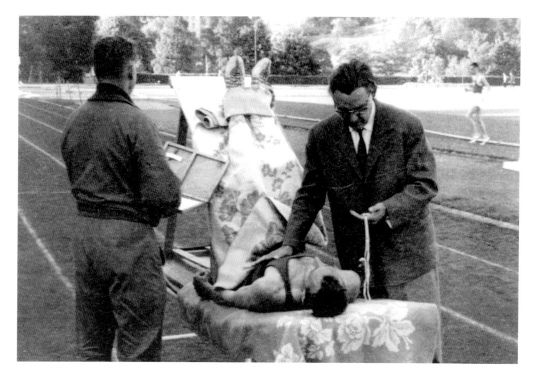

Mike Wiggs is tested by Woldemar Gerschler and Professor Reindell during a training session at Freiburg.
Mike Wiggs

times 100 metres), the recovery time, the weather, etc. I often drove with Pirie to the University clinic to see Professor Reindell, the head of the medical institute at the University. Competitive sportsmen and women from all over the world came to Freiburg principally because of the heart research."

Mike Wiggs, of Thames Valley Harriers who was guided by Pirie during the early part of his running career and who later broke Pirie's British record for 5,000 metres, paid a number of visits to Freiburg with Gordon. "Basically what we did there was to test out our different training drills, and agree on what we would do each week while we were away. We as athletes had to decide exactly what to do, in the light of our race programmes and conditions. Dr Reindell gave us a full test at the clinic and told us how we were shaping up and what we needed to work on."[6]

---

[6] Such tests and analysis were unusual in the 1950s. Today they are quite commonplace and some athletes wear heart rate monitors during training. Athletes can use devices which are strapped to the chest and which incorporate a stopwatch, heart rate display, upper and lower heart rate memory. The equipment also indicates the number of calories burned during a session. It does not make you run faster.

Pirie took note of Gerschler's assessment that his potential, particularly at that stage of his career, in 1953, lay over the shorter rather than the longer distances. In other words, he had begun his career the wrong way round, being saddled with running six miles or 10,000 metres for the team when he would probably have done better to concentrate on shorter distances. The balance between volume and quality, and between distance and speed, in his training began to switch towards quality and towards speed. There was, Pirie himself acknowledged, some loss to his great reserves of stamina as a result.

The main impact Gerschler had on Pirie in the first two or three years of their collaboration was this greater concentration on speed. Pirie began this process in the summer of 1953, undertaking more speed sessions on the track especially in the run up to the Emsley Carr Mile.

But there was no lessening of Pirie's commitment to an intensive, daily schedule of training. Indeed, his contact with Gerschler reinforced his belief that hard work, carefully planned, could take him to new levels of achievement. This meant a training schedule no British runner had ever attempted before. More than ever his whole life was revolving around running. Those brought up in a different school were often ready to challenge his approach. In May 1953, when Pirie was in the middle of a formidable training and racing programme, Norris McWhirter suggested in a London evening newspaper that his running had become listless and lacking in inspiration. "Would Pirie do better if he cut down his training to two days a week?"

The university men like Bannister and Chataway still spoke of their training in modest terms, and emphasised that they had other things they wanted to do with their lives. Roger Bannister had been asked a year or two earlier to write about his training in *Athletics Weekly*. He said he trained only three times a week and for 45 minutes at a time, and he was not able to say much about what he did because it all depended on how he felt.

This produced something of an outcry in the correspondence columns. Hadn't other athletes told their fellow runners what they did? Wasn't Bannister carrying all their hopes for the mile and the 1,500 metres and weren't they entitled to know how he was preparing for this? Bannister sat down and wrote a reply: he didn't want to set out exactly what his schedules were in case others, who were not suited to them, tried to ape them.

All this encouraged belief among some club athletes that "people like Bannister" (and Chris Chataway was usually lumped in here) weren't training enough or weren't being entirely open about what they were doing. In fact it was probably a bit of both. Bannister stepped up his own training a little after the 1952 Olympics, influenced in part by what was emerging about the preparation undertaken by Barthel, an indirect effect of the coaching Gerschler had undertaken. And Bannister was always doing a little more than he admitted. Chris Chataway recalls: "Roger went to great lengths to conceal the amount of training he did. It was a long time before I really understood that he did more than he said he did." At the same time Bannister and others – Chataway especially took this view – believed it was fast racing that really got you fit and that excessive training made you stale. Chataway tried running between 45 and 50 miles a week in training for several weeks in January 1952 but, he told *Athletics Weekly*, "… it produced boredom, tiredness and a tendency to get fit too quickly."

Of course, Bannister and Pirie were preparing for different distances. But there is no doubt that the early 1950s saw the final flowering of one tradition and the establishment of a new one. Chataway again: "When I got to Oxford and met Roger Bannister I rapidly fell into what is characterised as effortless superiority. We were anxious not to get too stale, but there was also a certain amount of intellectual snobbery. It would be impossible for thinking people, we felt, to spend all their time pounding out mile after mile. This was a hobby and we took pride in the fact that we weren't subjugating our lives to it."

Not all the university athletes took this view but inevitably they had things in common so tended to be friends. The Australians and New Zealanders, always quick to pick up any "Pommie" attitudes, noticed this in 1954 at the Empire Games, identifying it particularly with the Oxbridge athletes who ran together in the Achilles club. "The Achilles people did everything together. They even ate at a separate table," recalls Allan Lawrence, the Australian distance runner.

Pirie was taking things away from the amateur tradition – the tradition which had thrived particularly, though not only, in the

Pirie (right) takes an intelligence test.
Hildegard Gerschler

universities – just as sportsmen and women were in other sports. "If you don't do the training", he told a radio interviewer at the time, "you won't be the best. I train seven days a week, sometimes two or three times a day. I start with a one hour warm up, then put my spikes on and do repetition slow and fast runs on the track for an hour and a half and then a half hour warm down." In other words he was training for three hours a day. He was asked about the four minute mile. It was coming soon, he said, and he thought it could be done in 3 minutes 50 seconds. In 1953 this was an astonishing prediction.

World Sports invited leading distance runners to set out their personal training beliefs at the beginning of 1954 and Chataway put his view. He acknowledged the remarkable performances produced by the "sheer quantity" of work done by some athletes. But, he added:

"There remain a large number of athletes who either cannot or will not train every day throughout the year and who are not prepared to devote three hours to each training session. But I believe that a much more limited programme allowing, perhaps, an hour four days a week during the training months can produce good results.

"A careful balance between speed and stamina training, the maintenance of a fresh, aggressive attitude to racing, with a steadily graded increase in the intensity of work outs to produce peak form at the correct time, must be the characteristics of such a programme.

"It will never give the recovery rate nor the physical indifference to fatigue achieved by full-time devotion to training. But it may produce a fresher approach on the day of the big race – and that can, I think, be surprisingly important."

On the same page, Pirie took his stand, unrelenting in his commitment to the very highest levels of achievement, and hinting at what he was learning at Freiburg:

"To achieve a world's best performance in distance running during 1954 two qualities will be required by the athlete – superb physical fitness matched by superb mental fitness. To develop these qualities, the athlete must concentrate on training schedules unimagined a decade ago... the schedules of the modern distance athlete must be fantastic 'time and distance' devouring affairs, which will produce a 'machine' – not an ordinary machine but one capable of sustained 'plateau performance.'"

The differences in approach at that time were plainly set out. Within a year or two both runners could claim their views had been vindicated, but Chataway knew that the world was moving to a new approach. In 1955, when the Achilles Club revised again their standard book on *Athletics*, Chataway wrote "I have no hesitation in saying that the rapid general improvement in the standards of long distance running in Britain since the war is due solely to the acceptance of longer and harder training schedules."

Pirie was getting from Gerschler not only scientific assessment and testing and a new approach to his training, but also a sense of support and thereby growing confidence. Whatever the help Gordon had received from his parents, from Peter and from others in the athletics circle of the post-war years, he had done much of his pioneering work on his own. He had borne all the responsibility for deciding what to do himself, a critical load to carry on top of the physical work. He was once quoted as saying that "Gerschler does my thinking for me." Peter Pirie recalls the impact of the early visits to Germany: "Gerschler gave Gordon some confidence in the way he was going. Gordon was looking for someone who could advise him on training methods. Gerschler's role was to explain to him how he could maximise his vital factors, his lungs and so on. We were pushing up the threshold of achievement at that time." Pirie

told *World Sports* magazine in 1955: "Gerschler teaches you your body's capability – other coaches teach you how to run."

Peter Pirie remembers the coach–athlete relationship between Gerschler and Gordon as a "partnership of equals". It blossomed into friendship, helped by the hospitality Gerschler and his family showed to Gordon, and, later, to his wife. After he retired from competitive athletics Pirie continued to visit Gerschler, sometimes with athletes he was coaching. Gerschler spoke good English and almost faultless French. His wife had been a successful athlete. Peter Pirie went to Germany in 1955, in part to improve his German, and joined Gordon at Freiburg. "The hospitality was very good. I was going to stay in a Youth Hostel but they wouldn't hear of this – we lived as part of the family." Mike Wiggs and Pirie would often have tea with

Walking with Gerschler in the grounds of the University.
Hildegard Gerschler

99

the Gerschler family when the work outs were completed, and there they would all quietly talk over the findings and what might be done.

Gerschler visited the Pirie home at Coulsdon and learned more about the environment in which Gordon had grown up. "Gerschler was in London for a conference, I think, and came to the house," recalls Peter. "He went up on to the Downs where we did so much of our running. Once he'd seen the type of countryside he could understand what we'd achieved. He saw the kind of grass we were running on, the conditions under foot, the size of the hills – they were challenging but not impossible. He thought the whole area was visually attractive, and that was important to runners too."

Sometimes a fatherly tone surfaced in Gerschler's letters: praise, personal advice, and, just occasionally, rebuke. After the victory in the Emsley Carr Mile he wrote: "I am very proud of you! But, I hope, in spite of all these successes you will always be the same, the good sportsman." A few weeks later, when Pirie was disappointed about his races in Sweden and Germany Gerschler reminded him that he was still young and told him: "Be glad of it!" And, after an attempt to run a world best time on an unmodernised track: "If you have in mind to run the world record please prepare it much better in future. It is a nonsense to try it on a track of 350 metres."

Not everyone admired Gerschler, or thought he was good for Pirie's career.[7] Reservations were expressed in the press about a British athlete going abroad to seek help, and not just abroad but to Germany. Peter Pirie remembers that his father Alick was courteous and polite when Gerschler came to the house but expressed his reservations after he left. It was only ten years or so after the war. Later, when Pirie got to know the Gerschler family, he found that one of their daughters had been killed in the bombing of Dresden.

Some in the sport argued that since British distance running was so much in advance of German achievements at that time, Pirie might have done better to go to a British coach. In interviews Pirie was careful not to disparage British coaches but he pointed out that

---

[7] The 1982 entry about Gerschler in the standard German obituary archive, *Munzinger*, concluded: "The contributions of Prof. Gerschler to long distance training and medical care of top athletes are indisputable. Woldemar Gerschler was single-minded, possessed a trained eye for analysis of movement, was a teacher. He possessed a sense of mission, but he was also authoritarian and self-righteous."

Tea with the Gerschler
family.
Hildegard Gerschler

few if any of the small team of professional coaches had distance-running experience. Interviewed in Canada when he was running there with Peter in August 1955 he was asked what lay behind the revival of athletics in Britain. In his answer he paid tribute to the chief national coach. "If anyone deserves credit it is Geoffrey Dyson, he has worked magic, re-organising and developing an amazing programme."

There were other concerns. As reports came out of the intensive testing programme Pirie underwent in Freiburg, so foreign to British practice, there was some muttering that maybe Pirie was being used as a guinea-pig. This speculation may have been fuelled by the photographs in *Picture Post* of him undertaking tests in a laboratory with a mask on his face, and also by press accounts of what he said. Neil Allen, writing in *Athletics World*, reported that Pirie had told him that he was asked to pedal as fast as he could for as long as he could on the cycling machine and went on so long that Dr Reindell had to stop him. Bob Harvey, of Croydon Harriers, went to Freiburg in 1958 with Pirie and saw how demanding some of the exercises were. "Dr Reindell had Gordon on the treadmill and really worked him to exhaustion. I was standing there in my kit and I thought I was next on. Thankfully, just when my turn came, Dr Reindell announced that it was time for lunch. I didn't argue."

Pirie always stressed that the schedules he followed under Gerschler's guidance were arduous, and that he needed time to recover from them, but they were manageable. Years later he was fond of recalling that when he started on his sessions at the university track, full of energy and ready for some fast running, Gerschler would often be at the side of the track saying "Slowly, slowly…" And Gerschler's letters are consistent in the advice they give to combine hard work with sensible caution, advising rest the day before a competition, restricting training to mere jogging during a cold ("Be more careful…," he remonstrated at one point), and advising Pirie not to take his training sessions too far: "You can be tired but never exhausted."

Pirie implemented some of Gerschler's suggestions assiduously. For instance, the coach advocated a one hour warm up of very easy jogging before a work out on the track. When Neil Allen visited Pirie at Tooting Bec in November 1953 to watch him train, Pirie took Allen with him on his warm up jog, explaining Gerschler's advice as they ran. "We had left the dressing room at 10.48. We arrived back at 11.40 but in order to accomplish the full hour's warm up we jogged round for a further eight minutes." (*Athletics World*, November 1953.)

Something else was particularly important in the partnership between Gerschler and Pirie. It became clear to Pirie that the decisions he had felt impelled to take about his general life style, in particular his approach to work, to rest and to the routines of daily life, generally mirrored the philosophy of his German coach.

Gerschler may not have had day to day contact with his athletes, as some coaches do, and as Pirie had later with his. But he insisted on the need to know about an athlete's world, because other activities outside of sport can undermine the training, a conclusion Gordon Pirie had reached at an early age. Writing in 1956 of his work with rowers, but with reference to all athletes, Gerschler said: "An athlete's performance depends on his conduct during the period of rest… the way he spends his time, particularly his leisure hours, is vital in regenerating his ability to perform by day... Modern training is characterised by a comprehensive guardianship, strict routine and a planned arrangement of work, training and a way of life." When Pirie floated the suggestion that Gerschler might also be able to help the English athlete Don Seaman, the response was: "I should like to help Mr Seaman – but I must know him!"

Tony Weeks-Pearson, the Blackheath Harrier, had a number of discussions with Gerschler during the International Student Games which were held at Freiburg in 1954. He found that when Gerschler took an athlete under his wing he insisted on knowing all about the pattern of their everyday lives. "As proof of this he recited the daily routine of Gordon, which seemed to involve a knowledge almost as intimate as that enjoyed by his mother – what time he got up, had breakfast, how long it took to get to work, etc."

Gerschler also conveyed to the young Pirie something that Gordon had already begun to grasp intuitively, but not fully understood. That to train the body methodically, you had to free it from its inhibitions. To do that you had to free the mind from inhibitions too. This insight came to affect the way Pirie thought about the act of running itself. He became passionate in wanting to share the belief with others. And he developed a new and greater confidence in what he could achieve.

In 1953 Professor Reindell, the heart specialist who worked with Gerschler at Freiburg, estimated that Pirie showed the capacity to develop and run the 5,000 metres within three years in a time of 13:44, some way below the then world record. Soon afterwards, when the press asked Pirie what he thought he was capable of, he suggested 13:40, a time that to experienced observers seemed almost unthinkable. It was a measure of the contribution the Freiburg team made to his development as an athlete that Pirie was able not only to reach this time but surpass it.

THE SOUTH LONDON HARRIERS' GAZETTE
and
Club Chronicle.

FOUNDED 1871.

No. 1 Vol. LXIV   Edited by D. B. GRAYER, under the sanction of the Committee, and published by W. D. THOMAS, 8, Morella Road, London, S.W.12   **Dec., 1949/Feb., 1950**

EXECUTIVE

PRESIDENT—C. J. G. Hughes, 13, Selcroft Road, Purley, Surrey (Telephone: UPLands 1566).

HON. SECRETARY—W. D. Thomas, 8, Morella Road, S.W.12.

HON. ASSISTANT SECRETARIES—F. J. Frost, 50, Agincourt Road, N.W.3; C. E. Puddicombe, 8, Dover House Road, Roehampton, S.W.15 (Telephone: PROspect 1450); G. E. H. Roots, 56, Woodside Road, S.E.25.

HON. TREASURER—L. A. Pool, 25, Beech Avenue, Radlett, Herts.

HON. EDITOR—D. B. Grayer, "Crooklets," 1, Highbury Close, New Malden, Surrey.

CROSS-COUNTRY CAPTAIN—W. C. Young, Warren Lodge, Warren Park, Warlingham, Surrey (Telephone: Upper Warlingham 212); VICE-CAPTAIN—P. J. Pirie, 7, Meadway, Coulsdon, Surrey (Telephone: Downlands 3786).

TRACK CAPTAIN—A. T. Liffen, 57, Montholme Road, S.W.11.

COMMITTEE—C. F. G. Aldridge, H. A. Hathway, J. G. Harris, C. G. Herniman, S. R. Hill, H. B. Holder, J. C. Jewell, H. F. J. Read, P. D. Robinson, G. H. Sykes, C. H. Watson, J. C. H. Willett.

CLUB FUNDS.

Subscriptions, due on 1st October each year, are at the following rates: 15s. for members over twenty-one years of age; 10s. for those over eighteen but under twenty-one years; and 5s. for those under eighteen years on the date when the subscription was due.

Donations to the *Gazette* Fund will also be welcomed by the Hon. Treasurer.

25th FEBRUARY

THE SOUTHERN
(SENIORS, JUNIORS and YOUTHS)

AND THE SOUTHERN SUPPER
at
EASTBOURNE

COME AND SUPPORT OUR TEAMS

Travel by Coach—see page 2

(Coulsdon Hall will be closed)

11th MARCH

THE NATIONAL
(SENIORS, JUNIORS and YOUTHS)
at
AYLESBURY

(See page 2)

(Coulsdon Hall will be closed)

25th MARCH

CLOSING RUN AND SOCIAL
EMPIRE GAMES FILM

1st APRIL

BRIGHTON RELAY
(SOUTHERN CLUBS ONLY)

Come with us to Brighton and support our team on the way

Leave Mitcham approximately 11.30 a.m. Reserve your seat now from the Track Captain. (Take a sandwich lunch with you.)

Return coach fare, 8/6.

We want to fill two coaches

8 The club

Travelling abroad to compete in international races or to see Gerschler brought new friendships and opened up new possibilities. But much of Pirie's running was still rooted in the life of South London Harriers. His years in the club, he always acknowledged, were the basis of his athletic success.

Club life was not only about running. It also had an important social dimension with its shared occasions during the year. Important among these was the first gathering each autumn, when people would come together for a new season. September 27th 1952 was one such day. It was a quiet, sunny afternoon and over 60 people were present for the club photograph on the Downs. The opening run was a gentle one led on this occasion by the club President, Alick Pirie, and captain, Peter. Gordon, who had done his serious training in the morning, jogged round at the back of the field, chatting to everyone. More members of all generations arrived for tea and then there was a social in the clubhouse in the course of which awards for the previous season were presented by Mrs Pirie, as President's wife.

The evening provided an opportunity for laughter and banter. Gordon, very much a joker when relaxed and with friends, liked to join in. There were songs and dances, and a magician. Then Gordon, along with Peter Pirie, Mick Firth and Peter Driver, dressed themselves up in club kit, past, present, and future. They set out a little catwalk in the hall and paraded like models before their cheering club colleagues.

But membership of South London Harriers was also about competition and about rivalry with other clubs. The club had, and still has, a tradition of cross-country running and the pinnacle of the

Facing page: Front cover of the *SLH Gazette*.

SLH club photo, 1956. Alick front row in kit; Peter centre of third row. (Gordon in Melbourne.)
SLH

winter season for the best runners was the National English Cross-Country Championship, "The National". This more than anywhere was where Pirie helped SLH make its name.

In Pirie's day, and for some time afterwards, the men's races for The National were held on the first or second Saturday in March, the women's a week later. The numbers competing were large, often four or five hundred in the senior race, and well over a thousand finishers in total in the three men's races, seniors, juniors and youths. All the best runners from England and many of the best from Scotland were there and top club runners would give an arm or a leg to get in their club team. To come home first was a matter of the greatest pride, both to the individual and the club and for many years the first nine home in the men's race were chosen to form the team for the International race two weeks later. If you got into the top 20 or so you had a chance of being picked for a representative team in races at home and abroad which were much prized.

In the 1950s the senior race was over nine miles or so –old timers describe it as "a long nine – good value for money," and it was generally run over three laps. Nine men could run for each club, which entered the race, and of these nine the first six home scored in the senior team competition. Juniors' and Youths' events both involved teams of six so that big clubs might have as many as 21 runners competing on the day.

Spectators who organised themselves well could see the runners pass five or six times and get some notion of the drama of the race as it unfolded. Unless there was a Pirie or a Hesketh killing off the field, there might well be a leading group of ten or 12 at the front early on, down to five or six at half way and then two or three people struggling to assert themselves over the final mile. All the way down the field there were races within the race as clubs fought it out for team positions.

In the immediate post-war years the national cross-country courses were generally over a mix of heavy, uneven grassland and ploughed fields, sometimes with ditches to jump. On a muddy day the ground became increasingly difficult as the runners came round each time. In the 1957 event at Parliament Hill in London the first mile and a quarter became a quagmire of mud and water six to eight inches deep.

And facilities were sometimes fairly primitive. Alan Brent of Blackheath Harriers ran in a number of the 1950s events and in later years was championship secretary, and also President of the English Cross-Country Union. "I remember at Bromford Bridge race course in 1949, the first year that Hesketh won the junior race, we changed in horse boxes and when we got back after the race we had to wash down in little tubs in the stable yard. In 1954 at Birkenhead we had a school to change in but we had to bathe in canvas water tanks out in the school playground. They had screens round the tubs, but it was a snowy day and windy and the screens soon blew down – it was excellent entertainment for people watching from nearby houses."[8]

Pirie's involvement in cross-country went back to his childhood: it was the earliest type of running he did. There was always, and still is, debate among athletes and coaches as to whether a runner can combine top class performance over the country during the winter with success on the track in the summer.[9] Pirie thought you could, but nonetheless he knew that he had to make a choice about the balance between stamina and speed in his training. Soon after he began to write to Gerschler he sought his advice about cross-country and the advice he received was unequivocal:

[8] Ferdie Gilson suggests that these tanks were probably the canvas "sportapool" dams originally issued to the fire brigades during the war.

[9] Looking back on his career in 1999 Sebastian Coe put his view: "... Winter is a good natural protector. You shouldn't run that hard or quickly all year round." (*Athletics Weekly*, 20th January 1999)

"It was my habit as a cross-country runner to settle the question of who would win as early as possible..." (Pirie). *Susan Prout*

"I don't like the cross-country races for a competitor who is one of the best of the summer races [sic]. It is not possible to be the best in the winter and in the summer. Only one of it is possible. You need the whole time in the months of October till May for the training, still more you need the whole strengths for this training. By the competition in winter you are loosing too much strength. . . the preparation during the winter must be accompanied by rest and not by hard competitions." (letter to Pirie, 27th June 1953)

A few weeks later, cautioning Pirie against the idea of running the indoor circuit during the winter Gerschler returned to the same point: "For every athlete there is only ever one season, never two." On this front, it seems, Pirie did not share Gerschler's view. In the winter of 1956 Pirie however had to abandon much of his cross-country running because of injury. In the following summer he had the best track season of his life, but he did have several seasons of good cross-country work to draw on.

Pirie won his first "National" title in 1953, in what was his sixth race in the championships over different age groups. Once that victory came, he promptly repeated the performance not once but twice, in 1954 and 1955, starting each race at a murderous pace. "I was well known during those years for destroying the competition with insanely fast starts," Pirie wrote towards the end of his life. "It was my habit as a cross country runner to attempt to settle the question of who would win as early as possible, leaving everyone else in the field to run for second place." (*Running Fast and Injury Free*)

In 1954 the race was held at Arrowe Park, Birkenhead, and a day or two before Pirie travelled up by train to Warrington, where he was met by Bill McMinnis, his old running chum from RAF days. By this stage Pirie had already become quite fussy about what he ate. Like his father he would chat to anyone about athletics, but he had no illusions that he was becoming well known. "He had his honey with him, and all he wanted for breakfast was some nice thick bread to put it on," recalls Bill. "I'd told the lad next door that Gordon was coming so he came round for his autograph, and Gordon invited him in for a natter. They sat talking for a couple of hours. Next morning, the day before the race, Gordon went down to the main road to hitch a lift to Birkenhead so he could run round the course and get the feel of it. I was worried he might not get picked up. 'Don't worry Bill', he said, 'they'll know me – I'll get a lift in no time'."

The Birkenhead course was a relatively flat one with only gradual slopes and Pirie covered the opening half mile in just over two minutes. Most of the other top runners thought he had got away but the young Ken Norris, who had begun to distinguish himself on the track in 1953, did not give up. Here was another young runner who had been inspired by the 1948 Olympics and had come up through the club ranks, this time under the tutelage of Alec White at Thames Valley Harriers. Norris caught Pirie and ran with him for a while. But Pirie pushed ahead again at around three miles and finished over half a minute in front of the field. Norris was second and Frank Sando third.

In 1955 the championship was organised at RAF Cardington, Bedfordshire in the shadow of the two great airship hangers. John Lyne, a contemporary of Pirie's in SLH teams for many years, remembers the day and the course: "We had to change in big wooden RAF huts but Gordon managed to find a storeman's room where the SLH team could change on their own. He saw I had the wrong shoes for the ground and lent me a spare pair he had with him. It was flat course but there was plenty of rough grass and one stretch of very heavy plough, it was muddy and fairly heavy and there were some quite deep ditches to cross."

Leading Frank Sando
in the Southern Cross-
Country Champi-
onships at Aylesford,
1953.
David Thurlow

This was the test of stamina and pace that Pirie enjoyed. And let
there be no doubt about what was involved. To run fast for nine
or ten miles is one thing. A number of the best club runners could
do this. But this was not roadwork, with an even, predictable surface – this was rough country, potholes, furrows of mud, all breaking up the rhythm of your stride, jarring the body and sapping its
strength.

It was a windy day and the runners stood shivering in their pens
at the start. Pirie looked ominously well prepared. Hair short as
usual, SLH vest over a long sleeved top, (with brown paper between
the two to help keep the wind at bay), trimmed shorts, his cross-
country shoes laced up with fastidious care, he stood a little apart
from the team, limbering up. As soon as the gun went, he was away
from the field, escaping at speed from the great mass of runners
behind him. After 30 seconds, he was 20 yards clear of the rest of the
field, hundreds of runners in narrow formation behind him, the
back markers already struggling with the conditions. He stayed
ahead for the full nine miles. When he lost a shoe at six miles, he
simply discarded the other one and ran the last part of the race in
bare feet. His victory margin was 26 seconds. This time Pat Ranger
was second and Ken Norris third, of 462 finishers.

These were important team days, which brought distinction to
SLH. They were now becoming very much the top club in British

cross-country. Peter Pirie's victory in the Youths' race in 1947, Gordon's series of races against Hesketh, and then his great wins in 1953, 54 and 55 helped to raise the profile of the club. The two brothers, with Mick Firth and John Lyne, formed the backbone of the team that won the seniors in 1955, and Firth and Lyne were also members of the SLH winning team in 1957 and 1958.

Inspired by Gordon Pirie and the others, a new generation was also coming through in the club; they included Roy Darchambaud, Ferdie Gilson, Roly Langridge and Laurie Reed. SLH won the Youths' race in 1954 and 1955, and the Juniors' in 1955 and 1956. Most remarkably, in 1955 SLH won all three men's titles – Seniors', Juniors', and Youths' – on the same day. It was a unique achievement, and one that was regarded with some awe, and envy, across the country.

Tommy Thomas, club secretary and team manager, marshalled the support around the course, ensuring that club members knew where to stand to have the greatest impact. And he also ensured that messages were passed to the club's runners, informing them how Gordon and others were doing, and what extra effort was needed to keep the club in front. "We've got four in the first 20," he might stay to encourage those further back to press even harder for top places; "Stay ahead of the Coventry man," if a close tussle was developing with another club.

Peter Pirie captained the team from 1951 to 1956, and was twice in the first 25 to finish. He inspired great loyalty, so that club runners found themselves running for him as well as the club. Mick Firth remembers his support and influence. "He taught us youngsters a lot – things like how to take fences, and he would also help us sometimes in races by running alongside and pulling us through the field, rather than going to the front himself. He had a calm authority and we all respected him." Peter's rivals must have been glad he never trained as hard as his younger brother.

The three consecutive victories that Pirie had in The National in 1953, 1954, and 1955 were important in cementing his reputation within the sport. Not only was he racing successfully at international level on the track but he was taking on the great body of outstanding club cross-country runners at their own game and leaving them in his wake. During those years the position was clear: in England, over the country, he was unbeatable.

Tommy Thomas, SLH club secretary for many years.
Kevin Kelly

If The National was the prestige race of the cross-country calendar, the National Road Relay from London to Brighton was the nearest event on the road. It was run just a few weeks later, on a Saturday in April before the main track season got fully under way. Coaches would come with runners and their supporters from all over the country and even at the height of his international career, Pirie hated to miss it. "What is this 'road relay'?" Gerschler asked once. "Must you run it?" When Pirie explained, he responded: "It would be a great mistake to disappoint your friends. Run the 'road relay' and stand with them wherever you are." And that is what Pirie did.

Twenty clubs usually entered the race and each had to provide a team of ten or 12 runners to cover one leg of the road between London and Brighton, a total of 54 miles. The legs varied in distance and in terrain. The shortest were just over two miles and the longest over six; some were flat and others undulating. The winning team was not simply the one with the fastest runners but with those most skilfully matched to the demands of individual legs, bearing in mind the psychological advantage of taking a lead. Peter Pirie remembers the challenge SLH faced in choosing the team in a strong club with many desperately keen to run: "It was very important to make the correct selection for each stage. You had to be dead sure that the 12th was the 12th best and not the 13th. Our success came because the guys knew that if they dropped off the pace there would be someone to replace them next time… "Jack Heywood recalls that in Herne Hill Harriers competition to get in the team was intense: "We seemed to talk about nothing else for weeks."

This was another *News of the World* sponsorship and the relay began at the paper's sports ground in Mitcham for many years. The race start was moved to central London in 1954. The first two runners took the baton from Westminster Abbey through Clapham Common to Mitcham. Then they moved on through suburban London to Purley, the beginning of open country, then through the centre of Redhill. Down into the Surrey and Sussex countryside they went, on the arterial road built in the 1930s, on through Crawley, and then some testing, undulating stretches through Handcross and Hickstead. Finally, on the last leg, the lead runner had a police motor cycle escort to take him from Patcham past crowded pavements to the sea front at Brighton. Says Ferdie Gilson: "In my running career there was nothing to compare to that moment."

Pirie on the Brighton road.

Many of the country's best middle and long distance runners ran in the National Road Relay over the years.[10] The event produced not only great battles between clubs for the overall trophy but great individual contests within the race as runners struggled to keep their position, or sought to cut down the lead of the man in front. Chris Chataway ran for Walton Athletic Club: "It was just about the most exhilarating race I ever ran. If you were on the last lap it was unforgettable, running down hill those last three miles you felt you were absolutely flying, you'd go round a corner and there was another runner, you'd get past him and then start to chase another. It was an amazing experience."

It was most of all a club day. Gerry North was a fine young distance runner from Blackpool, who had moved south after completing National Service in order to get better competition. He had a number of fine runs in the relay for Belgrave Harriers. The slogan

SLH winning team London to Brighton relay, 1955.
Left to right.
Back row: Mick Firth, Colin Wilson, John Lyne, Johnny Prince, John Humphreys, Roy Darchambaud, Phillip Ll Morgan.
Front row: Peter Driver, Peter Pirie, F T Thew, Gordon Pirie, Ray Ashworth.
SLH

---

[10] Increased traffic flows began to cause problems for the event in the early 1960s and the National Road Relay was last run on the London to Brighton road in 1965. The equivalent event is now held in Sutton Park, Birmingham.

on their coach was "Gerry and the Pacemakers" . "For some club runners," says Gerry, "making the team was not just the highlight of the year, but the highlight of their running career". George Knight remembers the importance of the event to Essex Beagles. "I think the London to Brighton really held a lot of clubs together – it seemed to unite the whole club. Track people would come along in the coach. The half-milers would train hard and aspire to do the short leg. It was a great social occasion as well as a hugely exciting athletic event."

The 1954 race was one of the best with SLH favourites to win. The club had puts its strongest runners, Gordon Pirie and Peter Driver, in the second half of the race and needed its early men to stay in touch with the leaders over the opening legs. The general view was that Belgrave would take the lead early on and that if they could get two and a half minutes up by leg seven they might be able to hold off Pirie and Driver. But Peter Pirie and John Lyne upset those plans by fine runs on legs three and five.

Pirie took the baton at Lowfield Heath and faced a new six and three-quarter mile stretch through Crawley to Handcross, a combination of two shorter legs used on previous races. His target was Charlie Smart of Belgrave – no mean runner himself – some 90 yards ahead. Bit by bit and mile by mile he caught his man and then on the hill up from Crawley pulled away to give Driver a lead of over a minute. Despite great runs by marathon runner Jim Peters for Essex Beagles and Alex Olney for Thames Valley Harriers, SLH got home first. Pirie's time for his long leg was faster than the combined records for the two old stages. (A year later it was beaten by his old rival Frank Sando.)

So in 1954 SLH were second in The National and winners of the London to Brighton. The following year they went one better and won both, and Pirie was in all four races. It's no surprise that when he signed his autograph he often wrote: Gordon Pirie – South London Harriers.

9 Celebrity

During the 1950s no man or woman in British sport made headlines more consistently than Gordon Pirie. Crowds flocked to the White City to see him run. Pirie was never hiding in the pack of runners, somewhere down the field. He ran to win. When he took the lead early he liked to do the job properly, "grinding 'em" he called it. When he was a place or two back, he was always ready to pounce. And then there would be that powerful lengthening of the stride as he drove towards the finish.

By the end of 1953 he was the best known athlete in Britain. In recognition of this his wax image joined those of other celebrities on display in Madame Tussauds. The Amateur Athletic Association made Pirie their "Athlete of the Year." There was widespread coverage of his achievements, not just in the daily press but in the large circulation magazines such as *Picture Post*. The cinema newsreels made him familiar to millions of people who never went near a stadium. Like a film star, he was instantly recognizable in the street. Almost everything he did was deemed to be newsworthy. For a while his races in local events received more coverage than some national events in which he was not competing. The press wanted to write about what he ate, what he drank, when he went to bed, his hair cut. Everything about Gordon Pirie was news.

Soon, Pirie found he was being stopped in the street by people who wanted to greet him. He tried to be courteous, but all the encounters took time. After he received one award from the BBC, a film crew came to the bank and filmed him turning the pages of a ledger. He was interviewed on *Woman's Hour*, he appeared on *What's My Line?* And as the publicity grew so Pirie became more and more public property, and he began to be appropriated for purposes that went beyond sport.

In 1953 sportswriters named him, along with Alec Bedser, Don Cockell and Henry Cotton one of the four sportsmen to have contributed most to Britain's international prestige. In 1955, in a poll by *Daily Express* readers of their "Personality of the Year" Pirie was voted into fourth place behind only Princess Margaret, Churchill and Eden. At one civic reception, the local MP told him: "You carry far more goodwill among foreign countries than most British representatives. You are not only a great athlete but also a great national asset. The goodwill that you have created abroad will help our ambassadors." Pirie was not keen on these wider social ramifications of fame. To him it was how good a runner you were that mattered. But his successes were important to other people for all sorts of reasons.

His first great run of races had a particular resonance in a country emerging from war and from austerity. Hazel Ryder came into international athletics through a local club in Surrey at the same time as Pirie. She remembers it as a special period. "We'd been through the war and gone without things. We'd lost friends and relatives. Then there was the rationing after the war. When things started happening in London we had to make the most of them. Looking back now, Gordon really epitomises the best of those times."

Pirie would have been pleased that people held that perspective. But his approach to being an athlete was more personal. "I run," he said once " to prove myself to myself." (Article by Pirie in *The Road to Rome*, published by the International Athletes Club, 1960).

He had to establish himself in a family of runners, of which he was the youngest. "His father and his brothers had been there, and he wanted to prove he could do it," recalls Martin Crickmore, who was a regular training companion with Pirie for a number of years. Gordon knew that his brother Peter was a better natural runner and that he, Gordon, would have to work hard to reach the same standard. But he believed that if he did add a lot of hard work to his talent he could be the best. To get that hard work done he had to isolate himself for much of the time and put himself first.

In early 1954 Pirie was in the news for another reason. Newspapers made great play of reports that he was considering an athletics scholarship to a college in the USA. This was the route a number of young athletes were taking to pursue their careers in sport. The story caused

Leading Kovács of Hungary in a cross-country near Brussels, 1954.
Hildegard Gerschler

some alarm. The public had just taken possession of this new hero and it was clear from letters to the press that they were not ready to let him go and live overseas.

"One cannot blame Gordon for thinking of going," said an editorial in *Athletics Weekly*. "He has almost reached saturation point as far as time for training is concerned." Yet, although the arrangement would certainly have given Pirie more time for athletics, he was not convinced that he would be able to race when and where he wanted and he did not follow it up. It was decision he later regretted.

Pirie was exploring the boundaries of amateurism. He did not see athletics as something you excelled at briefly before you went off to earn a living, as some of the best university athletes did. Nor was it only an enjoyable leisure interest, to which were added the social dimensions of club life, as it was for his brother Peter. For Gordon it was the thing he was best at, and something in which he could excel. But to do well at an international level, and not just within the confines of British athletics, was difficult.

From 1953 onwards he found it increasingly hard to manage both the demands of a full-time job and the demands he placed on himself as a runner. He became increasingly dissatisfied with the way the sport was run, and the rewards it offered. "If I was a brilliant mathematician," he said to Derek Johnson a year or two later, "I would be able to make a lot of money. Why can't I make money from being a brilliant runner?"

Advertisement for running shoes, *Athletics Weekly*, 1952. No mention of the star runner's name.
Athletics Weekly

Many of the other sports stars Pirie met were professionals, and the most successful could supplement their wages by endorsing products. The man advertising Litesome socks on the back of *Athletics Weekly* was not Pirie or Sando, it was Len Hutton, the England cricket captain. The man endorsing the hair gel Brylcreem on the back of *World Sports* was not Chris Chataway but another cricketer, Denis Compton.[11]

Athletes by contrast were not allowed to make a penny from running. They could claim the costs of travel to and from international meetings at the White City, and some out of pocket expenses on overseas trips but they could not be paid for races. The rule was broken from time to time of course, but it was applied quite rigorously during the first half of Pirie's career. Manufacturers of running shoes would mention that their shoes had been worn in a particular record-breaking race but not say who had worn them, because that would have infringed the athlete's amateur status. At this stage Pirie was assiduous in observing the rules. The *SLH Gazette* reported regular donations to club funds of the fees Gordon received for appearing on radio and TV programmes, for example the £3 he was paid for an interview on the radio programme *In Town Tonight*.

Pirie's own contacts with shoe manufacturers, notably Adidas, began at this stage but they were never lucrative. He first met Adi Dassler, one of the founders of Adidas, through Herbert Schade the German athlete who ran in the 5,000 metres at Helsinki. Dassler offered Gordon a pair of the red spikes Schade had worn and Pirie used Adidas shoes for the rest of his career and made a number of

---

[11] Compton received £1,000 a year from the Brylcreem advertisements; 40 years later the young soccer player David Beckham was said to be getting £1 million for endorsing the same product.

suggestions to the firm about how shoes could be improved. But he received no endorsements or sponsorship.

At this stage, in 1953–54, Pirie wanted to remain as an amateur but by the end of 1953 he was beginning to look at alternatives to working full-time at the bank while he tried to become a world class athlete. Pirie could see that, like his East European and American counterparts, he needed some kind of special arrangement which enabled him to train at a high level and get plenty of rest. Pirie always acknowledged that Lloyds treated him well, so much so that, although he was well liked by his colleagues, there was, remembers Henry Teague, "a measure of good tempered resentment among us because we had to do his work during his frequent absences to attend athletic meetings away from the area."

Derek Collins, another SLH member who worked for Lloyds, recalls how the bank tried to persuade Pirie to stay. "He was asked to an interview in Lombard Street where I was working at the time and he called in on me beforehand. I understand that it was suggested that he might go to the Bank's training centre at Hindhead where Bill Sykes was the bursar [Sykes was another SLH member]. The routine there was that one worked nine to 12, lunched, worked four to seven, dinner, then further work. This would have left the afternoon free." It seems likely that Lloyds also offered Pirie the chance to work at the bank's sports ground at Beckenham where he could have flexible hours for training. But neither of these openings was quite what he wanted.

In the end a journalist obtained for Pirie an opening he felt would suit him best. In the spring of 1954 he began work as a sales representative for Wilkinsons, a medium size paint firm in South London. The firm hoped that his "name" might help with sales. They gave him a car (his first, an Austin Somerset) and came to an arrangement about his working hours which gave Pirie the freedom to train in the way he wanted. He told a conference of coaches a few months later that he worked for Wilkinsons each day from 8.30 a.m. until 4.00 p.m. This allowed him a three hour training session before seven in the evening; he could eat at 7.30 and go to bed two hours later. Few people believed he sold much paint, but for a while the arrangement with Wilkinsons suited everyone.

All the attention put Pirie's personality under the spotlight. He had from the start chosen his own way of doing things, and it had brought him success, and fame. He displayed an apparent self-confidence. But it was hard for him to please everyone, and there began to be friction between him and officials and also with the press. Journalists without a background in the sport who tried to interview him in the immediate aftermath of a race found he could be distinctly spiky. He found it particularly frustrating to be asked ill-informed questions about his races by people who had no knowledge of athletics.

Many of Pirie's races were over the longest distances and he ran many of them at the front. They required careful preparation beforehand and then great concentration during the race itself. Afterwards Pirie needed protected time to regain his composure and ensure a proper recovery. All this meant he had to separate himself out from others. It was the only way he could do it. He did not want the additional burden of official receptions and the like, sometimes requested of the British team.

Track and field athletics is a sport which is governed by detailed rules and regulations. It is a way of ensuring fairness. But Pirie often found the rules were interpreted rigidly and no allowance was made for the needs of individual athletes performing at a high level. Tommy Thomas, the SLH secretary, sometimes found himself acting as a buffer between the demands of officialdom, of which he was a part, and the needs of his club's most outstanding athlete.

Once for example, he received a pompous and long-winded letter, written as if some great secrets of state were involved, about some transgression of the rules which Pirie was said to have committed. It transpired that Gordon had failed to return to the "competitors' enclosure" immediately after a race. What he had done, of course, was to jog round to wind down. Thomas managed to persuade the administrators of the sport that the matter was best dealt with by a quiet word. But after a number of these incidents Pirie began to feel that some people were out to get him.

Jack Crump had a soft spot for Pirie but he had marked him down as a potentially difficult customer fairly early on. He began to find it difficult to cope with Pirie soon after Gordon came onto the international team. Crump was generally discrete enough not to talk to one athlete about another but he confided to Walter Hesketh

Advertisement in
Athletics Weekly, 1953.

one day in 1953: "The trouble with Gordon is – he's got such a swollen head." Hesketh himself had already begun to find Pirie less approachable, more and more in his own world. "There was the team – and there was Pirie." Press interest added to the problem, because when Pirie did find time to talk to journalists his teammates were sometimes kept waiting. Frank Sando, who never found it difficult to chat with Pirie, remembers that, after the Stockholm run in September 1953, the whole team sat on the bus for some time while Pirie finished some interviews.

Pirie's apparent self-assurance was in marked contrast to the unassuming demeanour adopted by many sportsmen and women of his day. Albert Agar worked at another department of Lloyds in Croydon but in the same building. He knew about sport, having been an international rugby player but he found Pirie "cocky and arrogant" about his running. What was the phrase Jack Crump had used in 1952, "an unusual degree of confidence"?

Pirie was well liked by most runners who knew him. Indeed, his solid club background and loyalties made him something of an "athlete's athlete". And Pirie himself enjoyed the company of athletes, and sharing stories about the sport. He often invited them to join his training sessions, and many did. Fellow-runners understood why he was obsessive about his training and preparation. Most of them were obsessive to some degree too. That was what being a distance runner was all about.

They also knew that he was opinionated. In October 1954 *Athletics Weekly* persuaded him to supply the answers in their "Questionnaire column". Asked to include brief details of his athletic career, he included every race he had ever run. He added a number of suggestions for improving the organisation of meetings: "have a new set of young officials" and "remind officials they're there to serve the athletes and not themselves." Athletes might go on strike when the facilities at meetings are poor, he suggested.

All this was "pure Gordon". A week or two later a Surrey official wrote to *Athletics Weekly* to put Pirie in his place. "I don't pay 9d a week for four and a half pages of Pirie… if his attitude ever becomes popular it will be time to pack up and hand over to professional promoters." But however provocative Pirie's remarks may have seemed he was developing some serious and constructive views about the sport. In 1956 he argued the case for a Ministry of Sport

"Pirie the problem athlete".
World Sports, 1955.

and for a national centre through which profits from meetings could be ploughed back into athletics.

Pirie had a lot of time for sportswriters who knew their sport, but he distrusted those who came from outside to write about athletics. Fabricated stories were a particular bone of contention. Henry Teague, who worked at the bank in Croydon with Pirie, recalls: "I was with Gordon on several occasions when he was interviewed fairly informally by various journalists and on many occasions he was mis-quoted or quoted out of context so that a contrary view was implied. The British press seemed to go to great lengths to cook up antagonisms between him and other athletes." Dennis Crookes, a cross-country veteran with Blackheath Harriers, remembers another incident after a cross-country match between his club and SLH. "After the race the reporters were hanging round Gordon and he told them to clear off because he wanted a bath. He never spoke to them that day, but one paper still carried an interview with him in the morning."

There is no doubt the press capitalised on Pirie's willingness to speak his mind and he felt he was sometimes tricked into providing headlines he did not want.[12] Some sportswriters, on the other hand, felt that he quite valued the publicity he was getting. It all began to get to him. He deeply resented the way he was sometimes presented to the public, and at points it led him to consider giving up the sport. On occasions however, he chose to answer back.

In December 1955 the *Daily Mirror* flung a banner headline across its back page:

"The poison in the heart of Gordon Pirie." Pirie, wrote Peter Wilson, was a man of "overweening conceit". His speech, at a cele-bratory dinner, was "mawkish, intolerable and outrageous rubbish". The article appeared to reveal a well of pent up antagonism. "I for one am sick and tired of trying to cover up his arrogance when he wins and his excuses when he loses." Peter Wilson was the journal-ist who secured for Pirie a job with the Wilkinson paint firm.

---

[12] In a television interview in 1998 Steve Ovett, the British athlete who twice broke the world record for the mile, acknowledged that after some bad experiences with journalists early in his career, he decided never to talk to them again. Asked if there was anyone in the media he trusted at the time, he replied, "No, no one".

★ PETER WILSON *on why he stormed out of last night's big event*

THE POISON IN THE HEART OF GORDON PIRIE

LAST night, among the lush comforts of London's Savoy Hotel, Gordon Pirie was announced as the Sporting Record's tenth annual Sportsman of the Year and also as B.B.C. television's "Sportsview" personality of the year.

Pirie clearly found nothing to quarrel about in this double award to himself.

Then, after he had been presented with the Sporting Record award by Iain Macleod, Minister of Labour and National Service, Pirie made what I consider to be one of the most unpleasant, ungracious and utterly outrageous speeches it has ever been my misfortune to listen to.

WHAT RUBBISH!

Among other things, he pointed out that neither he nor Don Cockell had been selected as sportsmen of the year by the Sports

☆ Gordon Pirie and show jumper Pat Smythe, the Sporting Record's Sportsman and Sportswoman of the Year, with their trophies last night. Pirie was also named as the B.B.C. Sportsview personality of 1955.

What a cracking start by MCC— openers top 100

By BRIAN CHAPMAN

GOOD news from Pakistan! True, Young England failed to force the win against Karachi Cricket Association.

tings, staved off any fear of Karachi's defeat.

But Peter Sainsbury's left-arm slows earned him three for 24. That should give the Hampshire boy stacks of confidence.

The *Daily Mirror*, December 1955. *Mirror Group*

The dinner in question was held in the opulent surroundings of the Savoy Hotel in central London and the occasion was the presentation of two national awards. One was from the *Sporting Record* for Sportsman of the Year and one from the BBC for Sports Personality of the Year. There was a full house, sportswriters, sportsmen and women, TV executives, and sports legislators. Under the arrangements for the *Sporting Record* award journalists first met and agreed a short list of seven names, with a recommended winner, in this case John Disley, the steeplechaser. The names were put to the public, who were invited to send in their choice, if necessary nominating an alternative to the preferred seven.

Pirie was not on the short list for the *Sporting Record* trophy. His star, so high at the end of 1953, had fallen somewhat. He had had two major setbacks at the White City, both in big six mile races. Quite unconnected incidents, but two years in succession, it was enough for some people to write him off. Once personalities are established in the public eye, of course, failure can seem to be as interesting as success. Pirie's great successes in 1953 had raised great expectations of him. When those expectations were not fulfilled he discovered that only one thing made as much newspaper copy as success and that was defeat.

But in the second half of 1955 he had come back, and regained his place in the psyche of the sporting public, most notably by a resounding victory over his old rival Emil Zátopek, just a few weeks before voting began for the two awards. When the votes were counted he was in first place – for both. So he went to the dinner to receive them.

When Pirie stepped up to take his trophies, the hubbub of voices in the great dining room of the hotel began to subside and, as he prepared to say a few words, there was quiet. He spoke of his surprise at winning and the thrill he got from the occasion. Then, as he went on, the silence in the room seemed to deepen. "Public opinion has vetoed sportswriters' opinion," he said. "Fleet Street sportswriters do incredible damage to British sport. In an Olympic Year they should boost not denigrate British sport. A few unkind words will inflict more damage than they realise. I hope they will be kinder in the future." As he sat down, one person could be heard clapping.

Only a few months earlier Desmond Hackett in the *Daily Express* had called on British sportsmen and women to show more of "the Pirie spirit." Now he was almost as critical as Peter Wilson.

But Hackett talked to Pirie and the *Daily Express* offered Pirie space to develop his views. He apologised for implying that all sportswriters were in the wrong but largely stuck by what he had said: "I am unrepentant. I wanted to make a protest and I made it." He confronted the negative reputation he had acquired in some quarters head on: "I resent the constant impression the Press gives that I am difficult, conceited, a bit of a Bighead. I don't mind what it says but when people meet you in the street or at business and repeat these things, well, it's most embarrassing." In reply Hackett told Pirie to stop thinking everyone was out of step except him.

Some years later Pirie described what he said that night as "one of the rare moments of truth". He had felt an increasing irritation about press treatment of some British sportsmen and women, particularly himself. "There was a bit of Yorkshire bluntness about Gordon, an honesty," recalls George Knight, "he couldn't help but stand up and say what he felt."

A year or so later Chris Brasher, who by then had become a leading sports journalist, assessed the impact all the news coverage was having on Pirie. "Ever since he was 20 (he) has had the publicity of a film star without any of the material benefits that compensate for the assumption by the public that they own part of anyone in the news. Nobody of his age could emerge unaffected. He has had to fight a long battle against constant criticism. It has forced him into such isolation that it is almost impossible for him to trust fully the advice of anyone…" (*The Observer*, 5 May 1957)

10 Magical evenings

At the start of 1954 Pirie seemed to have the world at his feet. He had established himself as an international athlete. He had justified his unique training regime. He was so well known that when he got on a London bus one day the conductor refused to take his fare. But he entered now on a period of injury and misfortune, setbacks so severe that some believed his best days were behind him.

When he began the summer of 1954 his eyes were firmly on the Empire Games in Vancouver and the European Championships in Berne. Early in the season he had a fine victory over a mile, in 4:05.2, at the Lloyd's ground in Beckenham. However, Pirie had begun to be troubled by a foot injury. He should have stopped racing for a while but he was probably goaded by some press reports that he was avoiding competition. He ran in the six miles at the AAA championships in June, aggravated the injury and was forced to drop out with two laps to go. His season was more or less over.

The injury required long and painful treatment. He and Zátopek had developed their friendship through correspondence and in August Pirie wrote and told the Czech runner that he would not be able to compete against him in the European championships. Pirie had to listen to the races on the radio. Kuts won the 5,000 metres in a new world record, with Chataway second. The 10,000 metres went to Zátopek, with Frank Sando third.

It was Bannister's season. He ran the first four minute mile in May and then won gold medals at both Vancouver (the mile) and Berne (1,500 metres). While Pirie was stuck at home in Coulsdon recuperating Bannister twice wrote to him with letters of encouragement. For Pirie it was the most frustrating time in his career.

Perhaps 1955 would bring better fortune. Pirie went to Freiburg in May and he and Gerschler discussed what his racing programme might be. They agreed that Gordon should concentrate initially on speed, even though that might involve some loss of his great powers of endurance. Peter Pirie, who was on holiday in Germany, joined his brother at Freiburg and they ran in two local races. Gerschler felt that during the first the half of the season Pirie should try the middle distance events. After July, said Gerschler, "we will try for the longer distance".

Gerschler's view was that Pirie was at the stage in his career when he must go for distances like the mile and 3,000 metres. Pirie also knew that speed was needed for an extra fast 10,000 metre race, and the shorter races were good preparation for that. At this time Zátopek was asked in an interview, reported in *Athletics Weekly*, about Pirie's prospects: "Pirie is still very, very young and, at his age, one shouldn't force the longer distances too much. Pirie is also extremely good over the shorter distances. But if he really wants to achieve something sensational over the longer distances, *he must become still better over the shorter ones*." (Author's italics).

In various races during May, June and July Pirie tried out different lap times as part of an attempt to get a fast time for the mile. He undertook a series of record attempts: over 2,000 metres in Brussels, three miles in Manchester, one and a half miles in Paddington and then 2,000 metres again in Croydon. In the event only the Paddington race produced a world best time – 6:26 – but it is a rarely run race and the distance is not recognised for world record purposes.

This intense period of racing over shorter distances certainly established Pirie's position as a challenger to the best milers. The press reported that Chataway was planning an attack on the world record over a mile at Aldershot on July 2nd, that he had recruited Chris Brasher and Derek Johnson to help him and that he would have liked Pirie there too. But Pirie ran a three-quarter mile race at Southgate that day (in 2:58.2); Chataway's time at Aldershot was 4:00.8.

In July Pirie moved to the longer distances and to the six miles at the AAA championships. It was the distance, and the meeting, at which he had first made his mark on the track. He had had to retire from the race in 1954, so there was now great interest in how he

The AAA Six Mile
Championships, 1955.
Pirie and Ken Norris in
the lead.
Kevin Kelly

would perform. Did he still have the old stamina, or had he lost it
in the search for speed? For the first time the TV cameras were there
to cover the race.

There was serious competition. It included Frank Sando his old
friend and rival, Peter Driver, the young SLH runner who had won
the six miles at the Empire Games in Vancouver and Ken Norris,
who had taken over from Pirie as national cross-country champion.
There was also an outside threat from Jack Heywood of Herne Hill
Harriers who had been improving rapidly that year and who had
run a good three miles at Southampton the previous weekend.

Jack remembers that week well. "Ken Norris was at Southampton
that day and I told him afterwards – 'I could repeat that next week
in the six miles'. 'You'll need to', he said, 'I'm going for 28 minutes.'"
(By this stage Zátopek had reduced the world record Pirie had set in
1953 to 27:59.2). Jack was studying science at University and had a

127

vacation job working in the Zoology labs at Queen Mary's College. "It was hot that day, so I took plenty of fluid on board."

It was Friday evening as usual, but it was still hot at 7.00 p.m. – almost 80° F – and it was humid too. Crowds of people had rushed in from work to catch the race.

Early on Pirie tried to shake off the others with fast bursts but Norris held on to him and he and Gordon led through the first two miles and then began to drop the field. During the third mile Norris tried several attempts to get past Pirie but each time Gordon quickened his pace enough to stay in front. Finally Norris did take the lead, but with Pirie remaining just behind. The sultry conditions were preventing a very fast time, but the race between the two men was a great struggle, taking them away from all the other fine runners. By the end of the fifth mile Pirie and Norris were over half a lap ahead. The heat was telling on everyone. "It wasn't just hot," recalls Jack Heywood, "it was really airless. People started doing funny things. I remember Andy Brown staggering into the kerb several times."

At the front Norris and Pirie were faltering from time to time but hanging grimly on to each other. Pirie did once more get in front, with just over half a mile to go, but Norris soon led again. Then, as they entered the home straight with about 500 yards to go, Pirie, looking exhausted, and swaying slightly, gathered himself and sprinted past Norris as if he was heading for the tape. Instead he heard the bell announcing one lap to go.

Pirie could not go on. As Norris pressed on to the final lap, Gordon stumbled across the track towards the fence. When Heywood came through he saw Pirie wandering around in the outside lanes. Norris went on to win (29:00.6), with Sando just beating Heywood for third place. Peter Driver was last of only six people who finished the race.

The humid conditions were partly to blame but Ken Norris remembers the real problem. "Both Gordon and I had decided not to drink too much before the race, but he'd overdone it and hardly drunk anything all day. I knew by the time we got to five miles that he was more dead then me – he was swaying about." Pirie admitted later that on that day he was already thirsty by lunchtime, because he was rigorously following advice given him by Mal Whitfield not to drink on the day of a race. He never did it again. Ken Norris had run one minute slower than his original target but in the conditions his achievement surely came close to world record standard.[13]

So again Pirie had failed to complete the six miles in front of the White City crowd. This time he recovered within a few days, but the events of that Friday evening reinforced the views of the cynics, who were muttering about when Pirie would manage to finish a race. The comments hurt him.

In August Gordon and Peter flew to Canada for a series of races arranged by their friend Ken Thomson. Gordon did not run particularly well and after finishing third in a mile event he was reported by the *Globe and Mail* in Toronto as saying: "Frankly, I'm not a miler. I prefer longer distances. Six miles is more to my liking."

He returned to England to finish the season with a punishing schedule. Kenneth Doherty, one of the leading track coaches in the USA, reported seeing Pirie training on September 1st: three fast miles with 30 minutes jogging between each. Doherty was struck how such a workout must have contributed to what he called "fortitude", in the sense of "firmness of mind, despite fatigue." Pirie was going to need it. In the space of five weeks he now ran eight long distance races, taking in trips to Moscow, Prague, and Turku.

In Moscow, Kuts beat him convincingly over 10,000 metres. But three days later Pirie had his first victory over Zátopek, in a 5,000 metres race in Prague. The Czech runner gained his revenge over the longer distance the next day and his performance brought a glowing tribute from Pirie: "It was a great run for such a cold night and certainly too fast for me. Not only has Emil got such pace in his legs, he has got such intelligent running sense."

In early October at the White City Pirie finally beat Zátopek over 10,000 metres. It was Zátopek's first run in London since the 1948 Olympics. It was a misty night and the lead runners – Zátopek, Pirie and Ken Norris – were picked out in the darkness by the spotlight. For five miles the lead kept changing until the decisive break came. Rex Alston described the key moment for radio listeners: "Now Pirie opens up with an enormous spurt. Pirie is running magnificently, a tremendous performance, a magnificent Bannister-like burst."

---

[13] There were similar conditions a few days later for the AAA marathon at Reading and six runners were taken to hospital. The winner, at the age of 40, was Bill McMinnis, Gordon's PTI friend in the RAF.

These performances in 1955 suggested that Pirie had the speed to run world class times over a mile and 2,000 metres, and the stamina to perform at the highest level at longer distances. Zátopek was past his best at 5,000 by now but he was still a great champion over 10,000 metres.

However, Pirie will have kept his performances in perspective. He knew Kuts had the better of him over 10,000 metres at least at that stage; and that his own 5,000 metre times were some way down on both Kuts and Iharos at their best. But he had now got that "Bannister-like burst."

No runner can have raced quite so much over such a variety of distances in one season: 13 races at distances up and including a mile, six races at six miles or 10,000 metres, and quite a few in between. Some journalists, and some of his fellow-athletes, felt that for Pirie to reach the world class times he was capable of he would need to concentrate at one end of the range, or in the middle. There were those he felt he was really a long distance man, whose strength was built round cross-country. They feared that the trips to Germany, and the "dashing about" to try various shorter distances, were undermining his natural talent as an athlete with great stamina. Others simply thought he should stop experimenting, and "sort himself out." In the event, Pirie finished the season by going outside his previous range of distances altogether.

The Road Runners' Club was a group of running enthusiasts who organised periodic attempts on long distance records, sometimes over rarely run distances. In the autumn of 1955 they arranged for an attack to be made on two long-standing track records, that for 20 miles (removed from the world record schedule in 1938), and that for two hours running. Both records dated back to pre-World War I days, but had been rarely tackled since. The occasion required careful organisation, including a team of lap counters and timekeepers who could ensure accurate records were kept as each runner went by. Pirie was one of eight runners to be invited and the race was set for the Walton track in Surrey on October 22nd, after the end of the track season proper, but before the weather got too cold. Jack Heywood, who had been in the six miles at the White City that summer, was in this one too. "I liked a long distance epic at the end of the season," he recalls.

Zátopek leading Pirie
and Ibbotson, White
City, Manchester, 1955.

It is not quite clear what Pirie had in mind by competing. Was it an end of season "epic" for him too, or was he flirting with another idea? One of the favourites was Joe Lancaster, a 28-year-old from Manchester. Joe was a railway worker who regularly covered 25 miles a day by running to and from his work. He had met Pirie during the Manchester v Prague meeting in September. "In those days everyone knew everyone in running," says Joe. "I had heard on the grapevine that Pirie was thinking of trying to emulate Zátopek by going for three golds at Melbourne – 5,000, 10,000 and marathon.

Also that he was thinking he might do the Walton race. So when I saw him at the stadium I asked him. He said, yes, he was thinking of it."

The morning of the event was cold and damp but at four minutes past 11 off they went, many eyes on Pirie, an intriguing guest if something of an interloper among the "ultra distance" specialists. Miles had to be completed in 5 minutes 30 seconds to better the 20 mile figures and Pirie, on schedule as ever, took them through two miles in 11 minutes. On they went for nearly an hour, the leading group close together at the front. Pirie took a short lead at ten miles but was caught, and by 15 miles he was joined by Lancaster and Heywood as they began to pick up the tempo. It was Lancaster who broke away, during the 18th mile, appearing to take Pirie by surprise. Heywood, more or less content to let the man in front go, called to Pirie: "You've got two miles to catch him, Gordon."

But Pirie could not quite get back to him. Lancaster went through 20 miles just over four minutes inside the old record, with Gordon 17 seconds behind. As two hours approached, a gun was fired to warn the runners that they had one minute left and individual officials shadowed each runner so they could mark the precise spot every man had reached when the final gun went to mark exactly two hours. Lancaster was credited with a distance of 22 miles 418 yards 1 foot 7 inches. (Judges have to be precise on these occasions.) Pirie and two others also surpassed the previous world best performance. But Gordon's legs seized up as soon as he stopped running and he was reduced to hobbling about in agony.

He managed to drive over to Coulsdon to watch an SLH match on the Downs but when he got out of the car he could barely walk. The experience probably put paid to any thoughts he had of doing a marathon. Next day, in Budapest, Sándor Iharos ran 13: 40.6 for 5,000 metres – the third world record at that distance within six weeks. But Pirie was out of the headlines for a while. It was four months before he could run again.

When 1956 began Pirie was still in the midst of a painful period of recovery after the 20-mile race, which had damaged his achilles tendons. For three months he received physiotherapy at St Thomas's Hospital in London and did virtually no running at all. Fortunately the Olympics were to be held at the end of the year, in November.

Lancaster after the 20 mile race.

During 1955 Gordon had become friendly with a young woman athlete whom he had met on the athletics circuit, and whom he had known for some time. Shirley Hampton was four years his junior, but already an experienced athlete. She had shown great talent as a schoolgirl, winning the junior 100 yards at the Kent championships at the age of 13. In 1952 she was a member of a Southern counties team that broke the world 4×200 metres relay record and her times over 200 metres justified her inclusion in the Olympic team for Helsinki. However, the official view was that she was too young to run what some considered to be a demanding sprint distance for a 17-year-old. In the summer of 1954 she won bronze medals at both the Empire Games and the European championships.

The women's relay team that set a new world record for 4×220 yards in 1953. From left: Anne Pashley, Ann Johnson, Shirley Hampton and Jean Newbolt.

Shirley was a tall, vivacious and attractive 20-year-old, naturally good at most sports and someone who enjoyed the company of other athletes. She had her own ambitions but she also understood and supported Gordon's desire to do well. Her natural gaiety nicely complemented Pirie's rather drier, laconic sense of humour and her presence both off and on the track was important to him. At the end of 1955 they became engaged. It may help to explain a comment he made in an article for a business magazine at that time: "Happiness is very important if you hope to become a champion and I can't emphasize it too much."

By Easter 1956 Pirie was back to almost full fitness. He began training twice daily. Much later in life he recorded that on some days in 1956 he ran three times a day, a thirty minute run at seven o'clock, and interval sessions at noon and in the early evening. Weight training had become an important part of his programme. John Disley, who trained with Pirie from time to time during this period, remembers how this began. "My coach Geoffrey Dyson believed that muscular legs needed to be balanced by strong arms and upper-body. Gordon was very impressed when I pressed my own body-weight (152 lb) one day at Motspur Park track in the winter of 1955. He could only manage 95 lb. From then on he used to weight train with me on occasions." Pirie also brought some basic weights which he kept at home in Coulsdon and used in the back garden.

At this time Pirie and other runners were working out from time to time at the Duke of York's Barracks track near Sloane Square. It was an old track, five laps to the mile, but the surface was reasonable, there were showers and it was convenient for people in central London who wanted somewhere to train at lunchtime, people like Chris Chataway, Chris Brasher, Brian Hewson, John Davies and others.

Brian Hewson was an elegant half-miler and miler who had come into athletics through the Mitcham club, and who went on to win a gold medal at the European championships in 1958. He and Pirie found they had something to give each other in training. "Gordon said he gave me distance, while I gave him speed. We did some good sessions together at the Duke of York's and occasionally I went over to Coulsdon and ran with him on Farthing Downs. We both listened to the *Goon Show* and we used to enjoy telling it back to each other the next day." Pirie was deadly serious about his running but like many serious people, humour mattered to him too. He loved to share stories, particularly about people and, especially later in his life, could tell good tales against himself.

When Pirie left for his "fishing holiday" in Bergen in June he felt in good shape. There, after so many setbacks during the previous two years, everything seemed to come right. Beating Kuts and setting a new world record in the 5,000 metres was his finest performance to date. *Athletics World* said it was "considered the greatest track performance of all time." Pirie soon had a letter from Gerschler saying that his whole family and all the staff at the Institute in Freiburg were very proud of him. But there was more to come.

A day or two after his Bergen victory Pirie flew to Trondheim, in northern Norway for a 3,000 metre race. By now the impact of his run in Bergen, particularly the size of the chunk he had taken off the old world record, was beginning to sink in. To come down a distance, to just under two miles, rather than around three, must have given him particular confidence. Everything he had learned about athletics told him that, once you were running at your best, you had to capitalise on your form. This was the time.

At Trondheim the main opposition came not from Kuts but from two Polish athletes, Jerzy Chromik and Zdzislaw Krzyszkowiak. They were the leading runners in a sudden upsurge of Polish athletics and Chromik already held the world record for the steeplechase.

Pirie and Chromik met at the small Dalgard stadium an hour or two before the meeting began and chatted about the race. They were both 25, approaching the peak of their careers and they knew they were well matched. This was not an explicit world record attempt but Pirie and Chromik wanted a fast time and they did agree that whenever one slackened the other would force the pace. Pirie told Roy Moor that they had a target of beating eight minutes. Iharos held the world record in 7:55.6.

It was a fine warm summer evening, the day before midsummer, and the stadium was full to capacity with 5,000 people. Pirie had worked out for over an hour that morning and felt in excellent shape. When the race began, the shorter, dark-haired Chromik took the lead and held it to the 1,000 metre point, with Gordon close behind. Pirie went in front for most of the second kilometre but all the time the two men were within a stride or two of each other, handling the pace comfortably. They ran that second 1000 metres in exactly the same time as the first and they were just on world-record pace. With just over two laps to go Chromik, running with the balance and cadence of the good steeplechaser, took the lead again. At the bell he was still in front and down the back straight he began to lift the tempo still further. But Pirie was boosted by what had happened in Bergen. Just off the final bend he began to accelerate. Chromik, unlike Kuts, responded and for 50 metres

Training at the Duke of
York's track, Chelsea,
1956. John Davies,
Gordon Pirie and
Chris Chataway.
John Davies

they were almost stride for stride. Then, imperceptibly, Pirie edged away. He finished five metres ahead.

Soon came an announcement that it was a new world record, Pirie's second, it seemed, in three days. There followed ten minutes of cheering and applauding, Pirie did a lap of honour, insisting that Chromik accompany him and the organisers called for "three cheers", in which Pirie himself joined. He was surrounded by hundreds of young enthusiasts and then carried round shoulder high by two of the other athletes.

But it was not a "new" world record. In those days the times on three watches had to be submitted for the record to be ratified and the three timekeepers had recorded 7:55.4, 7:55.5 and 7:55.5. The regulations required the time to be rounded up to the nearest one-fifth second, giving 7:55.6, exactly the same as Iharos. So, officially, Pirie had equalled the world record. The watches at Budapest when Iharos ran had shown 7:55.4, 7:55.6 and 7:55.6. Pirie probably ran fractionally faster.

It had been the most exciting four days of Pirie's life. He slept little, marvelling at the shortness of the Norwegian nights, and anxious to see Shirley. She was to run in Amsterdam two days later. Next morning he rang Jack Crump and sought permission to race there. Crump agreed. After a reunion with Shirley and a 1,500 metres in Amsterdam, it was back to Coulsdon, the fishing trip over. In his suitcase he had the sweatshirt Kuts had given him as a souvenir.

Prompted in part by a suggestion from Zátopek, Pirie now had his eyes on the 10,000 metres record and a race was arranged during a meeting at Croydon on July 4th. The track at Albert Road was not in good condition and Pirie himself spent some time on the morning of the race trying to improve it, by raking loose cinder from the inside lane. He was one of the best-known athletes in the world and here he was doing the groundsman's job at his local track.

It was a windy night, conditions that long distance runners dread, but Pirie attacked the record aggressively. He went through the half way mark in 14:20.4, some seven seconds inside Zátopek's schedule but, running on his own at the front, could not sustain the pace. His final time, 29:17.2, was the fastest so far recorded in the UK, and equalled his own best time set three years earlier in Stockholm.

Then, next day, he pulled a muscle and had to ease off in running and abandon other plans for racing for three weeks. When he did return it was to run a new personal best time for the mile (4:02.2) before travelling to Freiburg for what was to be his last consultation with Waldemar Gerschler before the Olympics. The general assumption was that Pirie would be picked for the 5,000 and 10,000 metres at Melbourne. A Swedish paper reported in September that he had been toying briefly with the 1,500 metres as well but had decided it would involve too many races. On August 16th Pirie was informed that he had been selected for the two longer distances.

He had envisaged one more race over 10,000 metres before the Games. The Russians sent a team to London at the end of August, and Pirie and Kuts were expected to meet again. But one of the

Sándor Iharos.

137

Russian athletes was arrested for alleged shop-lifting in a West End store and, following some diplomatic tantrums, the match was called off. Pirie was all keyed up but had nowhere to go. It was then that the Achilles Club rang him to suggest another race in Scandinavia.[14] The club arranged overseas tours, occasionally taking guest runners with it, and one of these trips was set up for Sweden in the first week of September. Seeing Pirie somewhat at a loose end, the club invited him to join them.

The MAI club in Malmö organised a two day international meeting each year, the forerunner of today's Grand Prix events, and it was to this meeting that Achilles sent a small team. So Pirie experienced for himself the sweet smelling, peaceful early autumn evenings which make southern Sweden such a favourite with distance runners. Gunder Hägg had broken the world record for the mile on the Malmö track in 1945.

In 1956 there was a special attraction, the presence of the Hungarian runners, Sándor Iharos, István Rózsavölgyi and László Tábori. All three were members of the Honved Sports Club, and first got together in 1953. Budapesti Honved was an army club and provided facilities whereby sportsmen could devote themselves to training and competition, while nominally serving as full-time soldiers. They had to do about six months of army work and they then moved into the sports section so they could concentrate on that.

Under the supervision of their coach, Mihály Iglói, these three Honved runners started to dominate middle and long distance running from 1954 onwards. Within the space of a year all three of them broke the world 1,500 metres record. At the time of the Malmö meeting in 1956 it was Rózsavölgyi's turn to hold it. And at that time too Iharos held world records for two miles, three miles, six miles, 10,000 metres and, jointly with Pirie of course, 3,000 metres.

In reality Rózsavölgyi – his friends called him Rozsa – was the 1,500 metres specialist, a man with an 800 metres time below 1:50 to his credit but someone who had run a competitive 3,000 metres only once before in his life, and that four years earlier. Tábori was also immensely strong over 1,500 metres and a mile and his times

---

[14] The Achilles Club was formed by athletes who had studied at the universities of Oxford and Cambridge.

over two miles indicated his great potential over 3,000 metres. But it was Iharos who had the widest range of distances at his command.

Iharos was just three months older than Pirie. He had begun serious athletics at the age of 18 and, like Pirie, had run in the Helsinki Olympics, where he was eliminated in the 1,500 metres. He was almost six feet tall, but weighed under 10 stone, and standing in his vest and shorts at the start of a race he looked a frail and vulnerable figure. But, as someone said, he moved over the track as if he had wings. In a golden period in 1954–55 he broke seven world records within 13 months. For a brief period he had held the world record at 1,500 metres and at 10,000 metres at the same time. Only Nurmi had ever done this before, and no one has done it since.

Mihály Iglói, the coach, was a key person in all of this. Like Gerschler, Iglói used interval training but he supervised the details of each work out more closely, believing that this enabled his athletes to concentrate on their running. He was helped by the fact that in the army environment in which the group worked there were few social or other distractions. But, army or not, his athletes were all individual people and they brought their own personalities to the track. Tábori remembers that there were differences between him and his fellow runners and that he often acted as "the peace-maker". But he had no doubt that they all did as Iglói said. "When we ran we didn't ask questions." Later in life when Iglói was coaching in the USA one of his athletes had the temerity to raise a query about the work out he was given. Iglói's reply became legendary: "You run – I think".

But Iglói also knew he could not programme a complete race, against another world record holder. That night, in September 1956, he gave his athletes a schedule with times to aim for over the first two kilometres. After that, said the guidance, "run at will."

Pirie had with him in the race Roger Dunkley, a student at London University and one of the best young milers in Britain, but Roger was there for the experience not to help see off the Hungarians. And although he had support from the Achilles team – both Peter Hildreth and Derek Johnson were great admirers and able to give him encouragement – they did not expect Gordon to win. Pirie, despite his great run over 3,000 metres in Trondheim in June, may not have expected to either. His postcard home to Alick and Marnie read: "Running against the Hungarians tonight. Saying prayers."

That evening, September 4th, the crowds packed into the old Idrottsplatt stadium, lying in gentle parkland not far from the centre of Malmö. There were 10,000 in all, filling the little stands that lined the home straight, and crowded ten deep on the grassy banks that surrounded the track. Extra seating had been placed in front of the stands and late arrivals squeezed in here, often with young children on their laps.

On the back straight, just after 7.30, with the daylight beginning to fade and lights being switched on in the stand, the six athletes took off their tracksuits – the three Hungarians, Pirie, Roger Dunkley and a young Swedish runner, Stig Nilsson. The Hungarians revealed stylish white "tracksters" under their tracksuits, and then they stripped down to their red Hungarian vests and white shorts. The spectators picked out each in turn. Tábori with the dark, slightly wavy hair, Rozsa slighter, with those deep-set eyes, and the distinctive blond hair. And Iharos? There seemed so little to him. Had he really beaten Zátopek's world record for 10,000 metres? Pirie was in his white English international vest, with the red and blue bands across the chest, and white shorts. He was wearing his favourite Adidas shoes and, inevitably, as the starter called them to the line, he was re-tying his laces.

Unusually there was a false start, with Iharos breaking from the line before the gun. "Take it easy," advised Pirie, as the athletes lined up again. When the race did begin it was easy to see why Iharos was tense. His task was to go straight into the lead and ensure a fast opening kilometre. As the race unfolded the Hungarian plan became clear. First Iharos and then Tábori would dictate the pace, so that Pirie was never in control. Rozsa's task was to finish the job.

And indeed Iharos took them through the first 400 metres of the seven and a half lap race in just under a minute, with Pirie on his heels. They went on through 800 metres and then, earlier than planned, Tábori was in the lead, with Iharos second and Pirie third. Rozsa was holding back, behind Dunkley. They strode elegantly behind each other as they came in front of the stand. Pirie was the tallest, and all in white, standing out from the rest. It was clear by the one kilometre mark that they were slightly up on the times Iharos and Pirie had run in their record-breaking races. Then, just before the half way point Iharos again assumed the lead, and Tábori began to fade.

The Malmö 3,000 metres
race: Iharos leading Pirie
and Rózsavölgyi.
Running Wild

At the 2,000 metre point the runners had slowed but the spectators sensed they were gathering themselves. The shouts of support
and encouragement from round the track merged into a united
chant, urging the runners into one last effort. With two laps to go
Pirie made an effort to move ahead, but Iharos responded and held
him off. Then, just before the bell, Rozsa went into the lead and
began a long sprint for home, while Iharos fell back. On the back
straight Rozsa got three yards clear of Pirie and briefly Gordon felt
he might have lost contact. But he gathered himself, and got back
with Rozsa again, on his shoulder. The others were out of it – at the
top of the final bend there were only Rozsa and Pirie left.

As they came to the straight Rózsavölgyi turned to look but Pirie
was already up to him. Gordon's stride quickened, and he was past.
First Bergen, then Trondheim – now again at Malmö the strike from

141

behind had worked. The crowd rose to him from the side of the track as he strode powerfully to the finish. Rozsa had made his effort and had nothing left – he was some three to four yards down at the end. There were no tenths or fifths of a second to argue over here. Pirie was almost three seconds inside his Trondheim time: 7:52.8.

Pirie was exhausted but he knew he had to keep moving to help himself recover and he jogged on from the finish, round the top bend and back to where his tracksuit was, on the back straight. Then came the lap of honour, the crowd standing and cheering, throwing their programmes across onto the track, some reaching out to shake his hand. The photographers followed him round, flash bulbs popping in the darkening air and then Rozsa did his lap of honour, for he it was who had helped make the race. "It was a most thrilling run," recalls Derek Johnson. "There we were in the gathering gloom, with just a few lights, like one of those magical evenings in the theatre, when a crowd of people gather round to watch a spectacle – only here no-one, not even those taking part, knew what would happen. The crowd was ecstatic."

Looking back years later Pirie remembered the commitment he had made back in 1948 and how it had born fruit in 1956. "I had made up my mind to be one of the best runners in the world. It took me eight years of ultra volume running to get to the top." Some who had trained with Pirie that year, Laurie Reed and Brian Hewson among them, were convinced that he owed this great performance in part to enforced rest. And indeed he had had a three month lay off during the winter and a break from competition for three weeks in July. In the four weeks prior to the Malmö run (including three weeks or so when he thought he might be meeting Kuts over 10,000 metres in London) his training was arduous, if not always at his most intensive level. But he did very little running in the six days before the race. Perhaps he got the preparation just right.

Rózsavölgyi had beaten the previous world record, but he had made a mistake on that last lap, a mistake not unlike the one Landy had made in Vancouver in his race with Bannister. "In the last bend I turned, looking for Pirie. I couldn't see him, I thought he had fallen back six or seven metres. I had quite a bit of energy left and began to push forwards round the bend so that Pirie wouldn't be able to catch up with me again. Coming out of the bend I saw a shadow behind me – I realised Pirie was still there, had been right behind me all the time. He had moved onto the next lane – if I had looked to the right rather than the left I would have seen him."

Pirie, who was in the race only because someone was thought to have stolen a hat, valued the victory as much as the record. He was the first, it was generally accepted, to beat all three Hungarians in one race since they had reached their best and the Swedish press reported how much this meant to him: "To beat them today, achieve victory, that means more to me than the record. That won't last long. Records get broken – mine may disappear before the year is out, or next year, but the victory endures."[15]

The newspapers wanted to know how much faster people might go. " The same speed as we ran over the first kilometre over the whole distance would give a time of 7:48, and it ought to be possible to achieve that," said Pirie. "I haven't said I can do it, but it doesn't seem to me to be a time that is beyond the capacity of a human being." In fact the record lasted longer than Pirie expected, until Michel Jazy broke it six years later in France.

Pirie remembered later how demoralised Iharos and Tábori seemed after this race. It made him feel quite uncomfortable. Things were never the same for the Hungarians, in part because of the revolution in their country a few weeks later. Iharos lost his 10,000 metres world record to Kuts within a few days, and Rozsa lost his 1,500 metre record to Salsola and Salonen of Finland the following year. None of the three held world records again and between them these three great runners secured only one Olympic medal, a bronze. (Rozsa in the 1,500 metres in Rome). Eastern Europe was not finished but the balance of power in distance running was about to switch towards New Zealand and Australia.

After the setbacks of the two previous years, 1956 was certainly Pirie's year. He had set two outstanding world records and beaten several of the world's best runners. His critics in the press were silenced. He had invested much in working with Gerschler and it had paid off. Now for the Olympics.

---

[15] The Hungarians were, for a while, the Kenyans of their day, sweeping all before them. Pirie had taken on the three best in one race, and beaten them.

11 Melbourne

ordon Pirie was the first competitor in any sport to arrive in Melbourne for the 1956 Olympics. He was at or near his best as an athlete but he wanted to leave nothing to chance. He had left his sales job with Wilkinsons so that he could get to Australia early, to acclimatise. He and Shirley Hampton were married on September 25th at what was then a popular venue among celebrities for weddings in central London, Caxton Hall registry office.[16] Keith Whitaker came down from Yorkshire to act as best man and, according to one newspaper, it took ten policemen to hold back the crowds outside. Shirley and Gordon had a brief holiday on the Isle of Wight, and then he flew out to Melbourne. Shirley travelled to Australia by sea, arriving just before the Games began.

There was much talk that Gordon and Shirley might be emigrating. Gordon never lost a love of England but he felt its constraints quite severely at times, particularly those imposed by people he later called the "elderly dictators" of British athletics. In addition, emigration was a popular option. Pirie knew that two of the English sportsmen who travelled to Auckland for the 1950 Empire Games decided on the spot to stay there. Another, who was a member of SLH, returned to New Zealand to stay two years later. Both Peter Pirie and David Smith, one of Gordon's training pals in SLH, were actively considering going abroad. In the event Peter went to Canada and David Smith to Australia in 1957. At this time too Shirley's parents were in the process of arranging their emigration to New Zealand.

---

[16] Gordon a kept a diary of his training throughout the 1950s, recording a punishing workout almost every day. The entries for this week in 1956 were unusual:
September 25th – Wedding. September 26th – rest. September 27th – rest.

Facing page: Shirley timing Gordon Pirie during a training session. *Fox Photos/John Rix*

Roy Moor was certainly convinced that the Piries would not come back. On September 7th he reported Pirie as saying: "I will just look round before making up my mind." But three weeks later, when Pirie flew out, Moor wrote a piece in the *News Chronicle* ("Good luck, Gordon,") saying farewell.

Whatever his longer term intentions Pirie wanted to get to Melbourne early. This involved the British Board in extra expense, but Jack Crump recalled in his own book a few years later that he felt it was worth it.

"Some athletes found it possible to be away from their work and studies for several months, and they, and in particular university students, asked that they should be sent to Australia in advance of the main body in order to acclimatise and finish their Olympic training in Australia itself. It seemed a reasonable and indeed a wise procedure if the extra transportation cost involved could be permitted." (Jack Crump, *Running round the World*, 1966)

Crump cited in Pirie's case an additional reason why he be permitted to go. He was "in any case going on to reside in New Zealand," and Pirie was "experienced and well able to look after his own training requirements." Others who went early included Chris Brasher, Chris Chataway and Derek Johnson, in part to spend time with their advisor Franz Stampfl, who was now resident in Australia. Sando's employer (Reed, the newsprint firm in Maidstone) paid his expenses and this effectively allowed an extra team member to go. Sando was also given additional time off, and was met by Pirie in Melbourne when he arrived two or three weeks before the Games.

Other runners, like Ken Norris and Harry Hicks, were less fortunate. Harry Hicks, unbelievably, had to run two marathons that summer to get his place: he dead-heated with Arthur Keily in the selection race in June so the two men, and others who might be contenders, ran a marathon six weeks later, which Harry won. There was a three day delay after the main party assembled in London before they could fly out and the journey took the best part of two days.

Melbourne invites the world.

Since being awarded the Games in 1949 the city of Melbourne had gone to great trouble to prepare for the event. At Heidelberg, some eight miles out of the city, they had built perhaps the most comfortable "village" for competitors yet seen. Billy Holt, who had been in charge of athletics at Wembley, had spent almost three years in Australia helping set up the event. The vast Melbourne Cricket Ground (MCG), scene of test matches between England and Australia for years, had been chosen as the venue for track and field. Its already large capacity was enlarged to 104,000 by the erection of a new double tier stand. The playing surface which had a nine foot drop had to be remodelled and a 400 metre cinder track installed.

But the Games were beset by difficulties. The two international political crises that autumn, the conflict over the Suez Canal, and the uprising in Hungary against Soviet domination, overshadowed everything else. Partly as a result of the conflict in Hungary some athletes from Eastern Europe never got to Australia and others came with half an eye on possible "escape routes" to the West. There were 5,000 Hungarians living in Melbourne at this time and there were some emotional scenes at the airport when the team arrived from Budapest.[17]

There were media problems too, with the Organizing Committee caught up in one of the first major conflicts over payment for the rights to televise sport. The main dispute arose over the release, and sale, of film abroad. In the end news and entertainment companies agreed together not to take film and the organising committee set up their own arrangements, selling the film later. As a result British television viewers got virtually no coverage at all.

For the British athletic team tensions which had been simmering beneath the surface for some time, came to a head, both between athletes and officials and between coaches and officials. Some athletes complained about the low level of pocket money or subsistence allowances that they received in comparison with other countries. "They wouldn't give us the two dollars a day allowance other people were getting," recalls Derek Johnson, "and they made us pay for our own laundry. Another small thing that annoyed us was over the little Union Jack lapel badges. These were big currency

---

[17] Sándor Iharos did not go to the Games. He fell in love with a fellow athlete and, as John Rodda put it in an obituary, "his dedication to training wavered." During October he took part in the uprising against the Soviet Union, helping in the defence of a telephone exchange near the city centre. Later in life he became a coach but gave it up because, he said, "I do not feel I have a talent for leadership and for teaching." Things went badly for him. He had a drink problem and ended up in a number of low status jobs. He died in 1996.

Wedding Day, September 1956. Shirley and Gordon centre; Keith Whitaker on their right; Laurie Reed on right of photo.
Laurie Reed

in the athletes' village, but they said they didn't have any. When we pressed them, they came up with another two each, showing that they had been hoarding them for their own purposes. It was all so typical." Despite the investment made in the construction of the village there were few recreational facilities for the 4,000 competitors.

Ian Boyd, the 1,500 metres runner who went on to captain the English team at the 1958 Empire Games recalls the wider issues at stake: "In those days managers and team officials were still not fully supportive of the coaches. They were running the sport as an amateur business, after all they were voluntary officials and also running their own lives. But sport was getting bigger and bigger and it needed a professional organisation. That's what we were saying."

There was a climb down, and concessions were made. But by now a group of athletes got themselves organised in a way they felt could help the modernisation of British athletics and established the International Athletes Club (IAC).

Pirie was not personally involved in much of this. It was not that he did not share the views of the other "rebels" or that he was on the

148

side of the officials. But he was very much his own man and not one given to committees and organisation. In so far as he was developing ideas about the organisation of athletics in Britain they went at least as far as the IAC, and probably much further. But his relations with Crump seemed to have been quite warm at the time. The British team manager lent him the team car so he could meet Shirley at the docks when she arrived.

When he first arrived in Australia at the end of September Pirie had about eight weeks to get properly into shape and he went to Sydney to get some competition. There he and Sando did some training sessions together. Then he returned to Melbourne to greet Shirley. With that good training behind him, and Shirley safely installed with friends nearby, Gordon felt more relaxed and confident.

As always the 10,000 metres was the first big track final of the Games. It looked like a duel between Kuts and Pirie. This was certainly the view of the other two British entries in the race, Ken Norris and Frank Sando. Both had excellent six mile times to their credit that year but both went into the race thinking that the bronze medal was a realistic target for them.

In Pirie's favour was his fine run at Croydon that summer, his long-established record as a six miler and cross-country runner, his immense determination and will. But was he really in Kuts' league over this distance? His best time was some 47 seconds slower than Kuts' fastest and, even allowing for the wind and the lack of opposition on that evening in July, it was a big gap. To win Pirie would either have to run faster than he had ever run over the distance before, or outwit Kuts tactically. Pirie had said in March that 28:40 would be needed to win, well inside what was at that point the world record. But by September Kuts had reduced that world record to 28:30.4.

And what of the others? The Australians were beginning to look threatening: Dave Stephens had beaten Iharos during the previous Australian summer but there was some doubt as to his fitness; Dave Power and Allan Lawrence both ran well in Australia in the run up to the games, though with times a little outside Pirie's. On times alone the real danger was József Kovács of Hungary. Ken Norris certainly saw Kovács as his main competitor for the bronze medal.

149

Kuts had been preparing with great dedication and single-mindedness. After the 1956 Olympics Kuts wrote of his respect for the Hungarians and the Australians, but the man "who had to be watched most of all," was Gordon Pirie.[18] Kuts recalled that when he met Pirie at the training ground before the Games Gordon had told him that one month of living in Australia had been sufficient for him to become fully acclimatised.

Pirie probably knew that his best chance was not to beat Kuts during the race but at the end, by outsprinting him as he had done in Bergen. He needed, above all else, to be within reach of Kuts at the bell. Vladimir Kuts and his coach Grigor Kikiforov thought this too. "I knew," wrote Kuts, "that the English runners would follow hot on my heels, and would be in a position to pull out the win shortly before the finish by utilizing their greater speed." Pirie's greater speed was indicated by the fact that over 1,500 metres he was some seven seconds faster than Kuts. Kuts and his coach therefore devised a new approach, and they implemented it ruthlessly.

On November 23rd the great tiered stands were full. Enthusiasts had travelled from all over Australia to be there, among them the 18-year-old Herb Elliott whose father had brought him on the three day train journey from Perth to Melbourne. In Britain athletics enthusiasts woke early to catch the radio commentary on the race.

At ten to six on a cool, spring evening the 25 runners lined up three deep behind the white curved line that marked the start. Kuts, easily recognisable as always with his red vest and blonde hair, was in the front row, crouching slightly near the inside. Pirie was in the middle of the same row, tensing himself a little as he waited for the start. Frank Sando and Ken Norris were there too of course. The home crowd had three to cheer for: Allan Lawrence, Dave Power and Dave Stephens. Those in the know also picked out the small Hungarian Kovács. Twenty-five laps to run.

Kuts ran a fast first lap, almost four minute mile speed, and the field was quickly strung out behind him in a line. Ken Norris sensed the pace was fast and tried to hold back, but found he went through

---

[18] Comments by Vladimir Kuts in this chapter are taken from an article entitled "Return to Melbourne" which he contributed to the book *The XVI Olympiad* published by the AAA in 1960.

Melbourne: the 10,000
metres. Kuts strides on
into the sun, dogged by
Pirie.
*British Olympic
Association*

in 64 seconds, way ahead of what he had planned. Up front, for the
first two miles or so, four runners tried to stay with Kuts: Pirie, the
other Russian, Chernyavskiy, and two of the Australians, Power and
Lawrence. The new red cinder track was quite loose and sandy and,
as the race progressed, some runners moved out towards the second
lane to get a firmer purchase.

Kuts ran those two miles just inside his own world record schedule, averaging around 68 seconds a lap. What must have alarmed
the men behind was the way the Soviet runner played with them,
sprinting down the back straight on one lap to take an eight yard
lead, and slowing on another and then moving aside as if to let
someone past. That someone of course was Pirie but Gordon was
not ready to take the lead and as he slowed to stay behind his feet
almost touched Kuts' heels. On the ninth lap the pace, and the
seesawing tempo, proved too much for all except Pirie and the
others dropped back.

151

Now, for the long central portion of the race, for around 13 laps, there were two races for the crowd to watch. At the front Kuts and Pirie continued a prolonged and desperate test of courage. They were alone, and they knew that in going for gold they were surrendering the chance of silver or bronze. Behind them a trail of runners followed in what seemed to be a separate competition.

To sustain him Pirie drew on eight years of hard work, a lifetime almost of effort and exhaustion: those lonely runs across the Quantocks when he was at Watchett, a thousand meticulous sessions on the track, the hill runs on the Downs in Surrey. And indeed, for the first half of the race, Pirie ran easily behind his rival. From the eighth lap to the 13th, Kuts poured on, always under 70 seconds a lap, sometimes putting in short bursts, sometimes slowing a little. The stockier, shorter figure always in the lead, his face taut with determination, shoulders slightly hunched, leaning slightly. The taller one behind tracking his man and, as they came down the home straight in the evening sunlight, throwing his long shadow over the runner in front. They went through 5,000 metres in just over 14:06, fractionally outside Zátopek's Olympic record for the distance. But they were only half way.

Now something unusual was happening. Pirie was tiring. He, more than anyone, had prepared his body so that it could go on even when fatigued. But he had never run the first half of either a six miles or a 10,000 metre race at such a pace. Kuts could not see his rival and he could not tell from the shadow how fatigued Pirie was, only that he was still there. On the 16th lap he tried a fast burst on the back straight and briefly pulled ahead, but then the shadow was back again. He slowed and moved out a little, almost waving Pirie past, but Pirie hung back. The cruel changes of pace continued, Kuts choosing the tempo, Pirie responding. One hundred thousand people watched.

Then, in the 20th lap, with little more than a mile to go, Kuts moved aside again to let Pirie through. Unbeknown to Pirie the older man might well have surrendered the race at this point. He felt he had reached the limit of what he could do but he knew that if he could find one more spurt it might be decisive. "I had to have a look at his face," he wrote later, "to see whether he was running lightly or finding it the same hard going as me. Suddenly I slowed down so much that it seemed I had almost come to a complete stop. I looked round and gestured for Gordon to go ahead."

Pirie came up to him and momentarily he and Kuts ran side by side, before Pirie briefly held the lead. But the damage had been done. Kuts had looked across and seen in Pirie's face not the expectation of victory, but the pain of defeat. "For the first time I was able to get a look at the tired, limp figure jogging in front of me." Kuts gathered himself for one final effort, and passed Pirie again. In one moment, the struggle was resolved.

Pirie was not to suffer defeat quickly and suddenly in some final spurt. There were four laps left, four laps in which inevitably, once Kuts had got away from him, Pirie went backwards through the field. It was hard for him to run, and almost impossible for his friends to watch.

At the front Kuts, finding a new store of energy, motored on until at one point he was 200 metres clear, but over the last two laps Kovács and Lawrence began to catch him, and in the end the Hungarian finished less than seven seconds down, with Lawrence a few yards behind. Kuts' time was 28:48.6, just outside his world record. Ken Norris finished in fifth place in a new British record, although he never really got the credit for such a fine run. Frank Sando, who had a rare off day, was 11th.

For Pirie the last five minutes of the race must have been the longest of his life. One by one six other runners caught and passed him. He lost over a minute on Kuts during those four laps. His legs had gone and he could run only on memory, but even then he finished ahead of runners such as Frank Sando, Schade, Mimoun and Bolotnikov.

Kuts' greater experience over 10,000 metres and perhaps his greater raw, physical strength had seen him through. He was greeted with a tremendous ovation as he circled the track, jumping up and down with uncharacteristic exuberance and raising his hands in celebration. There were no congratulations from the Hungarian, Kovács, but when Pirie finished the two great rivals embraced.

The race was all too much for the officials. There were 19 lap scorers on duty, 11 judges and 11 time keepers but, after the first three men came through, it proved beyond them to decide which runners had actually run 25 laps, the order in which they had finished, and, most of all, the individual times. But, like Zátopek's run eight years earlier at Wembley, the race inspired at least one young man to greater things. Herb Elliott said later that he saw nothing that week which matched the magnificence of Kuts in the 10,000 metres.

It was the fast burst in lap 17 that had killed Pirie off, Gordon himself said afterwards. "Those last four laps felt like the end of a marathon race, I hardly knew how to keep going. I hope I never have to meet Kuts over this distance again." Kuts put his success down to the tactics he had worked on in the preceding months. "I intended to take the lead at the start and then unexpectedly change the pace sharply, with intermediate spurts and by this means to break down the strength of my opponents. I varied the pace so often and so unexpectedly that there were times when Gordon Pirie almost ran over me."

Pirie knew that there was much talk of his great courage in taking Kuts on, rather than settling, at some point in the race, for the silver medal he might have had. Others might have been able to draw some consolation because they had earned the admiration of the crowd. But Pirie was brutally honest with himself. He made no excuses. "Kuts murdered me – that's all there was to it." he said. "I don't think I could ever beat him over 10,000 metres."

Many, including Roy Moor, who was perhaps the best judge of Pirie's form, had said that it was difficult to make any predictions about the 5,000 metres until after the "ten". Some of those who had come to Melbourne thinking Pirie was favourite for the 5,000 (if only because of his victory over Kuts in Bergen) now wondered perhaps if he could recover and compete effectively in the next race. Harry Carpenter, writing in the *Daily Mail*, thought the "thrashing" Pirie had received would "leave its mark on him for the rest of his life. Kuts not only ran Britain's long distance prima donna into the ground, he tore apart Pirie's psychological fabric and left it strewn on the harsh red dust of the cinder track." But things could work the other way of course. Pirie might be steeled by defeat into an ever-greater effort, while Kuts would be off his guard.[19]

---

[19] Years later we saw something like this happen between Coe and Ovett in Moscow, though over shorter distances.

But in the 5,000 metres more than the 10,000 there were other important contenders. Both Derek Ibbotson and Chris Chataway had their backers, Ibbotson because of his fine mile and three mile times that summer, Chataway because he was a former holder of the world record, and because at the end of September he had beaten both Iharos and Ibbotson over 5,000 metres in Budapest. The other dangers included the Hungarians Miklós Szabó and László Tábori, and Mugosa from Yugoslavia. Chromik, who at best would surely have been a contender, was ill and could barely finish his heat.

Many felt it came down to Kuts against the three Englishmen, if only because the Hungarians had been through so much emotionally. But it was never going to be a team effort by the British

Melbourne: the 5,000 metres. Kuts leads Pirie, Ibbotson and Chataway (obscured). British Olympic Association

runners. Some hours before the race Pirie and Derek Ibbotson had a conversation in which they discussed Chataway's form. Ibbotson suggested that their rival was not really fit. "You can never be sure with that guy," was Pirie's reply. Chataway was under no illusions that he was on his own. "If Derek and Gordon were completely honest," he said many years later, "they wanted to beat me as much as they wanted to beat Kuts."

After the 10,000 metres final on the Friday Pirie had taken a sleeping tablet provided by Roger Bannister, and it was Sunday afternoon before he really came to. But the heats for the 5,000 metres on the Monday were relatively straightforward. All the top names came through, apart from Chromik. Pirie looked in good enough shape, winning his heat, hand in hand with the Yugoslav runner Mugosa. The runners now had a two day break before the final, held at half past four on the Wednesday afternoon, November 28th.

Pirie was by now in reasonable physical shape. He had been shattered by the 10,000 metres but he had great resilience and powers of recovery. Nonetheless, he had to decide what to do. He had no plans to spend another four years preparing in quite the same way for another Olympics. He and Shirley were talking about their holiday plans, about sightseeing and going on to New Zealand. But he wanted to get the best out of the 5,000 metres. Should he go with Kuts again, and risk everything? Or should be settle for something less? He decided to be cautious. Kuts was in such form, he wrote later, that he was bound to dictate the race and "all we could hope to do was to try and keep up." (*Running Wild*, 1961)

At the start Tábori made a burst and went in front but Kuts simply demanded to have the lead, and he took it, red vest again, shoulders tight, slightly bobbing head, chin stuck forward in determination. Before long Pirie and Ibbotson had positioned themselves behind him and now responded to his bursts. Chris Chataway moved up in the sixth lap to just behind Pirie and then, on the next lap, when Kuts accelerated again, Chataway went past the other Britons into second place. It was a decisive move, but to Kuts' advantage. Chataway could not sustain his challenge and fell back, and by the time Pirie and Ibbotson got past him to take up the chase Kuts was away. At ten laps he was ten yards clear, and by the bell the gap was 50 yards, with Ibbotson leading Pirie in the fight for the silver medal. Kuts finally finished in 13:39.6, equalling his Bergen

Melbourne: Kuts and
Pirie embrace after the
5,000 metres.
Time-Life

time. Pirie pulled past Ibbotson on the final bend but he finished 11
seconds behind the winner.

While all around him other runners collapsed onto the grass, Kuts
did his lap of honour, standing here and there to respond to the
crowd's applause, hands clasped above his head. He turned to the
camera afterwards and in repose, looked like a young sailor again –
after all, he was only 29. Like Zátopek in 1952, he had won two golds;
Pirie had one silver, Ibbotson a bronze. Chataway, the papers said,
had stomach cramp – he finished 11th. The silver medal was less
than Pirie came for but more than many thought he might get a few
days earlier. And he made no excuses: "My legs weren't fresh… I
shouldn't have done the 10,000."

When Pirie was interviewed by a Melbourne newspaper 15 years
later on a visit to Melbourne he took a similar view. "Kuts and I had
come here knowing it would be a life and death struggle. We knew
one of us had to go, and it was me. The 10K wasn't really my
distance. I should have been in the 1,500 and I should also have saved

157

myself for the 5,000." It was a view he reiterated towards the end of his life: "I reckon I was in with a chance to get in the top 6 (of the 1,500) or even the top three." (Alistair Aitken, *More than Winning*, 1990)

It is true that prior to Melbourne no British runner apart from Brian Hewson had run faster in 1956 over 1,500 metres than Pirie, though Ibbotson's mile time was faster. But Pirie had been Britain's first choice 10,000 metres runner for years, ever since he first went to the White City in 1950 and tackled the six miles. And was it not Pirie himself who has said a year earlier: "The mile is a bit short for me?"

Over the years Pirie continued to wrestle with the circumstances of his defeats by Kuts, and frequently attributed them to perform-ance-enhancing drugs. Allan Lawrence remembers: " When he was with me no matter what the conversation was about Gordon would steer it around to his defeat by Kuts... 'Did you notice the colour of his face when he was on the victory dais? And I had to turn him the right way round on the stand for the 5,000-metre ceremony. He was in a stupor, really confused!' he used to say."

Some years later in a radio interview Pirie was asked publicly whether Kuts was "helped" in any way. "I think he was influenced by hypnotism or drugs – even in Bergen," said Pirie. "His career was suddenly cut off... he was said to be ill." (*Frankly Speaking*, BBC Radio, April 1962). The point, Pirie clearly implied, was not so much that Kuts had cheated but that he might have done something that was dangerous to himself. The speculation about Kuts continued for years. After a series of heart attacks, the first in 1960, Kuts died in 1975, aged 48.

Whatever Pirie believed he knew that in the 10,000 metres he and Kuts had run a great race. "In my heart of hearts," he told the Melbourne paper in 1971, "I know I did my damnedest." But there were regrets. Discussing it all a few years later with Jim Hogan, the marathon runner, Gordon acknowledged how near he was to victory: "If only I could have lasted one more lap."

12 The road to Rome

While most other athletes flew back home to an English winter and to their jobs in offices or factories, Gordon and Shirley began a delayed honeymoon. They had bought a scooter in Melbourne, and now they made their way to Sydney, driving beside sandy beaches and lakes, through bush fires and miles of forest to the city where, over 40 years later, the Olympics would return to Australia. Twice they crashed but each time they got themselves patched up and pressed on, catching the boat to New Zealand at the beginning of January.

After a few days in Wellington, they drove over the mountains and up the coast to Palmerston North. Here Gordon worked for a while at a filling station and he and Shirley went potato picking, but all the time they were able to enjoy themselves, basking in the warm sun, swimming in the surf and laughing about what it was like in London in January. Then they moved on over the desert road to Lake Taupu and eventually to Auckland, "an Englishman's dream come true", said Pirie later. Altogether they had two months of sunshine, were welcomed with little formality into people's homes and by earning a little money here and there were able to live comfortably. This was the New Zealand of the 1950s, when, someone wrote later, "you could get milk shakes in silver tin containers" and the pubs closed at six in the evening. (*Arthur's Boys* by Joseph Romanos, Moa Beckett 1994).

During these months away from Britain Pirie ran a few races, including five or six in New Zealand during January. These were mostly on grass tracks, five laps to the mile, and his times were not good. Pirie was not doing the level of training he had done and he was putting on a bit of weight. He was more relaxed in talking to the press. The New Zealand sporting papers found him quiet and thoughtful "an intelligent sort of bloke who analyses what he is about" (*New Zealand Sportsman,* February 1957).

Gordon and Shirley seriously considered staying in New Zealand. But a Swedish promoter Pirie had met in Melbourne offered to pay their fares back to Europe and defray their expenses for a tour in Scandinavia. Gordon and Shirley left New Zealand towards the end of February 1957, but the country had made a great impression and Pirie often talked of going back.

Because of this break from serious training and from competition, and because of the pleasure he and Shirley got from their travels, Pirie seems to have put some distance between himself and the long period of hard training. Until 1956 his running career had been highly focused. He had demonstrated a relentless commitment to reaching and surpassing world standards. In the years that followed he retained his ambitions, continuing to visit Freiburg regularly for sessions with Woldemar Gerschler, and running in international matches and in one more Olympics. But he was developing his interests in the wider aspects of fitness and health, and also adopting a more relaxed life style. "I was never as intense about my athletics afterwards as I was in 1952–55," he said later.

In London Pirie had another spell in banking, working for some time for the United Dominion Trust, a finance company. His life no longer had the fairly domesticated pattern of his early days as an international, when he was still at Coulsdon with his parents. Now be began a more itinerant life style, one that he was to return to throughout his life and which he so much enjoyed. Spells in employment were mixed with periods of travel and racing, as and when opportunities arose. "We worked a bit, camped out, slept in the car – we roughed it," he recalled in a radio interview..

Doug Gardner tried to capture Pirie's life style in an article for *World Sports.* "He travels the world on athletics expenses, salaries from part-time jobs ranging from bank clerk in Oslo to garage manager in New Zealand, and a family legacy left to his wife. Pirie is indifferent to what the average man considers his main aims – 'settling down' and 'making a living.'" It remained that way for the rest of his life.

Recalling those days Shirley says they made no long-term plans. "We did one thing at a time as they came along." Shirley was often

to be seen holding the watch during Pirie's training sessions and she was also continuing with her own athletic career. She became one of the first British women athletes to tackle the 400 metres seriously and at the European Championships in 1958 she only just missed a bronze medal in the event.

Running with Mike Wiggs, Shirley and friend in Norway. Late 1950s. *Mike Wiggs*

Pirie was still training hard. He described his own day, when he was in employment, as working from 8 a.m to 12 noon, training at lunchtime, working from 2 p.m. to 6 p.m and then training again. He had found that the key was the quality of the training as much as the time you put into it. "You need two hours a day, but you must use it properly," he said in an interview a few years later. "I tried full-time athletics but got fed up with it. You can combine being either a professional or an amateur with doing a job, if you do your training for an hour at lunchtime and an hour in the evening." His views had changed from 1953 when he had predicted that in future athletes would need six hours a day.

Pirie was not slackening off, but he was maturing. The beanpole body of the boy and young man had given way to a well muscled, hardened tone, and the many years of training had made him tough. The use of weights had given him strength in his shoulders and arms. The callow youth who had run across the hills at Watchett had now matured into an immensely fit man, his skin tanned by many days in the sun. He seemed more at ease with himself, entertaining others with stories from his trips around the world. Occasionally, before a race, he would acknowledge that others might win. George Knight, who was in some awe of Pirie at the time, remembers Pirie's comment when they met in the changing rooms before a two mile race at the White City: "You should win this one, George."

Pirie was also, half-consciously perhaps, feeling his way into a new role as a mentor of young athletes and as a coach. Although he had always done many of his work outs on his own, Pirie enjoyed the companionship of training with others, both fellow internationals and club runners. Colin Young, the international walker, recalls the times when Pirie would come over the Thames to the Mayersbrook track in Dagenham, home of Essex Beagles. The groundsman at the track imposed strict rules, forbidding access during the dark winter evenings but one night when Colin was jogging past he saw flickering torchlight from the infield. He squeezed through a gap in the park railings and found two well-wrapped figures doing interval runs on the cinder track, illuminated only by the torch one was carrying. It was Pirie, who had come over from Coulsdon to train with one of the local runners.

John Merriman, who was to become British record holder over 10,000 metres, also got help from Pirie. When Merriman was stationed in Germany while doing National Service he was somewhat cut off from coaching and support and his father wrote to Pirie for assistance. Pirie sent him training schedules. John remembers Gordon and Shirley coming over to the Woodside track near Watford on a Sunday morning a year or two later and doing some sessions with him. "He was a real inspiration and a motivator."

Laurie Reed, who ran in the 1,500 metres at the Rome Olympics, trained with Pirie on and off for seven or eight years. "I was someone he could work with. At first I couldn't do everything he did in a session but I could stay with him part of the time. We would use the track at Withdean near Brighton sometimes, and on Sunday mornings do hill runs at Leith Hill near Dorking. Sometimes during the week he'd pick me up early and we would go to the Duke of York's track in Chelsea and then I would get the tube to work. I thought he was wonderful. He didn't have time for 'buddies' but he was a great friend. I was close to him because I could train with him. He was so easy to get along with – we never had a cross word."

Pirie's later years as a coach often grew out of these kinds of friendships at the track, where training partners who helped keep him going in his training also received advice and support. But the connection with Mike Wiggs began in a different way. Wiggs was a good cross-country runner at school in Hertfordshire but never did much on the track. At the age of 16 a "scout" from Watford Harriers called on him and pressed him to join the club, and within a year he had won the county youths' championships. Out of the blue he got a letter from Pirie saying that he had noticed his good performances and wondered if he would like any help with training programmes. "Gordon sent me some schedules setting out what I should try and do each day. But it was 18 months or so before we met."

Mike Wiggs joined Thames Valley Harriers and he continued to get advice through the post from Pirie. Then, in 1960, Gordon invited him to join a visit to see Gerschler. "At the national cross-country championships in West Bromwich Gordon was seventh and I was 11th and that got me a place in the English team for the international race. But Gordon would have none of it. 'Do you want to be a bum runner or do you want to be a world champion?' he asked me. He just told the selectors that neither of us would be running the international because we were both going to Freiburg."[20] Pirie carried this friendship and support, and firm control, into his later coaching of athletes around the world.

Gordon and Shirley spent more and more time out of England. They enjoyed living abroad, and the opportunities they now had to travel and run more or less where ever they were asked. Scandinavia

---

[20] Mike Wiggs eventually took the route Gordon had declined, an athletics scholarship to an American university. He was the first Englishman to better Pirie's 5,000 metres time set in Bergen. He did so in Helsinki in June 1965 with a time of 13:33.0, in a race won by Michel Jazy in a new European record of 13:27.6.

remained a special favourite. During the late 1950s they spent part of each summer in Sweden or Norway, where they worked in local banks or offices and built up a new network of friends. There was also some money to be made from racing. From the mid fifties onwards, the very top runners were being paid by Swedish and other promoters, the amount they could get sometimes depending on how much extra gate money the promoter thought their appearance would bring in. Sometimes there was a little to be made from airline tickets as well.

Pirie was increasingly attracted by the quality of the environment in Scandinavia and the life style that it permitted. One summer the Piries explored the Norwegian countryside with their friend Sverre Fjelstad the naturalist, swam in the fjords, ran in the pinewoods, and slept out under the night sky. They were the best of days.

Pirie was in Scandinavia for most of the Swedish season in 1957, for a short spell after the European championships in 1958, for several weeks in 1959, and again in 1961. If he had races in England during these periods he would travel over from Sweden for them. Sweden in particular offered opportunities to make money from races. He and some others could generally get £50 or £75 a race and he later estimated he made around £1,000 in his last year (1961). He produced some great performances on the track, and got into some legendary scrapes, one of them witnessed at first hand by the Australian runner Allan Lawrence.

The incident involved Pirie and the Swedish promoter Lennart Stromberg, or "Mr Moneybags" as the athletes called him. Lawrence describes how Pirie agreed to race a mile at the Gothenburg meeting but, the day before the race, was pressed by Stromberg to switch to the 5,000 metres, so that Roger Moens and Dan Waern could race the shorter distance. Such horse trading is the normal stuff of pre-meeting negotiations. But this particular dispute produced a stormy exchange between Stromberg and Pirie, each making accusations of letting the other down, and in increasingly violent language.

Next day there was another row between the two men in the hotel lobby, with Stromberg threatening to dock Pirie his hotel expenses. To effect this the hotel staff were asked to guard the lobby and prevent Gordon and Shirley getting away. Pirie had other plans however and with Lawrence's help he and Shirley literally broke their way out of the back door of the hotel and "escaped". Their flight was not made easier by the fact that Shirley, who had an achilles tendon injury, was on crutches, but they made it. The Piries left for Malmö but poor Lawrence had to turn out for the 5,000 metres and suffer the booing of the crowd. The announcer told them that Pirie had demanded money to run but that the meeting promoter had refused to be blackmailed. Whenever they met up later Lawrence and Pirie would refer to this event as "The Great Escape".

Scrapes of this kind contributed to the legendary stories that grew up around Pirie's travels and with which he would entertain his friends in later life. But his desire to run where and when he wanted, and not run sometimes where he was expected to, conflicted with the orthodoxies of the day. Roger Bannister felt Pirie had been given too much freedom: "No one can doubt the brilliance of Gordon Pirie as a runner at any distance from one mile to six miles… No runner has alternated such a bewildering succession of triumphs and disasters which, together with his startling frankness, have given him such a unique place in the affection of the public.

"Pirie is 26 and can undoubtedly improve further. Yet he darts about the world running very fast in unexpected places and then causing consternation among his supporters by failing to appear in important meetings like the British championships. An amateur runner must always have complete freedom to run where and when he wants to run; but in Pirie the normal latitude granted to athletes' idiosyncrasies has perhaps been exceeded." (Reprinted from *Modern Athletics*, edited by HA Meyer (1958) by permission of Oxford University Press, 1958.)

But his championship days, running for his country, were not over. In 1958 The Empire Games were to be in Cardiff in July and the European Championships in Stockholm in August. Pirie had missed both events in 1954 through injury and he decided that he wanted to be there this time.

Ironically, in view of what had been said about Melbourne, one of the first decisions the selectors made for Cardiff was to pick Pirie for the mile. His best that season (4:04.7) headed the rankings among English runners and he was chosen along with Mike Blagrove, Ian Boyd and Brian Hewson. Four were also chosen for the three miles – Pirie, Mike Bullivant, Peter Clark and Derek Ibbotson.

Of these four Peter Clark was the one with the best current form, though it had taken some years and much hard work to get there. He had grown up in Wiltshire some miles from an athletics club or a decent track and for many years he travelled 14 miles to and from school every day, and a similar distance to a track to train. He later took a long-term contract in the RAF as a radio fitter, joined Thames Valley Harriers and gradually worked his way through the running ranks until, 14 years after starting as an athlete, he got his first international vest.

Competitors at the Empire Games were accommodated in the RAF camp at St Athan and the authorities tried to ensure that there were some social diversions. There was a village social and entertainment programme and dances were arranged in the amenities block on two evenings. "There will be a number of partners, whose introduction can be effected through the lady hostesses," said the information card provided to competitors.

But Pirie found conditions in the camp difficult. He was disturbed by all the noise and he persuaded the English team manager that he be allowed to sleep in his camper van. Then there was a row about whether he should be present for the opening ceremony, and about his time of arrival. Pirie basically wanted to be left alone to prepare himself in the way he knew best, while team officials were reluctant to make a special case. In the end the dispute degenerated into farce when Pirie's "sleeping out pass" was withdrawn and he was instructed to move his van inside the gates of the camp. It was a classic clash between the rules of the day and the needs of an international sportsman, and a classic compromise.

The British sporting public already knew that there was a new generation of runners from New Zealand and Australia, and they were keen to see how their own heroes measured up against them. By the time Pirie lined up on a cool and blustery day for his first race – the three miles – Dave Power had won the six miles and Herb Elliott the half-mile. The favourite for the three miles was Albert Thomas, the Australian who had broken the world record a few weeks earlier. Things had moved on from Vancouver, where the Englishmen Bannister, Chataway and Driver won gold medals.

For much of the first two miles Thomas did lead the field, with Pirie and a cluster of half a dozen other runners still in touch. Then, with a little over three laps to go, the New Zealander Murray

Brian Hewson, Ron Delaney and Gordon Pirie running in front of a large crowd in Dublin, 1957.
John Davies

Halberg, helped by a slow eighth lap, burst into a ten yard lead. Thomas and the other New Zealander Neville Scott tried to stay with him but both Pirie and Ibbotson were dropped off the pace. Halberg steadily increased his momentum and finished 50 yards ahead. Thomas and Scott took the other medals and some way back from them Pirie just held off Peter Clark for fourth place. Pirie's time (13:29.6) was the best he had run for the distance, but it was some way down on his equivalent best over 5,000 metres.

The mile heats were held two days later and Pirie had little difficulty in qualifying. Thus on July 26th came his first and only final at this distance in a major championship. The weather was now very wet but there was great expectation among another capacity crowd of a tremendous race between Elliott, his Australian rival Merv Lincoln, Brian Hewson and a number of others. Few considered that Pirie was a serious contender. After Neville Scott had led the field through the first half-mile, Elliott made his move. He ran the third lap in under 59 seconds, showing a power of acceleration that other distance runners could not match. Only Lincoln and, to everyone's

167

surprise Pirie, were able to stay in touch but Elliott pulled steadily away and finished over 15 yards clear. Pirie hung on to Lincoln for as long as he could but then faded a little in the finishing straight and was overtaken by Thomas. His time (4:04.1) was the fastest by a Briton that year.

Pirie had shown that he still had the beating of his domestic rivals but he had ended up with two fourth places. Also he had seen at first hand the power and depth of the Australian and New Zealand contingent.[21] Of all the athletes he met in his career Herb Elliott was the one for whom Pirie felt something approaching awe: "unbeatable at every stage of almost any race," he described him much later in his life. Shirley Pirie tells of how Pirie came back from one race against Elliott, threw down his spikes in disgust and said: "There just is no way to beat him."

Pirie and Peter Clark were also chosen for the 5,000 metres in the British team for the European Championships in Stockholm. The rankings of course looked rather different. There was no Thomas and no Halberg, and Zimny of Poland led the list. But it was a most open race, without Kuts, who had taken Pirie's world record from him in October 1957 but had now suffered a rather sudden loss of form.

Pirie had made good friends with a bunch of the New Zealanders and Australians and after the Cardiff Games he lent his VW camper to Herb Elliott and others. They drove it to Sweden and met up with him at the European Championships. So he had some support from Commonwealth athletes watching at Stockholm.

With hindsight, this race was probably Pirie's best chance of a gold medal at an international championship. Despite all the travelling, he had kept himself very fit and must have fancied himself against a European field. It would have been some consolation to have taken a gold medal here, if only to show that he had kept his fitness longer than Kuts. But on this occasion the weather proved to be an unexpected factor.

---

[21] If there had been any doubt about that, Halberg ran a mile in Dublin on 6th August only three tenths of a second outside Ibbotson's world record of 3:57.2. Unfortunately for Halberg, he was more than 10 yards behind Mervyn Lincoln, who was 1.3 seconds inside the world record. And unfortunately for Lincoln he was another 10 or 12 yards behind Herb Elliott, who ran 3:54.5. "I was sprinting down the back straight when Herb just came straight past me," said Lincoln after the race.

The day of the 5,000 metres final, August 23rd, was one of heavy rain and the track was so wet that the race had to be run in lane three with a hose pipe and flags marking the inside lane. The water on the track was ankle deep in places. The lead alternated in the opening laps and at the mid way point at least eight runners were still in contention. With just over three laps to go Clark made a burst but he was held by Zimny and Krzyszkowiak, with Pirie not far behind. Both English runners were finding the sodden track conditions difficult but the Poles seemed to cope with it better and by the bell they had moved ahead. On the final lap both got further away and in the end Krzyszkowiak won easily in 13:53.4. Pirie came past Clark to take the bronze behind Zimny.

Pirie had finished ahead of all the British opposition again but from three championship races that summer he had just one medal, a bronze. He had justified his selection every time but he seemed to be slipping slightly as new runners came to the fore. He went on with what he called the Scandinavian "merry-go-round", racing not only over a mile and 5,000 metres but, without success, in a 3,000 metres steeplechase race. He began to look back on his career, rather than forward to what he might achieve. He was jotting down thoughts for a book on his experiences.

After the championships Pirie was approached about a possible trip to South Africa with Murray Halberg where they would run against local athletes and help raise the profile of the sport. It was an attractive proposition and it offered Gordon and Shirley a way of getting a passage on to New Zealand.

Murray Halberg remembers that Pirie wanted to run the length of Africa, with a support van. But the Piries went to Cape Town by boat, sailing from Southampton in the Caernarvon Castle. They were seen off from London by Jack Crump; despite his many disputes with Pirie, Crump was often around at crucial moments. During the long sea voyage Pirie started work on his book. He had decided that he wanted not only to write about his experiences but also to set out his views on the organisation of athletics.

The visit to South Africa was not a success athletically. Pirie ran 11 races over a seven week period and although he won seven of them his form was poor, and never approached Halberg's. Pirie had a cold for part of the time and he also had difficulties with the dry

Before Nadrolone.

169

air, the heat and, in Johannesburg, with the altitude. The South African press thought he might have made more of an effort in his races than he did.

It became clear too that there was a considerable difference between Pirie's approaches to training and those Halberg had developed under Arthur Lydiard's guidance in New Zealand. Halberg had been taught to keep the hard work to a minimum during the racing period and he could not understand why Pirie trained so hard between races. "The worse he did in races, the harder he worked out. He had his own beliefs, of course, but he could never improve on that training. He just ran worse and worse." Quite separately Pirie more or less came to the same conclusion: "I was training assiduously and getting nowhere."

The trip culminated in a race in Rhodesia. There was some dispute as to whether the local champion, Youtham Muleya, a 19-year-old car mechanic, would be allowed to run. The *Rhodesia Herald* put this down to a concern that Muleya had run for money in other meetings. Pirie was convinced it was because Muleya was black. In the end the race, which was over three miles, was agreed and 4,000 people turned up to watch. Muleya, running on Pirie's advice in bare feet rather than spikes which he had never worn before, won. Pirie, the first "official" runner to finish, was given the trophy but handed it to his opponent.

From South Africa, Gordon and Shirley flew across the Pacific to a reunion with friends in Australia and then on to New Zealand. Here they spent another two to three months enjoying the New Zealand summer, sailing, swimming and diving. Pirie worked in a brewery and got to know the favourite running spot of downtown Auckland – a city centre park called The Domain. They were on the point of buying a house and remaining in the country when yet again a promoter offered to pay their fares back to Europe for a further round of races. After some discussion and prompted by the thought of competing in one more Olympics, they agreed to return to England.

Pirie did very little running in Britain in 1959, the pre-Olympic year, spending much of the summer in Norway. The question being asked at home was "Is Pirie going to run in Rome?"

Facing page: Still winning after ten years' racing at top level. *Ken Finding*

171

He was keeping very fit and in 1960 he showed that he was still the most versatile distance runner in the country. At the beginning of June he beat Rózsavölgyi and Ken Wood in a 1,500 metres at the White City. Two days later he won a fast 3,000 metre race. In mid July came the AAA six miles, the event in which Pirie had first made his name nearly ten years earlier. Most of the top home distance runners were there, including Martin Hyman and John Merriman, but Pirie outsprinted them on the final lap. His time (28:09.6) was the best he had ever run for that distance, or its metric equivalent. And then, a fortnight later, he won a 5,000 metre race in an international match against France, running the last lap in 54.6 seconds, and finishing in 13 minutes 51.6, the second fastest time of the year.

Crowds at the White City had seen Pirie produce decisive wins at 1,500, 3,000 and 5,000 metres, and six miles, within the space of eight weeks. Mel Watman, in *Athletics Weekly*, described Pirie as "… the supreme runner, possessing the most awesome combination of physical and tactical prowess the world has yet seen." At 29 he was at his peak, his running more relaxed than ever before and there seemed to be no one who could out kick him at the end of anything but the fastest pace.

So, very quickly, Pirie's selection for the 5,000 and 10,000 metres at the Rome Olympics seemed to be almost automatic, and indeed there were growing expectations that he might win something. Peter Hildreth, who like Pirie was about to compete in his third Olympics, described Pirie thus: "The most experienced and distinguished athlete under British colours. No-one deserves the highest laurels more than he, and at his third attempt no-one is better poised for victory". (In *The Road to Rome, ibid.*). Some remembered that, even in the aftermath of the 1956 Games, Chris Brasher had suggested that Pirie could "mature into the dominant athlete of the next Olympic Games". So, after all the ups and downs, might Rome prove to be the climax of his long career?

In *Athletics Weekly* Mel Watman reviewed the fields and thought the 5,000 metres lay between Pirie and Halberg. At the longer distance Pirie was some way down the international rankings (12th in fact) but some still thought he had a chance of a medal. There was just under a month from the match against France to the 5,000 metres heats in Rome on August 31st and all that remained was to make the final preparations.

The situation was complicated by two factors: the fact that Rome was likely to be very hot, and that Pirie was keen to go to Freiburg and see Woldemar Gerschler.

There was a view at the time that athletes (not just runners) not used to the heat would perform best either if they had three to four weeks to acclimatise, or if they flew in immediately before their events. The British Olympic Association took advice from the British Medical Association (BMA). It is unclear what advice the BMA gave but writing in *Athletics Weekly* later Jack Crump said that "medical opinion was not unanimous." He acknowledged that the British Board did decide to send runners out 48 hours before competition, "but the consideration of aircraft didn't make this possible". In the end Pirie and the other 5,000 metres runners (Bruce Tulloh and Frank Salvat) ran on their fourth day in Rome.

Allan Lawrence, who had enjoyed various adventures with Pirie in Scandinavia, was in England that summer and saw Pirie's victory in the match against France. Next day they met in Croydon to train together. Pirie told Lawrence he was now off to Freiburg for a couple of weeks. Pirie had described to Lawrence in the past the strenuous work outs he did with Gerschler and the Australian told Pirie not to go: "You're in the best shape of your life. If you let Gerschler get his hands on you and work you over. . . you won't be able to jog… much less win an Olympic medal." Lawrence remembers Pirie putting an arm round his shoulder. "Gerschler's only going to test me to see where I am. Allan, I promise you I won't go full pelt at Freiburg. It's going to be very hot, and I'll take the opportunity to acclimatise myself before Rome."

So Pirie went to Freiburg. Midway through his stay Woldemar Gerschler rang Jack Crump to seek the British Board's permission for Pirie to run a 5,000 metres race at a meeting in Berne which the USA team were using as a pre-Olympic warm up. Crump's recollection was that Gerschler told him Pirie was in tiptop condition and might break the world record, and Crump agreed to the suggestion about the race. Three English journalists, Neil Allen, Roy Moor and John Rodda, were all at the meeting, on their way to Rome.

On the night in question – it was August 21st – Pirie eventually agreed to run in a 3,000 metres. Far from showing his best form, he was well beaten by the two Americans Beatty and Dellinger and finished in a time some 20 seconds slower than he had run a couple

Herb Elliott.

173

Rome: The Olympic
Stadium.
*British Olympic
Association*

of months earlier in London. Roy Moor discussed the race with
Gordon and reported his response: "I had no pace in my legs at all.
I was aware of it on the first lap. It's probably all the hard training
I've done, but there's still plenty of time to put things right." Moor
was so worried he took the unusual step of phoning Jack Crump in
London to alert him that Pirie had run badly and seemed stale.

There were ten days now to the first race in Rome and in that time
Pirie was required to return to Britain. The Board wanted the team
together in London before flying out. Pirie always believed that he
should have been allowed to go straight to Rome from Germany.

Pirie hated what he found in Rome. True, there was still the pleasure of meeting friends and rivals from around the world, and all the
exhilaration of a major international competition. But there was
now such national and civic prestige in hosting the Games, and so
many commercial and media interests, that the needs of competitors were beginning to take a back seat. Pirie knew he needed peace
and quiet to prepare himself. Instead he found the living conditions

in the village intolerable: the TV sets blaring out, people coming and going at all hours, the incessant whine of scooters. In the end, officials allowed him to sleep at a friend's apartment.

He still felt confident. These were his third Games, and he had no reason to feel overawed. He was not too disturbed by his poor time in Berne, in part because many runners find they race below par during a period of heavy training. When Allan Lawrence met him in Rome, Pirie announced: "I'm in the best shape of my life. I won't have any excuses if I don't do well." Derek Nicholls, Gordon's friend from Coulsdon, had driven out to Rome from London to give him support.

But on the first day almost everything went wrong for the British team. Arthur Rowe failed to qualify for the shot final, Mary Bignal finished down the field in the women's long jump and Brian Hewson was eliminated in the first round of the 800 metres. Then came the four 5,000 metre heats, with the first three in each to go through to the final. Frank Salvat went first but could not find his form. He was almost 40 seconds down on the time he was running a month earlier and finished seventh.

Pirie was in the third heat. The track was new and hard, and there were 60,000 people in the stadium. Pirie had checked the list the day before and, on form, knew he should have little difficulty qualifying. Of the four runners ahead of him in the world lists that year, none was in his heat. His best distance, the 5,000, was this time timetabled first. Everything seemed to be right.

The new Olympic stadium was in a magnificent setting, almost surrounded by hills and the track itself was slightly elevated to give the runners the sensation of running above the level of the first row of seating. It was one of the first truly modern European stadiums. The Games were being covered by BBC TV for the first time since the advent of large-scale viewing. In England people were watching in large numbers to see if at last Pirie was going to claim an Olympic victory.

But almost as soon as the race began Pirie knew he had nothing to give. Derek Nicholls had managed to come within sight of the runners on the outside edge of the track and within a couple of laps Pirie had given him a dismissive wave with his hands to signal that it was all over. For another ten minutes he had to struggle round in the burning heat, feeling emptier and emptier with every lap. The Roman crowd was not generous to losers and as he fell further and further behind the jeering and whistling started. The last lap must have been the loneliest of his life, lonelier even than the last laps of the 10,000 metres at Melbourne. At home, his friends watched in disbelief. Then, in the final heat Tulloh too failed to qualify.

Pirie was as puzzled as anyone: "I can't feel any difference in myself… but I just don't know what happened. I just didn't seem to run well. I can only apologise to the people back home. It feels hot. I'm quite satisfied that my training was right. I have no excuses. When the leaders started to increase the pace I could not hold them." Roy Moor – such a faithful friend and supporter – was sure he knew what had happened. Pirie had left the gold medal behind on his German training track. He was wrecked by over-training.

Pirie now had to face the interviews and inquisitions from the press, which he hated so much. There were eight days to wait before the 10,000 metres. He got some consolation from rounding up Salvat and Tulloh and taking them off to a beach where they could run together, telling them all this was not the end of the world and there would be better races to come. It was a gesture Tulloh always remembered with pleasure.

So came the 10,000 metres, Pirie's sixth and last Olympic race, but at a distance where he had few competitive races for some years. It was still very warm but there had been a cloudburst not long before the race and conditions were cooler than a week earlier. There was a large field of 33 runners, and the favourites among them were Murray Halberg, who had won the 5,000 metres a few days earlier, the European champion Krzyszkowiak, Dave Power, Hans Grodotzki and the Russian Pyotr Bolotnikov. Of the three Britons, John Merriman had the best recent record.

Pirie adopted what was for him an unusual strategy. Having seen his friend Halberg win the 5,000 so convincingly, he decided to shadow him in the longer race. But as it turned out it was Bolotnikov, watched by his countryman Kuts in the stands, who was the man to watch. The Russian runner moved into the lead just before the end of the first kilometre and led the field almost continually to the half way point. Pirie ran much of the first ten laps in lane two, apparently worried about being boxed in and losing contact but he went through 5,000 metres considerably quicker than he had run

the distance eight days earlier in his heat. At 6,000 metres there were 14 runners within reach of each other and all seemingly in with a chance. Pirie was still watching Halberg and still feeling reasonably comfortable.

But then it went wrong. On the 19th lap four runners began to pull away and within just over a minute had a 40 yard lead on the next group. With four laps of the race remaining Halberg was out of contention, and so was Pirie. Realising now that his strategy had failed, he lost what little confidence he had regained and fell further back. At the front, Bolotnikov went ahead with 600 metres to go, ran a storming last lap and finished less than two seconds outside Kuts' world record. The next six finishers, including Halberg who was fifth, all produced times which took them into the world's ten best. Behind them John Merriman ran a UK record (28:52.6) in eighth place, and Martin Hyman a personal best in ninth. Pirie was tenth. Over the last few laps he fell about 150 yards behind Halberg, and his final lap had taken 77 seconds.

It had been a much better race than the 5,000 and he had regained some sympathy from the crowd. But he was not satisfied. "I blame myself. I was convinced Halberg was the man to stalk and it was

Rome Olympics: Pirie (636) struggling near the rear of the field in his 5,000 metres heat. *British Olympic Association.*

177

a mistake," he told the press. "I had deluded myself with too many calculations," he wrote later.

At the time, his disappointment, and his anger with the press, was acute. "I've had enough. I feel I can't go on… because of certain sections of the press. Now all I want to do is get out of the sport and go back to New Zealand. I can't get there quick enough."

Although Pirie may have made a tactical error in the 10,000 metres he produced the fastest time of his career at the distance, though slightly outside his best for six miles. His hopes of a medal had really rested on kicking at the end off a much slower pace. Tenth place in a really fast race was about right for someone in his position on the world rankings in 1960. Although he got to within 16 seconds of the world record in 1953, and may have had the capacity to beat it in the right conditions, in the second half of his career he never produced times over the distance which matched the improvement in world standards.

In 1960 his times over 5,000 metres were still on a par with the world's best and he still had finishing speed in the straight. What went wrong over the shorter distance in Rome? Pirie always laid some, if not all, of the blame on the heat and on the failure of the British Board to make appropriate travel arrangements. He pointed to the success of the New Zealand and Australian runners who had arrived in Rome between three and four weeks before their races. He collected evidence about the number of competitors – cyclists and rowers as well as runners – who performed badly when required to compete three to five days after their arrival. Other runners in the British team, including Martin Hyman and Laurie Reed, found the heat a tremendous problem.

But there was another body of opinion which, having seen both his 5,000 metre run on August 1st at the White City and then his race over the same distance in Rome on August 31st concluded that something had gone wrong in between. Roy Moor, Armour Milne, Jack Barlow – all admirers of Pirie – attributed his failure in Rome to over-training in Germany, or to the staleness that it produced. It is not clear whether they knew what he had done in Freiburg, though Barlow reported that he had been doing sessions of thirty 400 metre repetitions at 66 seconds each in an hour. But they were doubtless influenced by Pirie's own statement in Berne that he had been working out very hard. Neil Allen reported in his book of the Rome Olympics that Pirie had acknowledged in Berne that he had over-trained in Germany, though Pirie dismissed this idea later.

In general Pirie did not ease off in his training before races as much as other runners. Laurie Reed thought this was a problem: "Gordon did too much of his training up to the event… he didn't know when to ease down." A Norwegian journalist put this to Pirie when he was in Bergen in October. "Weren't you a bit of an idiot, Gordon, training yourself to death when all you needed was to keep yourself in shape?" Pirie would not agree. "I did too little training… in the weeks before the Games I relaxed a bit and only trained once a day. But – it was the damned heat."

The problem with the over-training argument is that it does not fully explain why all three British 5,000-metre men ran below their best form on that day in Rome. Nor why Pirie ran well earlier in the season, or indeed at other times in his career. It may be that, at 29, he could no longer sustain peak form so consistently over a season. Arthur Lydiard, coach to Halberg and Snell, certainly thought peaking was an issue. "We were very glad that Gordon ran so well earlier that summer," he said. When Pirie was asked in radio interview a couple of years later to look back at Rome his comment was interesting: "I was getting too old – or it was too hot, I'm not sure which. We had only three days to acclimatise. We should all have reached the final." (BBC Radio, *Desert Island Discs*, 1962).

Some blamed this, of course, on the influence of Gerschler believing Pirie should have done less speed work and concentrated on the longer distances. Others thought Pirie's early involvement with six-mile running got him on the wrong track. We will never know for sure. But analysis of his times over a ten year period suggests that it is his performances around two and three miles (and 3,000 and 5,000 metres) which best stand the test of time.

Whatever he felt about that debate, Pirie had now had a series of disappointments at major championships. Some described them, unfairly, as a string of failures. He was aware that he might be remembered not as the person who did break world records, but as the person who did not win gold medals. It was going to be something to deal with, over the years.

Pirie did not retire and he did not return to New Zealand. He went on racing around the world for another year. On September 23rd in Dublin he achieved one outstanding ambition – his first four minute mile. Herb Elliott, who was revisiting the stadium in which he had broken the world mile record two years previously, helped pull him through and Pirie ran his best ever time, 3:59.9, beating Tábori, Snell and Thomas in the process. He was the only British runner to go under four minutes that season, and he duly received from Roger Bannister the tie awarded to all members of the four minute mile club.

In 1961 there was one more round of the favourite events, one more record, one more row, and then "retirement". In February and March Pirie ran a number of cross-country races for SLH, culminating in The National, where he finished 20th. He ran in the London to Brighton relay in April and the Southern track championships in June. Then in the middle of July he delighted the White City crowds with two fine wins. First he won his last AAA title, over three miles on July 15th, waving delightedly to the crowd as he finished. He was returning to New Zealand, said one report, confident that Tulloh and Hyman could fill the gap left by his departure.

A week later he turned out with Bruce Tulloh over the same distance for a British team competing against the USA. It was a misty, rainy day and in what looked like an agreed plan the two British runners shared the pace for the first ten of the 12 laps, in two lap shifts. Max Truex then took the lead until just after the bell when Pirie, nodding to Tulloh as he moved up, overtook the American. It was now a race for the finish, with Tulloh, short and frail, passing Pirie on the back straight. But Pirie, as so often, had the faster finish and won in a new UK national record (13:16.4), with Tulloh a stride behind. It was a sweet victory, designed to prove, said the newspapers, that he would have done better in Rome if he had not been sent there so late. Whatever the disappointments of the Olympics, there was a great welcome for Pirie at the White City in the summer of 1961.

Pirie now undertook two more months of racing in Norway, where he tried unsuccessfully to break the world two mile record, and in Finland and Sweden. Then came the final, inevitable row, the last quarrel between him and Crump. Pirie was due to run for Britain against West Germany in Dortmund on September 2nd but arrived late, having competed in a mile race in Stockholm the evening before. British officials now dropped him from the team for both the match with West Germany and one with Poland that was to follow.

Even the most ardent of Pirie's supporters did not try to justify his decision to compete the day before an international commitment. What concerned them, and many others, was that this might be the end of his running career in Britain without the White City finale all hoped for. Ken Norris, a friend of Pirie's but with his own views, wrote an open letter to Jack Crump and the British Board in *Athletics Weekly*.

Dear Jack

First let me say that I agree with your decision to ban Gordon Pirie, having joined the team late from Sweden. Gordon is his own worst enemy and a fool to himself. However, without doubt, he is one of the greatest if not THE GREATEST athlete this country has ever seen and in the past decade he has won countless points for us in international competition. Gordon has stated his intention to retire at the end of this season and one's memory flows swiftly back to the wonderful farewell appearance of Arthur Wint. Athletics today has too few characters, but Gordon is one of them and the public loves him. At least then, let him retire with some honour and invite him to compete in an international or invitation event in the Russian meeting. Quite apart from the thousands it will put on the gate, the British public deserves the opportunity to acclaim a truly great athlete.

To Gordon, I would say "Come off your high horse and apologise, and prove for the last time what an unbeatable athlete you really can be." To all parties I say, "Don't let pig-headedness spoil a great occasion."

Ken Norris

And that is what happened. Pirie was chosen for the floodlit match against the Russian Federal Republic at the White City on September 20th, where he ran in the 5,000 metres, partnered by the young John Snowden, against the Russian pair Naroditskiy and Yefimov. It was not a fast or exciting race. All four runners had spells in the lead and were in contention up to the bell, and some observers thought Pirie was shepherding his teammate to ensure they could get maximum points. The spotlights were able to capture the whole group as they circled and then, with a lap to go Pirie went in front and he and Snowden pulled away from the Russian pair, who were

Ken Norris.
Athletics Weekly

181

left in the darkness. John Snowden looked briefly as though he might challenge Pirie in the home straight but Pirie pulled away to win amid great applause. Some thought he had stage-managed it: "a theatrical show that would have made the Old Vic green with envy," said Desmond Hackett in the *Daily Express*. And why not?

It was Pirie's last amateur race. Over 13 years had passed since he had watched Zátopek at Wembley, ten years since he had set his first British record at the White City. He did a solo lap of honour, in his navy tracksuit trousers and white top, the spotlight picking him out again. All around the arena they stood up. He jogged past the main stand, shaking hands and making his farewells. A cluster of photographers followed him, their flash bulbs popping in the night air. Groups of spectators came down from their seats to the track-side to get his autograph. Then people began to leave, making their way out of the shabby stadium into Wood Lane to get their buses or the tube.

13 Running wild

Within days of Pirie's final race as an amateur a popular Sunday newspaper, *The People*, announced "a major exposure" of British athletics. It promised its readers sensational revelations about what really went on in the sport, and the man who was to spill the secrets was to be "the most outspoken athlete of them all" (see page 184). *The People* ran major articles for several weeks. The first ("Pirie confesses – I've been paid to run"; "Even the Russians tried to bribe me") was about illicit payments in the sport. Pirie told how he had earned about £1,000 in appearance money in 1961, negotiating with promoters, especially in Sweden, his "expenses" for racing in particular meetings. The next article tackled the issue of drug-taking, implicating Kuts and others ("Those supermen won on dope").

In later articles Pirie went on to attack the older generation running the sport and calling for athletes to be given a bigger say in its administration. "Strike now, you athletes, I'll lead you if you want me to", was the headline. In another piece Pirie complained about what the sport had cost him, in shoes and other kit, food and travel. "I would have done better as a builder's labourer" was the headline for that one. It was all well marketed. The story needed to be told, Pirie said, to help athletics get the new deal it so badly needed.

Pirie had been working on an account of his experiences for some time. He wanted to write something that would be more than the usual record of events that many contemporary sports stars produced. He wanted to set out his personal views, and justify many of the things for which he had been attacked.

He had begun writing the book on the sea voyage to South Africa in late 1958. When he visited Bergen in October 1960 he made it

PIRIE

TAKES OFF THE GAG!

At last—the most outspoken runner of them all has decided to tell all—and he really lifts the lid off athletics. Don't miss Gordon Pirie as he exposes:

❋ the sham of amateurism
❋ out-of-date British methods
❋ out-of-touch officials
❋ the "Good Time Charlies"

This is a hard-hitting, revealing story from a great athlete, a man who has dedicated his life to the sport he loved—and who ran to win! You might not agree with him but you must in fairness read *his story*, starting

EXCLUSIVELY IN

THE PEOPLE

ON SUNDAY

Advertisement in
Athletics Weekly.

clear to journalists that it would present things as he saw them and that he would "call a dog a dog". At that stage he was thinking of using the title *Races and experiences from many countries*. But before publication he sold serial rights to *The People* and they were looking for something more dramatic. The title chosen echoed a popular song of the time, and also hinted at Pirie's own rebelliousness: *Running Wild*.

Pirie opened *Running Wild* with a reply to his critics and a justification of his training. He paid tributes to Zátopek and to Gerschler, to whom the book was dedicated. There was then a fierce attack on the organisation of British athletics and "the hypocrisy of British

184

amateurism". Then came the more conventional, but entertaining, account of his travels and races. The book revealed a man determined to stand by his career and defend his corner, but also affectionate and generous to a multitude of friends and rivals. But much of it told of his struggle to succeed, with anecdotes about what happened along the way. The story was vividly told and some runners today still turn to the book for inspiration.

There was real anger in Pirie's book. That was the intention. He knew the sport needed shaking up and modernising. He did aknowledge in later years that he was "paid extra to put things in", especially to the newspaper articles, and he subsequently modified some of the views expressed in *Running Wild*. But Pirie never changed his fundamental views about the way the sport was organised.

The book evoked a mixed response. Some thought Pirie was tarnishing his good name by writing for cash in this way. Others thought there was less to the revelations than *The People* claimed, since most people in the sport knew all this already. Jimmy Green in *Athletics Weekly* thought that it was time for change, and that Pirie's book might help: "Alterations must come, and come they will, so if Gordon's revelations provoke the powers-that-be into action, they will not have been in vain and the sport may yet thank him for having written them."[22]

There was one other aspect of *Running Wild* that aroused the interest of athletics fans. Pirie knew more about the sport's statistics than most runners did and throughout his life he was able to reel off precise details about lap times and records. For *Running Wild* he compiled a list of the races in which he had run since 1950, well over 400 in all, drawing not from careful library research but from notes made in his training diary and from his own prodigious memory. He also made predictions for future standards in middle and long distance events suggesting what they might be ten years after *Running Wild* went to press, that is in 1971.

Pirie's predictions make interesting reading today. Indeed, looking back at past predictions is almost as interesting as making guesses about the future. Someone wrote to *The Listener* magazine

---

[22] *Running Wild* is not in print at the time of writing but copies can sometimes be obtained in second-hand bookshops.

The People, November 1961.
People – Mirror Group

in London in January 1951 and predicted that the world best time for the mile might be as low as 3 minutes 58 seconds in the year 2000. That time was reached in 1954, rather sooner than the writer expected, and it fell below 3 minutes 45 seconds well before 2000. At the end of 1985 Stan Greenberg, a highly experienced track and field statistician, stuck his neck out with predictions for the year 2000. There was a short delay before publication and two of the predictions he made were out of date by the time they appeared in print.

Pirie's expectations for the longer distances, for the 5,000 and 10,000 metres, were not far wrong. For the 3,000 metres, the distance at which in 1961 he was still the world record holder, he predicted an improvement from his own time of 7:52.8 to 7:45 and here be badly underestimated the improvements that would be made. Although his own record did last for six years, by 1971 the Kenyan runner Kipchoge Keino had brought the time down to 7:39.6.

Pirie was most off target with the shorter distances, where he vastly overestimated what runners could achieve. For instance he thought the 800 metres time might come down from 1.45:7 to 1.39:7, but by 1971 it had fallen to "only" 1.44.3. At the time of writing the record stands at 1:41.11.

Pirie knew his experiences, and his attitudes, were part of a wider change in British culture. He told *Bergens Tidende* in 1960 that he was in no way ashamed to say that he trained hard and that he was very pleased when he did well, and that he had received a huge number of letters and enquiries from people who felt the same. "That may be because new social classes are making themselves felt in the class society we have in England." When Shirley Pirie was asked in 1997 why Gordon had made such an impact in 1950s Britain, she commented: "I suppose he was a kind of Angry Young Man".[23]

The hypocrisy or "shamateurism", as it was sometimes called, was not new. Nurmi, Hägg and Andersson had all suffered suspension in the past. Some of Pirie's contemporaries, including Murray Halberg and Derek Ibbotson, have since talked about the money they were paid for racing at that time. There were probably half a dozen people getting money on a regular basis in 1957, but it afterwards it became more widespread.

All of this was part of the messy way in which the "real" life of athletics was bursting out of the structures and rules by which it had been constrained since Victorian times. This was so widely known to some that Stan Greenberg, in one of his periodic and trenchant letters to *Athletics Weekly*, accused Pirie himself of hypocrisy because of his claims that the sport had cost him money. Referring to Gordon's "revelations" about payments he asked: "Surely nobody with any knowledge of the sport could not have known that this was the case and that some athletes were making quite a bit out of the sport". He suggested Gordon keep his moans to himself and his accountant.

But Pirie was certainly not alone in the way he was thinking. Chris Brasher was one of those who were openly questioning the basis on which athletics was organised. He knew that it was becoming increasingly difficult to maintain the fiction of an old time amateur sport. In the book put together by members of the International Athletes Club before the 1960 Olympics (*The Road to Rome*) Brasher queried Lord Burghley's view that the amateur spirit was at the heart of the Olympic ideal. "No competitor will mind if his opponent is an amateur or not. If any athletes are barred because of the Victorian ideals of the International Olympic Committee, then the whole point of the Games vanishes."

Chataway joined him: "It may have been reasonable before the First World War to keep the professionals out: to pretend to do so today is hypocrisy." Derek Johnson criticised Jack Crump and

---

[23] Angry Young Man was a popular term in the late 1950s to describe writers and critics who were opposed to the stuffiness of British culture.

Harold Abrahams for "double standards" in enforcing amateur rules while getting money themselves for press articles. Interestingly, these criticisms were coming from the Oxford and Cambridge end of the sport, traditionally the home base of the amateur tradition.

Indeed, as Pirie knew, the sport was in growing crisis. Disputes between coaches and officials were coming to a head and in the winter of 1961–62 three leading full-time coaches, Jim Alford, Geoff Dyson and Lionel Pugh, resigned. A few months later a group of runners, coaches and senior ex-athletes, including Donald Finlay, John Disley and Robbie Brightwell, came together to promote the reform of the administration of British athletics. "Outstanding professional coaches have left in disgust, keen and capable ex-athletes have been discouraged from becoming officials and many athletes have retired too early and in bitterness," they said in their position statement. At the same time the International Athletes Club (IAC) was growing in influence and beginning to organise its own training weekends.

But despite his views Pirie did not play much of a part in this. Martin Hyman, whose athletic career had overlapped with Pirie's and who was involved in the IAC thought that it was probably because "Pirie was too much of an individual. Perhaps we thought there were particular ways of doing things that were right. But maybe we should have used him more."

Pirie's involvement in the organisational side of athletics was largely restricted to his activities in the British Milers' Club. The BMC was formed by coach Frank Horwill and others to provide up and coming milers with tough competition and thereby improve standards. "We wanted Gordon involved – he was a well-known figure, who wanted to shake people out of their complacency. He gave the club a lot of support, and was chairman for two years. Mind you, when Gordon was there, we didn't spend much time on business items – within ten minutes we'd be discussing training methods and Gordon would be laying down the law!"

Dust jacket of *Running Wild*.

In tennis, another sport with a long-standing amateur tradition, Jack Kramer was organising a fully fledged professional circuit and Pirie was asked in a radio interview if he could be the Kramer of track and field. He was cautious. "You need a lot of money to attract people to professional athletics. Herb Elliott was offered 80,000 dollars and turned it down. It could boom if the champions came… everything has potential if it has quality." (BBC Radio, *Frankly Speaking*, April 1962).

Pirie could see that sooner or later commercial pressures would force athletics to change its rules. He flirted briefly with the idea of professional athletics at home and abroad and tried to get one or two others involved. Ken Wood was one of those approached. But most athletes were pursuing their careers or their studies and not many were interested. It came to nothing.

Pirie went to Scotland in July 1962, and was paid £100 for competing in the Border Games at Jedbergh. He kept the crowd entertained with some spectacular warming up and the bookmakers made him favourite to win. But he was not used to running with the large numbers that compete in such races. Pirie found himself lined up on a small grass track against 50 to 60 other runners, all handicapped to start at different points. He was put 45 yards behind his nearest challenger in the mile, and 310 yards down in the two miles, and this proved too much. The standard of some of the other runners was higher than he expected and he finished some way down the field in both races. "I couldn't get any spark into my running", he said afterwards.

But he did get one fairly lucrative contract. In the summer of 1962 he ran two exhibition races in the bullring at San Sebastián in Spain against local opposition. The races were over 10,000 metres and involved Pirie starting on one side of the ring, and an opponent on another. It was essentially a betting occasion. Spectators gambled on when one runner would catch another and on the times individual runners would take to complete parts of the race. By the time of the second race Pirie was not fully fit and he was not disappointed when the organisers asked him not to try too hard. The whole thing, he reflected later, was "a bit of a joke".

Some other openings came his way. He contracted with the BBC to do some radio work during the Empire Games in Perth in the autumn of 1962 and, on the way out, found himself on the same boat as the English cricket team who were about to tour Australia. Ted Dexter was captain of that touring party: "Gordon Pirie was on board and I could not resist the temptation. He is quite the worst person to get involved with if you are not feeling fit. I thought, Ah,

Summer 1962. Pirie (far side of stadium) waits for the start of a race in the bull ring at San Sebastián.
Jing Guan Pirie

here is the man for us, he will stop us putting on bellies, and I enrolled him on the spot to help with our daily stint on board. Between us we got rather carried away. In no time the boys were running round the deck and doing all sorts of most punishing exercises." (*Ted Dexter Declares*, Stanley Paul, London 1966)

Freddie Trueman wrote later that Pirie told him to stop eating steaks and "go on a diet of nuts and lettuce like him". Colin Cowdrey has told how Freddie Trueman and Brian Statham, the two great fast bowlers in the team, slipped out of the squad as they were running round the boat so as to avoid doing the full distance. When Pirie reprimanded them Trueman told him in no uncertain terms what he could do with his fitness training. On arrival at Fremantle Pirie was reported to have described some of the team as "an unfit paunchy bunch of barflies".

The cricketers survived a long and intensive tour without many injuries but reports in *Wisden*, the cricket almanac, indicated that while the English team matched the Australians in batting and bowling they were not in the same league in fielding or running between the wickets. Today's top cricketers undertake serious fitness programmes as part of their professional routine.

On board the *Canberra*, October 1962. Pirie leads John Murray, David Allen, Donald Larter and Fred Titmus.
Rachel Brown

Pirie also got a little involved in the soccer scene, helping Dick Graham who was manager of Crystal Palace, then in the third division of the Football League. Pirie assisted with pre-season training at Selhurst Park for a couple of years and also took the players on training runs round the Metropolitan Police cross-country course at Hayes. "He certainly got them fit," remembers Dick Graham, "and he helped me get them into the second division."

During the late 1950s Pirie had continued his contacts with Adidas and developed his thinking about running shoe design. He had become convinced that runners were developing blistering and achilles tendonitis because many shoes had too much empty space around the base of the heel bone. He began in the late fifties to customise all the shoes he bought from Adidas to try and avoid this problem. Pirie was frustrated by his inability to persuade Adidas to

Pirie (sunglasses) gets Fred Trueman going.

do something about this. But his discussions with Adi Dassler did lead to one important innovation. When Pirie reported the problems he had because the spikes on his track shoes got worn down, they had the idea of screwing the spikes in and out rather than fixing them permanently. Spikes could then be replaced when worn, and also changed to suit different track surfaces. This became standard practice.

Since he was no longer an amateur athlete, Pirie was now free to accept advertising contracts. He refused to endorse products inimical to good health but in 1962 he signed a contract with the Glaxo company to promote Complan a new health product. Complan was a powder containing "all the nourishment necessary to maintain human life": protein, minerals, carbohydrates, vitamins and fat. It was originally designed for the feeding of those described at that time as "comatose" or for hospital patients who could not take normal food. Later it was marketed to the public at large as "a completely balanced diet" and as an aid to controlled slimming. Pirie promoted Complan for a number of years. In their advertisements he was shown coaching athletes and endorsing the product as "a complete scientifically balanced food that inspires medal winning performances."

But Pirie really needed a major challenge. He could sense the popularity of athletics falling. There was growing competition from other sports and from television. In 1962 there were barely 10,000 people at the White City for the AAA meeting, and the stadium felt empty. Pirie's retirement had left a hole at the heart of British athletics.

It had also left a hole in his life. Pirie had already found from his coaching links with runners such as Mike Wiggs and John Merriman that he enjoyed working with young athletes. Somehow he had to convert his drive and energy into substantial ventures, enterprises that would tap his ability to inspire others. He had pioneered new training methods, and showed how, contrary to the English tradition, you had to go out in races to dominate and to win. But he still had to find a role for himself now that competitive athletics was over. It was not going to be easy.

Athletics
WEEKLY

March 26th, 1960

9D

Vol. 14. No. 13

Gordon Pirie leads "National" field soon after the start

A.G.M. OF THE A.A.A.
AND HONORARY COACHES'
CONFERENCE

BEST BRITISH JUNIOR
PERFORMERS, 1959
(HAMMER & JAVELIN)

WALKING • ROAD RELAYS • LEAGUE RACES

THE OFFICIAL ORGAN OF ATHLETICS IN GREAT BRITAIN

14 Unfinished business

In 1963 Gordon and Shirley bought a house in the Surrey village of Nutfield, only a few miles south of Coulsdon where Pirie had grown up. The property was one of four created from the conversion of what was once the coach house on a large estate. Gordon and Shirley undertook a number of improvements and the house became a comfortable family home. The Piries' first child, Joanne, had been born earlier that year and their second, Sara, was born in 1965. There were spare rooms at The Coach House where people could stay and it became a popular stopover for visiting runners, just as 7 Meadway had been in Pirie's childhood.

This was a kind of "settling down". But Pirie had no plans for a conventional career. He was still running every day, he was keen to coach other athletes and he had some ideas about using his knowledge and experience as a consultant in the wider world of fitness and health. Some of his hopes were fulfilled, some were not. And he ended up doing some things that he had never imagined.

The first venture was the "Gordon Pirie School of Athletics", launched in December 1963, largely through advertisements in the athletics press. The "School" was not a building but a marketing device to establish some kind of nationwide coaching role. Individuals and organisations were invited to book visits or coaching lessons for set fees.

Shortly afterwards advertisements appeared in the press for new sportswear which Pirie had helped to design and promote: "Saxonclad" tracksuits and the "Gordon Pirie Sprinta", described as "the lightest and greatest track shoe in the world".

Pirie was by no means the first ex-athlete to coach, or to sponsor sports goods. But by promoting his services and charging for them

Facing page: Pirie leading "The National" at West Bromwich 1960. Basil Heatley was the eventual winner. *Athletics Weekly/Gerry Cranham*

he was breaking with the conventions of the time. In an amateur sport, with only a small cadre of full-time coaches, almost all coaching was done by unpaid volunteers and where ex-athletes were concerned it was very much a matter of "putting something back in", not making an income. There was some feeling, expressed in letters to *Athletics Weekly* and elsewhere, that by charging a fee Pirie was upsetting the status quo.

Pirie was certainly reaching for something new. He wanted to release the notion of fitness from its connections with the school gym or the parade ground. He was trying to open up a new market, by appealing to everyone, especially those in sedentary occupations, to think about their physical well being. This was well before what later became known as the "fitness boom".

Pirie was convinced that the process of keeping fit could be an enjoyable part of daily life but that people needed help in learning how to manage this. In 1965 he published *Fitness for Men*, a short guide for non-athletes who wanted to look after their bodies without giving up large amounts of time. The book included interviews with a number of people from different walks of like, including Sir Charles Forte, Norman Wisdom and Chris Chataway, in which they endorsed the book and its philosophy.

Inside the front cover was a small gramophone record on which Pirie talked to Frank Bough of the BBC about the ideas behind the book and the daily schedules that he was suggesting. The interview allowed Pirie to try and anticipate some of the popular fears that the word fitness might induce. The exercises were not going to be severe, like anything in Pirie's own training, they were not going to be like school PE classes, and they did not need special equipment. To prove the point Pirie and Bough went through one of the schedules in the room where they were recording.

This was one of the first books to offer simple fitness routines that could be carried out in the home and did not interfere with all the other things people wanted to do in their lives. It was unusual too in trying a multi-media approach. But Pirie's book went beyond daily "physical jerks". It presented fitness as something to do with health in general, with freedom from stress and with personal happiness. It contained advice and guidance on relaxation, breathing and diet as well as exercise schedules.

Young would-be runners
watch Pirie perform at
a training school.
Kevin Kelly

Pirie had acquired an interest in healthy eating as a young runner and this had developed, as he travelled the world, talked to people and read more widely, into a much wider commitment to a healthy life style. He now announced the existence of a "Health Food Department". This would advise on "the growing demand for natural foods which help to combat the ever increasing chemical and artificial ingredients included in many foods sold today."

Pirie's partner in some of these ventures was Derek Nicholls, the professional tennis coach who had helped him considerably during the later years of his athletic career. Derek and his wife Sheila were friends of Gordon and Shirley and the Piries sometimes retreated to the Nicholls' home in Purley when they wanted to get away from the attention of the media or the pressures of being in the public eye.

Derek Nicholls had learned from building up his own tennis coaching business that there was scope to provide a wider range of services relating to fitness, especially to business men and women. Together he and Pirie had the potential for a strong partnership – a big name, worldwide experience of international sport, coaching expertise, contacts in sport generally. But what they needed was to get some firms on board. Pirie often talked to friends about the need to get a major company involved, perhaps sponsoring an Academy, which would offer a range of services.

Derek had the idea of Fitness Lounges in big firms, rooms where executives could work out. It matched well with Pirie's notion that business people might want to do simple work outs as part of their daily routine. To help in the preparation of a brochure the two men went to Heals furniture store in the Tottenham Court Road and took pictures of modern office furniture with weights and exercise equipment lying about. They produced fitness schedules for executives in well-styled embossed covers and sent complimentary copies to major firms.

These ideas were the progenitors of the modern leisure industry, with its exercise rooms in office and hotels, and its spacious, luxury fitness centres, filled with state of the art equipment. But it would have a required a great deal of detailed administrative and business work to get the project going. Sustained negotiations were needed over a period of time with a number of major firms. Pirie was impatient to get results. He was not attuned to the disciplines of the commercial world. "Our plans were never realised," recalled Derek Nicholls. "Gordon understood that his name was important but he never really grasped what was involved in getting all this on a proper footing."

All the time Pirie was working on these business ideas, the running life continued. Runners came to the house to train and to talk, some, especially New Zealanders and Australians, seeking somewhere to stay as they passed through England. There was much telling of stories and reminiscing of good times around the world.

When it was time for a run, Pirie would round people up – "Come on, let's go, let's go!" – and the group would move off to one of the favoured circuits from the house. And in these training groups, Pirie was as competitive as ever. Mike Murray was a teacher in a local Surrey school and a fine miler who did a lot of training with Pirie at that time. He was called urgently to the phone from the classroom one day to find Pirie at the other end of the line: Gordon had just broken their best time for a one mile circuit both used in training.

A year after he announced the "Gordon Pirie School of Athletics" Pirie advertised the "Gordon Pirie Awards". These were to be made annually to the outstanding boy miler and girl half-miler. Six training scholarships would be awarded to the three top performers in each group who would like personal coaching. But athletes did not come forward for training in great numbers. Most of the runners whom Pirie coached during the next few years came to him through other connections.

Hugh Sweeney was living in New York when he saw an advert Pirie had placed in the American journal *Track and Field News* and sent $10 to start a correspondence course. "It was the only payment he ever asked for, although we wrote to each other for two to three years. When I told him I'd tried various things and they hadn't worked out he suggested I try four short sessions each day, running as hard as I could for 20 minutes. It seemed to work – I soon ran my best mile time."

Mike Rowlands was a junior international but lived in a part of Wales where he did not have easy access to a coach. "I used to send him money every month – about a fiver, I think – and he would send me schedules. I went up to the Coach House about once a month. There would be other runners there including one or two New Zealanders or Australians – maybe eight people in all, and many of them eating at the house too. We'd go to the track at Merstham, or do a ten mile loop from the house. Gordon was always running himself of course, he was very competitive and that made the training interesting. Gordon could contradict himself at times but he was inspirational and I still use what I learned from him in my own coaching."

Sometimes young runners living in the Surrey area were encouraged by their clubs, especially SLH, to try working with the Pirie group. John Rix started with Pirie when he was still at school. John won the mile at the London Athletic Clubs' schools meeting in 1966 and took a job near Nutfield and stayed with the Piries for two months before he went up to university.

"People came and went. Gordon seemed to be changing his ideas a lot, or maybe he was trying things out. Sometimes he'd criticise you for doing the very thing he'd suggested the week before. Some people may have found it hard to handle the criticism. Gordon was something of a perfectionist but he inspired me and made me take my running seriously. It did me good. It was refreshing to meet someone whose attitude was 'You can do it'." Pirie coached John Rix by post while he was at Cambridge and in 1967 Rix set a new UK Junior Mile record of 4:02.8.

The training runs that Pirie organised in Richmond Park or Wimbledon Common on Sunday mornings were well known, and attracted some of the best known up and coming runners in the sport. Gerry North remembers: "In the early sixties some of us would meet up on Sunday mornings and do some long runs. Sometimes Jim Hogan would come along, and Brian Fernee might be there and occasionally Ron Clarke. It was good steady running. To me Gordon was the athlete's athlete. He was always friendly, he loved his athletics and he lived for it."

The companionship of long-distance runners, Richmond Park, 1963. From left: Mike Shingles, Mike Kortennay, DAGP, Charlie Dabbs, Brian Fernee, Ano, Ano, Gerry North.
Gerry North

This companionship was important, and Pirie often spoke of the importance of groups of runners training together and raising each other's performance, something he saw the Kenyans do in later life. But the greatest challenge for any coach is to help an outstanding individual harness his or her ability and prove themselves a champion. So it was with Gordon Pirie and Anne Smith.

In 1963, when she was 22, Anne Smith was one of the best half-milers in the country. She had joined Mitcham Athletic Club in South London as a schoolgirl, at a time when there were considerable restrictions on the distances young women were allowed to run in competition. Pat Brown (now Pat Turmer) was the same age as Anne and joined the club at about the same time: "Anne and I both fancied the longer distances and even then you could tell how strong Anne was. But in those days you weren't allowed to compete over anything longer than 220 yards until you were 16. As soon as we got to 16 we started to try 880 yards."

Anne and Pat received encouragement to try half-miling and cross-country from one of the stalwarts of the Mitcham club, Jack Fitzgerald, and they both improved rapidly. When Anne Smith went to College of Education, to train as a teacher, she got help and encouragement from Diane Leather, who had held world records at 1,500 metres and a mile. In 1963, Smith ran three internationals for Britain, bringing her best time for 880 yards down to 2:07.2. But although she had improved considerably she did not have the pace and strength to win races at international level. Anne had reached the stage when she had decided that she needed to be a tougher racer. " I couldn't race to save my life. I used to follow everyone else round the track and then try to get to the front just before the finish. It worked in club races, but it certainly didn't work in international class half-miling."

Anne met with Gordon and Shirley almost by chance, had a discussion about her running and Pirie took her on. By now Anne had qualified as a physical education teacher, she was stronger and fitter and the ideal height, 5 ft 6 in, for a middle distance runner. Several nights a week in summer and winter she would drive her Fiat 600 from the school in Hammersmith where she was teaching to Nutfield for training sessions with Pirie. She benefited not only from his guidance and support but also that of Shirley, who could draw on her own experience of international athletics.

Her times improved. Often running strongly from the front, her hair billowing behind her, she won race after race setting, said *Athletics Weekly*, "her own fierce pace". By the time of the 1964 Olympics she had taken her best time down to 2:05.3 seconds and was fourth in the world rankings. But Tokyo proved a disappointment for her. She won her heat and then, next day, broke the British

Anne Smith winning the
Women's AAA 880 yards
championship in July
1966.
Kevin Kelly

800 metre record in the semi-finals with a time of 2:04.8. But in the
final she was outsprinted on the second lap. Ann Packer took the
gold medal in a new world record time of 2:01.1, over three seconds
inside the British record Smith had set a few days earlier. Anne Smith
was almost unnoticed in last place.

Some of the controversy which had surrounded Pirie's running
career now began to dog him as a coach. "Anne Smith had a
wonderful year of consistent top class performances. As with her
coach in 1956 and 1960 however she was over-trained and stale
when it came to the vital day of days," wrote one correspondent in
Athletics Weekly. Perhaps it was inevitable that, because Pirie had
a reputation as someone who had trained extremely hard, he would
be suspected of over-training his athletes. There were certainly
those, knowledgeable athletes some of them, who thought that

the training load Pirie designed was too heavy. The great Australian runner Ron Clarke visited Nutfield from time to time and concluded: "The trouble with Gordon was that he had too much passion, and he worked his people too hard. He was impatient. He wanted them to be too good too quick. Every so often he had Anne in tears. It needed Shirley to give the input that made it all work."

But this was a time when British women's track running was already beginning to turn towards harder work, to reach the standards reached by European competitors. Jim Alford was one of the first coaches to do this, and Madeleine Ibbotson one of the first athletes. It was the time too when longer distances for women were coming onto the schedule for international championships. In the Pirie-Smith case the story was complicated by the fact that Anne was, by her own admission, lazy and needed the incentive of training with Pirie, and particularly the sense of confidence and direction he provided. Pat Brown went on a coaching course for university athletes at Motspur Park and saw Pirie in action as a coach: "He certainly had a dominant personality. He made you aware that he knew what was best and some runners really gain from that sense of confidence."

The training regime that Pirie devised for Anne Smith was intensive but varied, with regular rest days. In the winter there would be as much running as possible, strong running with changes of pace. In the summer there was an emphasis on interval work, over a range of distances. Hill running was used to build up leg strength and stamina. Isometrics and weight training were also part of the schedules. Much of this was done from Nutfield, where Anne increasingly became one of the family. And Pirie did a lot of the training with her. Throughout his career as a coach he believed that running with his athletes brought a number of advantages, notably in giving him a better picture of their strengths and weaknesses.

The hard work began to pay off. In January 1966 Anne equalled Zsuzsa Szabo's world indoor best time for 880 yards of 2:10.5 and the following summer, in winning the AAA title she set a new European record of 2:04.2. With increasing experience, and helped by Pirie's guidance, she had become not only a faster but also a more competitive athlete. That summer they had two important targets:

Anne Smith running in a road race.

the Empire Games at Kingston and the European Championships in Budapest. The first was to be a disappointment, the second a disaster.

In Jamaica Anne led at the bell but was overtaken on the second lap and finished with the bronze medal, the winner the little known Canadian Abigail Hoffman. The European event a few weeks later provided a second chance and here, as at Kingston, Anne led the rankings. She travelled to Hungary with Gordon and Shirley, having obtained permission from officials to arrive a little later than the rest of the team.

Top performers need to have everything right if they are to perform at their best, and having everything right often means having things the way they are used to. But it is a feature of major championships – and was especially so then – that athletes have to take leave of their personal coaches and live in athletes' accommodation. This was a particular challenge for Anne Smith. Pirie was her mentor and motivator and she was used to having him by her side before big races.

At Budapest Smith, like many athletes before her, found the athletes' village noisy, with people coming and going at all hours. It was a problem Pirie himself had experienced at Cardiff in 1958. She and Gordon decided that she would move out and join Gordon and Shirley in their hotel. The team management wanted their athletes to be together to support each other as a team and they were furious at what they saw as a direct challenge to team loyalty. Pirie felt that all the careful preparation was at risk and that his athlete must have the conditions she needed to sleep properly and relax before a major competition.

The British officials took a hard line. They called Anne Smith to their office and, in a dramatic assertion of their authority, she was expelled from the team, sent home in disgrace and suspended for three months.

Jimmy Green, long an admirer of Pirie, used his editorial in *Athletics Weekly* to tear him off a strip. "On all sides people were asking just how Gordon Pirie could allow a young athlete, one who is obviously influenced by him to a greater degree than is usual, to do such a thing. The general consensus is that this must be the end of a very fine athlete's international career. You just can't do this kind of thing and get away with it."

The incident further soured the relationship between Pirie and some members of the athletics establishment. A few months later, Anne was disqualified for being "persistently paced" at the Southern Cross-Country Championships. The coaches of rival athletes alleged that Pirie, who was encouraging Smith from the sidelines and running alongside her at the side of the course, was giving her an unfair advantage. But, if Pirie and Smith needed any further incentive to prove how good she was, this incident provided it.

And indeed 1967 proved Anne Smith's greatest year. She had already begun to turn her attention to the mile and 1,500 metres and in May of that year she broke the world record for the imperial distance at the Surrey championships at Wimbledon Park. The conditions were windy but she had been taught by Pirie that this need not be a reason not to run hard. She moved away from Pat Brown over the last lap and finished in 4:39.2. Three weeks later at Chiswick she ran 4:37.0. The timekeepers had been alerted and this time there were watches at 1,500 metres too, giving her a time of 4:17.3, nearly two seconds inside Marise Chamberlain's world record for that distance. Pirie was elated. It was the first time that any runner had broken both records in the same race and Smith had brought the women's world time closer to the men's than ever before. No other British woman broke an outdoor world record for a track event until Sally Gunnell in 1993.

Those close to Anne Smith at that time have no doubt that the influence of Pirie was formidable. "His training was the clinching factor that got Anne to world record status," says Jack Fitzgerald. Looking back many years later, Chris Smith, Anne's brother commented: "It was the harder regime with Gordon that improved her performance."

Anne Smith was not picked for the Mexico Olympics in 1968, after injury trouble during the season and her career never quite touched the same heights again. But she had made a formidable impact on women's distance running. Some of Anne's contemporaries thought she became too dependent on Pirie's advice and presence, and that she could not produce top performances when we he was not there. Pat Brown, who started running with Anne as a schoolgirl, now has a successful career as a pharmacist. She reached international standard as an athlete but did not want to give everything to athletics, or to the demands of one coach. However, she saw

The coach. Holding the stopwatch while Anne Smith runs, Leicester, 1968.
Glaxo Wellcome

the advantages for Anne Smith: "In some ways the collaboration between Anne and Gordon was the start of the close coach/athlete relationship that we know today. It was very intense. It wouldn't have worked for everyone. But Anne had the ability and she responded to Pirie beautifully."

Frank Horwill tells of overhearing a conversation which illustrates what the coach expected of his athlete. Pirie and Smith were talking just before a mile race on a blustery day at Hurlingham. "Isn't it a bit windy for front running, Gordon?" The coach's reply was uncompromising: "Get out there".

And get out there she did. Nothing demonstrated this more than that day in June 1967 at Chiswick when she broke immediately from the gun and ran alone against the watch, faster than anyone had done in history.

But Pirie needed some other outlet for his competitive spirit and he found it in orienteering. He first competed one day in February 1965. After running through the Surrey woods for nearly two hours trying to find his way round the course he finally admitted defeat and knocked on the door of a country cottage to ask for help. The elderly occupant told him the way back to the village school, where the race had started. The result sheet must have made grim reading. Beneath the names of the 31 finishers were those who had "retired lost", and they included G Pirie and A Smith.

Pirie was not going to let this happen again. John Disley lent him a book about the sport, he learned to use his compass and a month later he turned up at Leith Hill, south of Dorking, for another attempt. There was snow on the ground, but it was a sunny morning for the 50 competitors to negotiate their way round. Result: D A G Pirie 2nd.

Orienteering originated in Sweden in 1918. The Surrey races, in which Pirie took part, were organised by John Disley, the former international steeple-chaser. They were not quite the first in Britain (there had been events in Scotland and Lancashire a few years earlier) but they led to the formation of an organised body for the sport. Disley and Chris Brasher brought into orienteering a number of other international runners, including Martin Hyman and Bruce Tulloh. Roger Bannister ran a number of the early races. Martin Hyman has remained active in the sport for many years both as a competitor and as a coach. Pirie in turn encouraged athletes in his coaching group to compete, some, like John Rix, with considerable success. But British orienteering soon produced its own champions, fine navigators as well as runners, who did not come into the sport with a background in athletics.

In 1965 some of those who came to the first orienteering races shared a history as athletes and enjoyed a kind of competitive reunion. Friends and rivals would meet up, but now in the forest. Pirie formed an orienteering club called the Nutfielders to compete in team events. It included Tony Walker, then working for the Surrey Association of Boys' Clubs, who went on in 1972 to become the first full-time professional officer for British orienteering.

The sport revived Pirie's career as a sportsman and provided a different kind of sporting experience. In 1966 he told a Swedish interviewer: "Invitations keep coming to me to run on the track but I actually have no desire to. Orienteering is without doubt the best sport I know. It gives everybody the chance to compete… a 1,500 metre runner has to train much harder and with professional ambition. Everybody can enjoy orienteering, it's not necessary to be able to run fast. It's the satisfaction from finding the red flag which is fascinating."

But when he competed in races, Pirie still wanted to win. He brought to orienteering all the determination, single-mindedness and fortitude that had made him a great distance runner. Chris Brasher recalls: "He was very strong and fast. He could run in circles for hours and still win. But he was let down in the end by his competitive instinct. He and a few others would indulge in personal races within the sport."

Less than 18 months after his first experience of orienteering, in the summer of 1966, Pirie won the English championships at Hindhead. Then, after the founding of the British Orienteering Federation, he won the first British Championships in 1967 and 1968. In 1968, at the age of 37, he was the first member of the British team to finish at the world championships in Sweden. In 1968 he wrote a short introduction to the sport (*The Challenge of Orienteering*) which Pelham Books published as a part of a series called *Sport for All*.

His success as an orienteer came despite the difficulties that successful athletes often have in adjusting to the demands of the sport. Very few good runners become good orienteers, partly because they find it difficult to stop and use the map. Pirie won his races more through speed and power than through his skill as a map reader. Mike Rowland went on a few orienteering runs with Pirie. "It was almost surreal. We ran striding through the brambles, counting our strides, getting from flag to flag. 'We must beat the bastards', he'd be saying."

Orienteering also opened up an opportunity for some business. Tony Wale was another athlete who took up the sport and he and Pirie went into partnership. "Gordon and I first got together when Stan Eldon got some new Tiger racing shoes at his shop in Reading, they were going like hot cakes. Gordon got hold of a lot so I could sell them at league meetings. They went well – and a year or two later we moved into orienteering gear." Tony Wale was in the army when all this started and he had to get permission from his commandant to do the trading. "Gordon and I had suits from Scandinavia and also Kompassrosen shoes, waterproofed and studded – specially made for orienteering. We got a bit of a buzz from all this. We had quite a lot of stock, maybe 15 or 20 thousand pounds' worth and took it to events. It went quite well. Gordon handled most of the invoicing and so on."

Dust jacket for Pirie's third book.

Pirie loved the sport, the competition, the travel, and the people. Tony Wale again: "Gordon got orienteering onto a higher plane of determination and dedication. He had an extremely professional approach to the business of winning. 'You'll have to stop me', he would say. That's how I remember Gordon."

In a number of different ways – interviews, books, media work, coaching, kit endorsements and other advertising – Pirie kept money coming in. He never wanted to be surrounded by possessions. But he loved cars. He developed a particular love of the open-top 230SL Mercedes, and he loved driving. His friends vary in their assessment of his skill as a driver but they all agree that he liked to get to places quickly and that he disliked being overtaken. When the first motorway opened north of London in 1961 he quickly went to try it out, driving north and then back again just for the pleasure. Foreign cars could be imported into Britain free of tax if they were more than a year old. He would buy his new Mercedes in Germany and store it in a garage near the French coast until it was ready to bring in.

But he did need some way of earning a living. By 1965 it was clear that the business ventures were not going to take off in a big way and John Disley suggested to Pirie that a teaching qualification might add another string to his bow. In September of that year he started a two year course to train as a physical education teacher at St Mary's College in Twickenham, south west London.

St Mary's was a college of Catholic foundation, but open to people of all beliefs. The head of Physical Education at the time was John Kane, who had himself been an athlete of some standing, and who became a leading figure in the field of Sports Psychology and Director of the West London Institute of Higher Education. He remembers that Pirie did not have the formal qualifications to enter but was given credit for his wider experience. "It was Father Hurley who interviewed Gordon about his general suitability for teaching. Father Hurley was not a sports follower but he reported to me: 'This man has done things like write books, he has represented his country, even I know about him. We should take him.'"

So Pirie joined the other students, many of them 25 years younger, studying to become PE teachers. One of them, Alex Mineyko, who had come to England as a 17-year-old from Eastern Europe, became a good friend.

Pirie orienteering.
Orienteering Federation of Australia

From left: Ano, Mike
Wiggs, Adrian Metcalfe,
Ron Clarke, Gordon
Pirie.
Mike Wiggs

Except that he came to college in a Mercedes, Pirie was in many ways just another student. He took part in many of the college activities, even playing the odd game of rugby. He organised an orienteering weekend to introduce staff and students to the sport, taking John Kane out on the Surrey hills and teaching him how to map read. When a biology lecturer illustrated how cardiovascular systems could be tested by measuring students' breathing he found that, ten years after his peak as a competitive athlete, Pirie needed to breathe only four times a minute. The average among the other students was 12.

But many staff and students remember Pirie's time at the college for one particular episode. John Kane had some connections with the government of Czechoslovakia through his role in the International Society of Sports Scientists. When, in 1967, he heard that Zátopek was coming to London for a BBC programme, he persuaded the Czech embassy that Zátopek should be allowed to come to the college, enjoy a reunion with his old rival, and speak to the students of the college.

211

The college duly sent someone to London to collect Zátopek by car, this duty being entrusted to Joe Jagger, a lecturer at the college (and father of Mick). On arrival Zátopek was given lunch and then a large crowd of students, some of them from nearby Borough Road College, assembled to hear the great man. There followed a long and entertaining account by Zátopek of his athletic life, including praise for Pirie who was given his own place of honour in the front row. The party then went out and walked across the lawns to the college running track. Zátopek and Pirie took off their jackets and their shoes, John Kane started a starter's gun and the two men jogged round the track, finishing to loud cheers, hand in hand.

At St Mary's Pirie was studying some subjects in which he had a lifetime's experience and a core of knowledge in some ways ahead of his time. But he found it hard to give to the course some of the things it required of him. He had to complete formal assessments, which required assimilating a number of set texts. Teaching practice, where he was placed in a school for several weeks, required careful preparation.

John Kane again: "He passed the physical education part of the course but, first time round, he failed the education. He hated our rules… he had to read things up and re-gurgitate them. I arranged for him to have special tutorials in the end and when he took the papers again he was given an Aegrotat pass.[24] So Pirie became a qualified teacher. But he was not cut out for the week by week daily grind of school life. It seems likely that he saw the teaching certificate as a useful paper qualification rather than as an opening to a new career. He never took a permanent post in a school. As so often happens, more interesting work was to come from an unexpected source.

In 1967 the Australian author Hugh Atkinson wrote a novel called *The Games*, about the efforts of four runners from different countries preparing for an Olympic marathon. The story was marketed as "faction – fiction based on fact". The runners included a Czech athlete brought out of retirement, and the Olympic Games in question was to be high in a mythical central American state situated at

---

[24] Awarded to students who have not completed all the examinations successfully but are deemed for exceptional reasons to have been worthy of a pass.

altitude (Mexico was the venue for the 1968 Games). One runner collapsed towards the end of the race, as Jim Peters had done at Vancouver. A central character – of dubious probity – was the international president of the Olympics, by name Kaverly. The real life president of the IOC was Avery Brundage.

Twentieth Century Fox soon bought the film rights. Michael Winner took on the direction and he recruited Pirie to be chief technical advisor on the running side.

For months before the start of the film Pirie trained the actors who had parts in the film as athletes, so that they had the stamina for the running sequences and could seem authentic, rather as Tom McNab did in later years for *Chariots of Fire*. Michael Crawford, one of the actor-runners, did much of his training with Pirie on Wimbledon Common and was praised by Pirie for his ability and his guts. Press reports said Crawford's mile time was around 4:20. For his part Crawford said that preparing for the film was "like training for the real Olympics". Some of the action was shot in England including some convincing scenes of Pirie himself running with Crawford and others through the woods in a big cross-country race. Great efforts were made to ensure that the stadium scenes were convincing. The White City stands were filled with 1,000 real people acting as extras and with 20,000 glass fibre models making up the rest of the crowd.

The filming also took Pirie to Vienna, Melbourne, Tokyo and Rome, where city streets around the Olympic stadium were closed off so that the final scenes of the marathon could be filmed. This sequence is lent conviction by Crawford's portrayal of a runner who has set off too fast and reaches the point of collapse within sight of victory. There is a moving sequence when, barely able to stand, Crawford leaves behind the roars of the crowd and enters the tunnel that leads to the stadium, staggering forward step by step in total silence.

The film, which like the novel was called *The Games*, received mixed reviews. The running scenes were praised – "Gordon Pirie did a creditable job," said *Variety* and the *British Monthly Film Bulletin* thought that all the actor-runners convincingly demonstrated the physical demands of the race. But in general the film got a poor reception in Britain, the worst criticism being reserved for the script. The *Daily Sketch*, a popular paper of the time, thought that "the dialogue developed a crippling limp from the starting line".

"Being yesterday's hero," Derek Ibbotson once wrote "provides no meal ticket." Pirie did not have the natural acumen for business activity and in some ways he was too early with his ideas. It was some years before the fitness industry began to take off. By the late 1990s there were over 2,000 fitness clubs in the UK with around two million members, and the gym and health club business was estimated to be worth around a billion pounds a year. Fitness had become big business. Pirie saw the start of all this, at the end of his life: "I have a chuckle every time I go into a health club," he said. "There are runners and tri-athletes playing silly games with puny weights, instead of getting 'stuck in' and doing something that would be really beneficial for them." (*Running Fast and Injury Free*)

Pirie explored briefly the possibility of managing the affairs of up and coming athletes. As the control exercised by officials began to weaken, it became clear that runners needed help in arranging and managing their racing programme. When John Whetton, who won the European 1,500 metres title in 1969, first broke through into top-flight athletics he received a letter from Pirie offering to manage his racing programme. Pirie would negotiate the fee and take a commission. John was interested and might have signed up if Pirie had been able to guarantee him the money, but Gordon was not in a position to do so.

Tony Wale and Pirie had hoped that their sales of orienteering gear might be the start of something. But then Pirie phoned up one day to say he was going abroad and someone else would look after things. In later years Tony Wale teamed up with Chris Brasher to form Brasher-Wale sports, and later that became Sweatshop, a major retail company in sports wear.

It was clear by 1968 that Pirie was not going to find a role in the British coaching set-up, nor were his business ideas going to take off. And he was not going to settle down as a schoolmaster in Surrey. It was then that he got a letter from New Zealand. Great changes lay ahead.

15 A dream come true

Three years later Pirie was writing home to England from New Zealand about a young schoolgirl he was coaching. Anne Garrett was 16, and in only her second 1,500 metre race, she had beaten Anne Smith in the Auckland championships. Pirie was right to be enthused about her. Running under her married name, Anne Audain, she became one of the finest distance runners in the world, and one of the first under the new rules of world athletics to be paid for her achievements.

At her peak Anne Audain ran with great fluency and power. Dark-haired and of medium height, she developed a blend of poise and aggression which intimidated many of her rivals. But she had started with few advantages, indeed she had been born with deformed bones in both feet. In an interview in 1978 she recalled how she came to start running:

"They had to wait until I was 14 when all my bones had formed properly before they could operate; then they cut off the excess growth and transplanted the tendons so that I could use my toes. I had plaster on both legs but instead of giving me crutches they gave me wooden boots, which made me rock instead of walk. I had the plaster taken off after six months but I continued to rock and finally they told me that instead of walking I had to run – on my toes." (*New Zealand Athlete*, March 1978)

Pirie saw Anne Garrett run in an 800 metre race as a 15-year-old. She was only third, but Pirie was impressed by her commitment. That evening, the President of the Otahuhu club in Auckland called at her house to ask her parents if the Englishman could coach her. A few days later she went down to the club on her bicycle, accompanied by Barbara Moore, who lived in the same road and attended the same school.

Pirie had already registered her potential and as soon as she began to train in his group he saw that she had the ability and the determination that could make her a champion, and he told her so. She began to train regularly and under Pirie's guidance she was soon winning races, on the track, on the country and on the road.

She did the qualifying time for the 1972 Olympics but was considered too young to travel to Munich for the Games. But in 1973, two years after starting with Pirie, she was in the New Zealand team for the world cross-country championships in Belgium. Still only 17 and competing against the best cross-country runners in the world, she finished 9th and was the first New Zealand woman home.

Anne Audain was coached by Pirie for nearly ten years, on weekday evenings at the grass track at Sturgess Park in Otahuhu, or at Mount Smart stadium, long Sunday morning runs at Woodhill Forest, hill runs at One Tree Hill or near the Piries' home in Arney Crescent. During her time with Pirie she was in the top ten finishers in the world cross-country championships in 1973, 1975 and 1977, and sixth in the Commonwealth Games 1,500 metres in 1974. At the Montreal Olympics in 1976, when she was still only 20, she ran New Zealand records in both the 800 metres and 1,500 metres.

In the early days Pirie did much to instill in her a sense of self-belief. Writing to England at that time he described one of her early cross-country runs: "She didn't believe me when I told her that she was the best – she spent the whole of the race hesitating, looking over her shoulder to see why no one was with her. Next time it should be different."

Pirie was always convinced that if Anne Audain followed his advice she would become a world beater. She did. But by then she and Pirie had parted company. They endured a series of painful and aggressive rows until finally, one day in 1980, she walked out on him.

Pirie had received the invitation to coach in New Zealand in 1968. The letter came from a small club in Otahuhu on the southern outskirts of Auckland. The club president, Barney Roberts, was concerned that Otahuhu was in the doldrums and he believed he could only revive it by bringing in someone with coaching experience from Europe or the USA. He knew that Pirie had already left the amateur ranks and also had some New Zealand connections, so it seemed

Gordon Pirie with the
young Anne Audain,
1972.
News Media (Auckland)

possible that he might be interested. Committee members and
parents got together and agreed they would try and raise $1,000 a
season (about £5,000 in today's terms) to pay him.

Pirie was interested. He had happy memories of his stay in New
Zealand in 1957 and had described the country in *Running Wild* as
"a dream come true". Shirley's parents had moved to New Zealand
about the same time. Gordon and Shirley had visited again after the
Perth Commonwealth Games of 1962, and their first daughter,
Joanne, had been born there. Shirley recalls that it seemed a country of clear blue skies, warm seas and a gentle pace of life, "… such
a contrast to the London city scene… " Pirie liked the way New
Zealanders welcomed people into their homes, without any fuss or
bother, and he liked the fact that there were many opportunities to
enjoy the outdoor life. Indeed he once said that there was so much
else to do that if he had been born in New Zealand he would never
have taken up running.

New Zealand also had one of the best-known track and field
coaches in the world: Arthur Lydiard. Three of his runners, Peter
Snell, Murray Halberg and Barry Magee, had won medals at the
Rome Olympics, and Peter Snell went on to win two gold medals at
Tokyo in 1964. Pirie had competed and travelled with New Zealand
(and Australian) athletes and he had come to like them.

In July 1968 Pirie wrote back to Barney Roberts, saying he was
interested. Roberts contacted some local secondary schools about

217

the possibility of obtaining a teaching post for Pirie. In the autumn the decision was taken – the family would go. The Piries talked it over with Anne Smith and it was agreed that she would go too. The move would give her chance to take up a teaching post in a new environment and perhaps give her a fresh start in athletics. She could continue her coaching with Pirie and perhaps qualify for the New Zealand team.

But Pirie was walking into something of a coaching minefield. So successful were Lydiard's athletes that coaches had come to New Zealand from all over the world to learn more about him. But Lydiard's ideas were not the European ideas of training, and certainly not the ideas Pirie had learned from Gerschler.

Arthur Lydiard was born in 1917. As a young man he had a good physique for long distance running but it took him many years of hard work to make himself into a decent marathon runner. He was a tenacious and independent man whose determination and single-mindedness was not unlike Pirie's. Indeed his account of his own training has distinct echoes of what Pirie wrote about his time at Watchett. "I ran and ran and ran. I wanted to find out what a man could do. While I was in this experimental stage, I thrashed myself so hard that sometimes I was running more than 30 miles through the Waitakere Ranges. Often I was so exhausted I had to walk the last few miles home." (Lydiard quoted in *Arthur's Boys* by Joseph Romanos).

Lydiard tested and evolved his ideas over many years. Because of the part he played in stimulating the jogging boom and because he encouraged people to do steady running as a way of improving their general health Lydiard became associated popularly with the idea of LSD – "long slow distance" as a way to fitness. As he later eplained in his book *Running with Lydiard* (1983), he believed athletes needed more than this. When the base of fitness was in place they needed a period of speed and interval work – but "four to five weeks is usually enough".

Pirie and Lydiard had much in common. Both demanded everything of their runners, and gave everything to them. Both often ran with their athletes in training. Pirie laid some stress on this, arguing that by running alongside those he was coaching he gained a better knowledge of them. But Pirie brought a different emphasis

Arthur Lydiard.

Auckland 1974. Pirie had beaten the local bus from home to work.
News Media (Auckland)

to training. He was not against steady running providing it was done at a decent pace. But for him repetitive speed work had a high priority, and those repetitions were most effective when run over specific distances, in specific times with specific intervals in between, to maximise the heart's recovery powers.

John Davies was an Olympic athlete who was coached by Lydiard and then became a leading coach in his own right. "When Pirie arrived in New Zealand the country was almost totally Lydiard," he recalls. Lydiard himself had fallen out with the athletics establishment (another similarity with Pirie) and gone off to Finland to coach, but his ideas ruled among runners. Pirie was bringing in ideas that had been learned and developed in Europe, and which had not been assimilated into the training regimes of New Zealand runners. "Gordon," said one of the Otahuhu members years later, "was the first one to teach speed."

219

Lydiard's published comments on Pirie's own achievements added spice to the situation. In his book *Run to the Top* written with Garth Gilmour and published in 1962 he had said:

"Gordon Pirie is a typical example of a runner who could break world records but at times could not win his national title, let alone Olympic or Empire Games titles because he was always ready at the wrong time and either short of his peak, or declining from it when he needed to be at his peak. Don't let any runner kid you he'd rather have a world record than an Olympic, Empire or national title… on the day when Pirie's records are erased from the books, he will be gone forever…"

(The comments perhaps explain an exchange that took place during a run in Richmond Park a year or two after the book was published, and remembered by Charlie Dabbs. Another runner in the group, chatting as they went round, mentioned he had been enjoying reading Lydiard's views on running. "You know what you can do with that kind of rubbish," said Pirie, and pointed to the nearest litter bin.)

So Pirie knew when he arrived in New Zealand that in some people's eyes, if not his own, he had to prove himself as a coach. He was an intruder into what was a relatively stable environment. He was a Pom, too, who thought he was right and would rarely admit he was wrong. Not everyone took to him.

In 1969 Auckland was a relaxing, low rise city of about a quarter of a million people spread comfortably between its many bays and harbours. Pirie and his family settled in Remuera, a prosperous residential district near the centre. He got a temporary teaching post at a local school and began his coaching job. It took only ten minutes for him to drive down the Southern Motorway from the centre of Auckland to the thriving township of Otahuhu and the club headquarters at Sturgess Park.

Here, there was a 440 yard grass track set in a shallow bowl, with some gentle banking around, and a small changing and refreshment area. It was not one of the area's major tracks but it had seen some good races. Both Peter Snell and Murray Halberg had run there in their prime.

For Pirie, things started slowly. Anne Smith was there at the start together with about six others. Among those who joined Pirie first

Sturgess Park, revisited
by Anne Audain in later
years.
Anne Audain

was Shirley Somervell, a young half-miler at another local club who
had read in the newspapers of Pirie's arrival and phoned to ask if he
would coach her. One of the first Otahuhu members to move across
from an existing coach to Pirie was the 14-year-old Barbara Moore,
one of the few runners of Maori origin in the club. Years later she
won a medal at the Commonwealth Games.

While he was getting started in Auckland, Pirie was nurturing one
other idea: the possibility of a long distance run across the USA. The
recognised best time for running from coast to coast was 73 days
and Pirie knew that his old rival Bruce Tulloh was making preparations to attack the record. Tulloh had calculated that if he could
manage 45 miles a day he would break the record.

Tulloh was five years younger than Pirie but their careers as three
mile/5,000 metre runners had overlapped, and shortly after Pirie's
retirement Tulloh won the 5,000 metres gold medal at the European
championships in 1962. He was a competitor Pirie greatly respected
on the track. "A damned difficult bloke to beat," he told Frank
Horwill once.

Tulloh was in many ways just the man for this kind of adventure.
At 35 he was greatly experienced, with an enormous amount of running behind him. Like Pirie he was wiry and tough with the mental
resilience to withstand hour after hour of monotonous running. He
began the run in April 1969, just before Pirie arrived in Auckland.

The whole thing appealed to Pirie. The run did not require amateur status and it set the kind of challenge he relished. Tulloh's time would make a good target. Pirie kept press cuttings of Tulloh's progress in his wallet and discussed the idea of the run with Hugh Sweeney, whom he had coached by letter in the USA. Sweeney helped him put together information about climatic conditions in different states and also advised him to run East-West, rather than starting in California as Tulloh had done.

Tulloh arrived at City Hall in New York on June 25th 1969, having beaten the previous record by eight and a half days. The news reached Pirie a day or two later.

Pirie wrote to Mike Rowlands, who had joined him at a number of coaching weekends at Nutfield a few years earlier, inviting him to run with him and suggested they think of a 50 miles a day target, which would enable them to "smash Tulloh's time". Pirie talked of doing three ten-mile runs in the morning (each taking about an hour), with a rest between each, resting in the afternoon and then doing 20 miles later. Mike Rowlands began to try this kind of training in Wales: an hour at 7.30 a.m, an hour at nine o'clock and an hour at 11 o'clock, then more runs later in the day. In May Pirie was still serious, occasionally trying 40 miles a day himself– and he was hoping for a September start. "One has to work at some damn thing," he wrote to John Rix. "But I still don't know if I'm keen enough. You try doing 50 miles every day – just for a week. I would need $5 a mile to make it interesting."

But the project was proving difficult to organise and potential sponsors like Glaxo, for whom Pirie promoted Complan, did not come through. In October he finally told Mike Rowlands that it had proved impossible to get financial support and that he had abandoned the idea.

The training group at Otahuhu which Anne Audain joined grew over the next year or two until it was sometimes 40 strong. Those at school would rush their homework and get someone to run them to the track in the car, cycle down or jog over as part of their warm up. Waiting by the hut for Pirie's car to come up the drive into the park, they could exchange the latest gossip, talk about what times their rivals were doing, and speculate what the session would be that evening. To get started they jogged around the college playing fields adjacent to the park, chattering with each other, and then did "stride outs" on the track infield. When the serious work began and the effort told, conversation would fall away. A popular Pirie session involved ten 880 metre runs, with a two lap jog between each. Every runner would take turns leading the group and learning the pace and Pirie would run too, carrying the watch and calling the times.

Anne Audain recalled later how much she enjoyed those training sessions in the early days and how Pirie protected her from over-training:

"What was so good about Gordon was his motivation and enthusiasm for us. Young athletes really do need a coach who is like that. He was great – training was always a lot of fun. Gordon's meth-ods were always very good for a young athlete. There was not a lot of stress, not a lot of mileage. He just let us enjoy our running and, because of that, we ran well. We weren't pushed at a young age." (*New Zealand Runner*, Jan–Feb 1982).

Barbara Moore, who had first joined the club when she was only ten, became a member of Pirie's group and stayed with him until 1977. Within a year of working with Pirie she was not only winning races in her age group but came second in the national road cham-pionships. She came close to selection for the world cross-country championships and may only have missed it because there were too many "Pirie athletes" in the team. Much later, coached by Arch Jelley, she won a bronze medal in the 3,000 metres at the Com-monwealth games in 1990. "Gordon Pirie gave me my foundations as a runner." she says.

But perhaps the schoolgirl with the greatest natural talent to join the Pirie group was Alison Deeds, who, as Alison Roe, went on to become for a while the finest female marathon runner in the world. In 1973 she was sitting at home watching an athletics meeting at the Mount Smart stadium on TV. All Pirie's athletes seemed to be doing well, so her father suggested she phone him. "Gordon arranged for me to join the group at Sturgess Park. Within a couple of sessions he told me I had the potential to be a world class runner – and I believed him." He coached her until 1979, though she was also helped by Max Golder.

Alison was tall and elegant and fair-haired, easy to pick out in races. In due course her photograph was on the covers of sports magazines all over the world. When she started with Pirie she was

Alison Roe winning the
New Zealand Cross-
Country championship,
1974.
News Media (Auckland)

quickly successful, winning the national cross-country championships at the age of 18 and running for New Zealand in the world
championships.

   She gives much of the credit for her success to this early training
with Pirie. He restrained her wish to do really big sessions before she
was ready for them, and she recalls today how she valued the struc-
tured framework that Pirie gave to her training. "I liked the discipline. You knew what you were going to do, and you did it." Like
others in the group she responded to his enthusiasm and the stories
he told about himself and his running career. " He inspired us by
running with us. That's why we did all our training. He was such a
great motivator. He used to say 'I know you feel tired, but this is what
I did when I was training.' "

Alison Roe's time in winning the Boston marathon (2.26:46) in 1981 was the second fastest ever by a woman, and in New York later in the same year she recorded a world's best time (2.25:29), though the course was later found to be slightly under distance. Her marathon successes made her internationally famous. "Even as a marathon runner I did two speed sessions like I did with Gordon. If it hadn't been for him, I would never have got to where I am." She found his presence running in the group a great motivation, and it is something she now does herself in her own coaching work with tri-athletes.

Both Gordon and Shirley had seen at first hand how low expectations had restricted the development of women's athletics in Britain. In *Running Wild* Pirie had called on women athletes to "break through the old-fashioned barriers which men have put up to hold them back." He made Otahuhu the strongest women's club in New Zealand – not only with Anne Audain, Barbara Moore and Alison Roe, but with the Vercoe sisters, Pauline and Bev, with Sharon Thompson, Vickie Marler and many others. Andrea Wade, whom Pirie coached from 1974 to 1984 was one of the best sprinters of her generation and she too competed in the Commonwealth Games.

In England Pirie had helped Anne Smith become the best woman mile runner in the world and he continued to coach her for the first three years or so that they were in Auckland. For a while she pursued her international career, running for her adopted country at both the Commonwealth Games in 1970 and at the international cross-country championships in 1971.

But Pirie was increasingly taking on other athletes, and using the competitive ethos of the training group to spur each runner on. Anne Audain remembers Pirie telling Smith: "I've got another Anne here who can replace you." Anne Smith felt that Pirie did not understand when she began to pull back from serious athletics. (She was now over 30). He complained that she did not show the independence and guts of some of the other runners. She moved to another coach and their relationship soured. Subsequently, she told friends that Pirie shouted abuse at her during races.[25]

---

[25] Anne Smith returned to England to live in 1986, took up a teaching post in London and ran regularly for the Bromley club as a veteran. She died in 1993 at the age of 52 after suffering a cerebral haemorrhage.

There was also a strong band of young male runners at the Otahuhu club. One of the first was a young student teacher, Perry Cunningham. Pirie spotted him at a meeting. "Come and have a run with us," insisted Gordon, a phrase he must have used a thousand times to people he met on tracks around the world. On Tuesday and Thursday afternoons Perry would go over to the Piries' house at about 5 o'clock and travel down to the track in the car with Pirie and Anne Smith. "Sometimes they would be speaking to each other, sometimes they wouldn't," he recalls. People came and went from the group, but they included Bruce Milne, now a senior coach in New Zealand, Philip Wilson, Robert Drum , Kerry Eustace, Kerry Pascoe, a whole cohort of good young runners who became caught up in the passion of the Pirie training sessions. "We ran on heart – only Gordon could bring it out of us," said Pascoe, looking back years later.

As the group grew larger, so the coaching expanded, first four days a week, then five or six. Great success came to the club. It began to win honours first locally and then at national level, stimulating some envy among its rivals. John Walker, who was on his way into the top flight of world athletics, occasionally did sessions with the Otahuhu group.

On some days the scene would move to the Domain, a hilly park close to the centre of down town Auckland, criss-crossed by driveways and pedestrian paths. Earlier generations of New Zealand runners had used it for training – Peter Snell did work outs there before the 1960 Olympics. By Pirie's time it had become a favoured spot for city centre running and jogging. At midday there might be three or four hundred taking lunchtime exercise. Pirie had his squad doing repetition runs up the steep footpath from Stanley Street to the duckpond or measured one mile runs on the grass. Perry Cunningham recalls a classic Pirie interval session of thirty 400 metre runs on the grass there in July 1971. It was a rainy day and Pirie stayed in his car with the stopwatch, shouting the times through the open window. The plan was that each run should take the pulse rate up to 180. Perry rested between each until his pulse was down to 120. This took about 50 seconds. Pirie had measured out the 400 metres meticulously – more than once he incurred the wrath of the park attendant for marking the kerb to ensure his data was accurate. The first twenty 400s were done in the low 70s but the last ten in 67 seconds. Coach and athlete went home satisfied.

One Tree Hill.
Sandra Nicholls

On Sunday mornings Pirie often took a group of runners to Woodhill Forest for a long run. Woodhill is a plantation forest of pine trees on sandy soil adjacent to the sea, about 30 minutes drive out of Auckland to the north-west. The group would assemble at the Pirie home, sometimes as early as 7.30 a.m. and drive up to Wood-hill in a couple of cars. Out in the forest paths Pirie would some-times run so hard that even a good runner like Philip Wilson could barely hold him, while those behind could hear Pirie puffing and grunting as he drove on through the trees. "It was eyeballs out all the way," Debbie Elsmore recalls "and some of the younger ones just couldn't take it. We would re-group at half way and run back together…" Some Sundays the group would take a boat to Kawau Island and run, then picnic on the beach. Once they found a load of jelly fish on the beach and had a fight with them, until they all collapsed in a heap laughing.

Kevin Hall remembers those great days. "Even though we'd crawl into bed, it was fun because we felt we'd achieved something – pushed ourselves and shared it with others – knew we were getting there – using hills, parks, beaches – and only tracks when fine tuning was required. So there was an aesthetical essence in blasting up hills surrounded by sweet smelling pines and firs, and often when I was under pressure to keep going my mind would latch onto the sweet smell of pine or fir and almost become engulfed in it, a form of escapism from not knowing if I could run another 10 yards."

Training with Pirie could be fun but it was tough. He was getting people ready to win. Steve McOnie, a young New Zealand runner in those days, was never in a Pirie training group and never warmed to him, but he could see what was happening. "With all his athletes Gordon instilled the aggression and competitiveness that paved the way for their future success. Gordon himself was a 'tough athlete'. Thus so became his progeny. Their aggression in races was always a delight to watch."

Pirie had a contract with the Otahuhu Club from 1969 to 1975. The family had a house in Arney Crescent which was well placed for the city and local schools (Joanne was seven and Sara four when they arrived in New Zealand). Shirley did some running, both 400 metres on the track and a little cross-country. Joanne and Sara

Woodhill Forest.
Sandra Nicholls

competed from time to time and showed they had the potential to be fine runners but Joanne recalls that her parents put no pressure on them to run.

It was a generally busy life. Shirley had a night job in a hotel and she and Gordon were also managing some property they had let out. Pirie described their routines in a rushed letter to John Rix. "Shirley works 11 p.m. to 7 a.m. Monday to Friday. I work 8.30 to 3.30 p.m. Coach 4 days a week in the winter, 7 days in the summer (5 to 7 p.m. weekdays) Sat/Sun in the forest and orienteer. We have bought 4 houses and let them to students. Make 100% or more. All spare time doing screws, doors, toilets, electrics, gases, gardens, write letters and visit bank to put in money. In between we train too and sleep together weekends. Shirley cooks. I sew. Swim in hot pools. Drive Mercedes. Pay bills."

Pirie had taken advantage of the tax laws to bring two Mercedes into the country and was keen to try and arrange for friends in England – Martin Crickmore for instance – to do the same. "I need someone I can trust to bring out a Mercedes Sports 350SL for me… I supply cash – you merely have name on papers as owners," he told John Rix. Later he and Shirley put some money into a mineral company which, they had been told, would do well. But they lost out.

Running was at the heart of it all. Home was always open house. There was often someone staying for a week or two on their way through New Zealand, or stopping overnight before a race or a training expedition, or just lazing around talking about running. Pirie worked for a while as a teacher and then as an accounts clerk but he was not interested in anything resembling a "career". He was still running himself every day, sometimes twice. He was as lean and bronzed as ever, but the old spiky crew cut had gone and his hair was longer. He was also busy with orienteering.

There was no organised orienteering in New Zealand when Pirie arrived in 1969. He knew it would be difficult to get people to start running out in the forests so he began by organising some very basic runs in Cornwall Park, a popular recreational area not far from the city centre. The *Auckland Star* had a photo of Gordon, Shirley and Anne Smith looking at a compass: "the perfect family sport", said the

Location of Woodhill Forest.

caption. People came along and as numbers grew Pirie began to take the sport further afield, to some of the plantation forests near the city.

Within a few months orienteers in Australia heard what Pirie was up to and asked him to try and organise a team to go to Melbourne for an international match.

Pirie negotiated sponsorship from Cerebus and before they left the team kitted themselves out in official blazers and ties, complete with the New Zealand silver fern. This was Pirie's first international competition of any kind for some years, and he was seen by the New Zealanders, and the Australians, as the top man in his team.

In Australia Pirie returned by chance to the scene of his two historic Olympic races with Vladimir Kuts, at the Melbourne Cricket ground (the MCG). The MCG had been chosen by the Australians as the venue for a full media event and journalists gathered to talk to Pirie about his memories of the ground, as it was 15 years, almost to the day, since his two races with Kuts. But in the empty stadium, and with no running track in sight, Pirie found it difficult to recapture his emotions from those days. He wanted to talk more about orienteering. It required, he said, more thought than track running. "People who run fast may still finish last. It takes brains to be an orienteer, and that rules out most athletes."

For the international match the Australians set a testing eight mile course in the bush at Tooboora, some 60 miles from Melbourne. It was a difficult journey just to get to the start and when they arrived the New Zealanders were a little out-psyched by the organisers. First, they were handed written advice on how to cope with snake bite and then they were given whistles to blow if they got lost.

The New Zealand team had some difficulty with a very flat course with few natural features and they were somewhat unnerved by the sight of kangaroos breaking out of the trees and running beside them. The terrain required particularly accurate navigation skills. The race was won by an Australian, Bengt Karlsson, and Australia narrowly won the team match. But the event was a disaster for Pirie. He lost nearly an hour at one checkpoint. "Control number 3 was wrongly drawn," he said afterwards "I was running round the point marked 3 on the master map for 55 minutes and nearly gave the whole show away and came back." The organisers would have none

Waiting for the race to begin.
Orienteering Federation of Australia

229

The first New Zealand orienteering team. From left: Perry Cunningham, Pirie, Beau Doherty, Colin Battley, Ralph King, Jack Ralston, Sverre Moen.
John Robinson

of this. "None of the other competitors failed to find it. Pirie should have seen the 3 bucket was smack on a small spur," said the course organiser.

David Hogg, who ran for Australia in the early races with New Zealand recalls Pirie's reaction to defeat in two races on the tour. "Gordon had also had a bad run in one of the preliminary races. Other competitors were mentally conditioned to making mistakes and having bad runs, Gordon was not. These two incidents established his reputation among Australian orienteers as someone who could not cope with being beaten."

Nonetheless the Australians valued Pirie's advice and support when it was their turn to visit New Zealand. An orienteering federation was soon established in Auckland and by the mid seventies four separate orienteering clubs existed in the city. Pirie was second

230

in the New Zealand championships in 1973 at the age of 42 and then showed his old competitiveness by turning round immediately and winning the veteran's race. He competed for New Zealand in two world championships. In 1978, in Norway, when he was one of the oldest runners in the field, he was first New Zealand man home. But by this time his interest had started to wane and he was making more mistakes. At the world championships in Finland a year later he was the last of his team to finish, losing over 50 minutes at one control. At Easter that year he drove down to Taupo with Dave Harkness for a three-day event. "We stayed in a tent," remembers Dave. "and intended to do all three races. On the second day, however, Gordon had some trouble on the course, which he blamed on officials and he ran through the control lambasting the organisation. He insisted on driving off and I didn't get my run on the third day."

But the seeds Pirie planted took root. When he was in Australia helping with the filming of *The Games* he gave a copy of his book on orienteering to one of the extras, Dave Lotty. Dave subsequently helped to get the sport started in New South Wales and since 1980 has worked full time for the Orienteering Association of the state. In New Zealand the sport has a national organisation and some 20 active clubs. In the match against Australia in 1997 Ralph King, who had run with Pirie at Tooboora in 1971, was a member of New Zealand's winning over 65 group.

The veterans from those days recall Pirie's early guidance in teaching them the elements of compass work, the techniques of getting in and out of control points easily and the value of accurate pace counting. Those who ran with him recall how frustrated he was by poor organisation and how angry in defeat. He usually blamed the maps or the organisers, but never himself. Most of all they remember the long determined strides, the incessant grunting as he bounded through the undergrowth, racing on and on. Whatever the terrain, his strength and speed took him on, contesting anything that stood in his way.

But things were beginning to go wrong, both in the family and in the coaching group. Pirie wrote to an old childhood friend in 1978 to say that he and Shirley had recently separated. Shirley and their two daughters, Joanne and Sara, stayed in the family home and Gordon moved to another house nearby.

Gordon and Shirley had met on the running track, trained and raced together and run open house for athletes for 20 years or more. The break up was painful. It also had an impact on Pirie's work as a coach. Dave Harkness, who was doing a lot of training with Pirie, remembers: "I really felt he lost his confidence at that time. He began to ask me questions about what we were doing. It wasn't like Gordon at all."

From the mid 1970s onwards the numbers in Pirie's coaching group had begun to decline. In part it was because he got involved with other things. He would often leave the family and go off on his own, travelling a lot to North America and Europe, especially during the New Zealand winters. Sometimes he left behind a training programme for his athletes in Auckland, written schedules, indicating the daily programme they should follow, what to do if they felt unwell, and the precise dates on which they were to write to him with reports on their progress. Nonetheless, a number of runners lost contact with Pirie while he was away. Alison Roe felt she needed to have regular face to face contact with a coach and found someone else who could provide that.

Other athletes left Pirie's coaching group because they found the competitive atmosphere too intense. His desire to beat his own athletes in training was a facet of this. And one athlete's progress was sometimes used to threaten the status of another in the group. Occasionally Pirie would rubbish other coaches in front of their athletes, to the embarrassment of his own runners. "There were times," says Debbie Elsmore, recalling her early years in the Pirie squad, "when I just wanted to be around something more positive."

Pirie believed that his runners would compete more effectively if they kept away from other athletes and their coaches. He did not want his athletes to fraternise with other runners. They were there to compete against others and win. This desire to give athletes a psychological advantage over other competitors meant that some were prevented from enjoying the company of runners from other clubs or countries – one of the attractions of the sport.

The biggest break, and the one that hurt most, was with Anne Audain. She was an athlete with the toughness and resilience to train hard and to compete at the highest level. She was also a winner. She and Pirie had all the difficulties that two strong people often have

Anne Audain in full flow
during a road race.
Tony Scott

when they work together. "They were both stubborn – and they were
both fighters," recalls Debbie Elsmore who knew them both well.

The foundations Pirie gave Anne Audain were important.
"Gordon Pirie brought out the fight in me, and my next coach took
over someone tough," she recalled in an interview a few years later.
But there were fierce arguments between them. She found herself
questioning his changes of mind. He complained that she was not
looking after herself properly, for instance that she continued to train

while she was taking medicine. She felt Pirie resented it when she got married. He disliked the fact that she began to socialise – and drink – more.

In the summer of 1980 she accompanied Pirie to Norway for the European summer with another New Zealand athlete, Rob Davies. The trip was a disaster. Drammen was the port where car imports came into Norway and Audain (dressed as a man) worked with Pirie unloading cars from the boats. There were arguments over the money she earned. Pirie felt that Audain's racing ambitions were getting in the way of the coaching he was trying to do with other athletes. She felt Gordon was losing his touch as a coach. In mid summer, feeling she was close to a breakdown, she left and returned to Auckland. She never spoke to Pirie again.

Anne Audain's view is that the aggressive element in Pirie's style of working, part and parcel of his ability to motivate runners, also had a destructive side. "He taught me a great deal that I have carried throughout my career. I travelled a lot and learned a great deal. But he was dogmatic and aggressive. Eventually I had to walk away."

Her greatest success came later, with the help of another coach, John Davies, a man whose coaching style was very different. Audain broke the world record at 5,000 metres in 1982. In the Commonwealth Games she won the 3,000 metres gold medal in 1982 and 10,000 metres silver medal (behind Liz McColgan) in 1986. For several years she dominated the road racing circuit in the USA. Pirie had put her on the path to success but it needed a different person, she discovered, to advise her in her later career. When she went on to her great victories there was little mention in the press of the part Pirie had played in her formative years.[26]

Pirie never found a role in the organisation of athletics, or orienteering, in New Zealand. Roy Williams, the great New Zealand decathlete, served with Pirie on the executive of the Auckland Track and Field centre but recalls that Pirie attended only one meeting. John Robinson, himself a fine athlete and orienteer, remembers Pirie's frustrations with meetings. "People like Gordon are on a fairly short fuse and they're hopeless on committees. They can take on a

---

[26] Anne Audain now lives in the USA. Her book *Uncommon Heart* is due to be published by Hodder Moa Beckett (New Zealand) in 2000.

Pirie the coach.
News Media (Auckland)

huge work load but they have to be let loose." Pirie's views on most
athletics officials were succinct and readily offered – "a pack of
bums". For their part, they would claim that he broke the rules. More
than once officials threatened to have him banned from a track
because he was passing information to his athletes about their
progress in a race, a technical infringement but quite common
practice.

235

Pirie made his mark on New Zealand athletics because, almost single handedly, he created a new tradition in New Zealand women's running. The best young women runners he coached acquired the toughness and self-confidence they needed to make their way in the world of international racing. They proved this in 1981.

In that year runners in the USA formed the Association of Road Racing Athletes. Road running had become a popular and lucrative sport, but the rules of international athletics prevented runners from taking the prizes on offer. The ARRA was determined to bring open competition to road racing and in June of that year organised their first race, in Eugene, Oregon. Anne Audain and Alison Roe (and Lorraine Moller, also from New Zealand) entered. Audain was first and Roe second, and they openly took the money offered as prizes, a deliberate challenge to the athletics authorities.

At first the sports governing body (the IAAF) tried to hold firm and the runners were suspended. But their bluff had been called and the runners were soon reinstated. Before long the rules about receiving payment for races – rules that had become increasingly out of date in Pirie's own running career – were changed. Audain and Roe had not only been good enough to win, they had been strong enough to stand their ground.

By then both had moved on from working with Pirie. He never saw any of his athletes through to top status and he never had a male athlete who became – even with another coach – a top international performer. Yet none of the runners who spent time in the Pirie squad will easily forget those days at Sturgess Park, on the Domain and at Woodhill. Barbara Moore remembers those years. "Gordon was a real maniac, but he had such a big heart. He put women's running in New Zealand on the map. He was light years ahead of existing coaches. He had visions, they didn't." As Kevin Hall put it years later: "We were like a family on our way to achieving something."

They were good days. But the family was changing and moving apart.

16 Ten summers in a row

Pirie spent much of the 1980s on the move, travelling, running, coaching. A number of things had gone wrong in New Zealand but the love of running, and the sense of physical well being which it provided, always sustained him. For some years yet that would not be taken from him. Increasingly he lived day by day, not for the job or for a pension, and not encumbered by belongings. Rather, a cheap flight here, a lift in a truck there, a friend who had a room he could stay in, a park nearby where he could run. Wherever he was it seemed to be summer, and most days he ran at least once, sometimes twice. By 1981, he calculated, he had run 216,000 miles (347,000 kilometres). And from that year he was inseparable from a new partner, Debbie Elsmore. They had great years of adventure together even though, at the end, things fell apart.

From the late 1970s Pirie generally spent only the summers in Auckland. When the weather got cooler, around Easter, he would be off to Europe or the States. Once, over a five year period, he managed to get ten summers in a row. Often he had one or two other runners with him on his travels. Sometimes he had coaching jobs to go to but mostly he had no great plans, except to run, or do an orienteering event, coach the athletes travelling with him, and see people, including his parents while they were still alive, but especially his old friends from running days.[27]

He would occasionally meet up with some of the new generation of New Zealand runners who were making such an impact on the European circuit, John Walker and Dick Quax especially. Pirie had given them advice when they were first planning to run in Europe.

---

[27] Pirie's father, Alick, died in 1975 and his mother Marnie in 1979.

Pirie got to some of the big European meetings, and saw Coe and Ovett run at Bislett. He greatly admired them both but it was in Ovett particularly that he saw somebody who was his own man, somebody he could identify with.

In the States he saw at first hand the explosion of the road running circuit, and the big cash prizes that came with it, some of those prizes going to athletes he had coached. All this helped him keep in touch with what was happening in the sport, and frustrated that he was no longer a part of it. He loved to train with younger runners who were competing at world level, and could still hold his own with them. But he was on the edge of what was happening, not a real part of it. Hugh Sweeney remembers that when he took Pirie to a 10K race in New York in 1981, only Nick Rose, the British international, greeted him. No one else knew who Pirie was.

Debbie Elsmore had joined the Otahuhu club as a gangly schoolgirl of 16 in 1974. As a youngster she was in awe of Pirie's reputation as an athlete and as a coach, the man who been to three Olympics and set world records. In the club she was overshadowed in those days by the achievements of Anne Audain, Alison Roe and others, but her slight frame concealed an immense determination to succeed.

When Debbie first became friendly with Pirie she was still completing her training as a teacher and there were almost 30 years between them, so there was considerable family resistance. But although there were some fierce fights between them the partnership, both personal and athletic, grew. It saw them through some tough times. "A lot of Gordon's toughness rubbed off on me. I became more and more strong-minded and in the end when we had arguments I wouldn't give in," she recalls.

Their trips overseas were not carefully organised: "We would just throw some kit and a few overnight things into a bag and take off." Pirie knew that travel need not be expensive. Occasionally he found a sponsor, for instance New Zealand Airways, to get him to an event and to do promotional work. But he had learned how to get around cheaply during his time as an athlete 25 years earlier. "He was a smart traveller," one of his daughters remembers, "and he could just talk his way round the world".

In 1978, when he was in Norway for the world orienteering championships, Pirie was approached by Per Andersen, a member of the Sturla club in Drammen: would he come and coach some young athletes at the club?

Drammen was a pleasant town, on the coast some 30 miles west of Oslo, and the Bislett meeting at Oslo was one of the great events of the European track circuit. A base at Drammen during the European summer would give Pirie the chance to bring over some of his athletes from New Zealand and perhaps get access to some of the big track meetings. He was greeted as something of a hero in Norway because of his 1956 world record in Bergen and of course there were the links with South London Harriers. He agreed to go, and spent the summers of 1979, 1980 and 1981 there.

The Sturla club gave Pirie a small retainer and he supplemented this with odd jobs, unloading cars from the boats or clearing up forestry land in the hills behind the town. Friends of the club or parents of athletes helped with accommodation, bicycles or free haircuts. One year a local Honda dealer found him a small car to use.

The Sturla people never knew quite when Pirie would arrive – or leave – but he came. "The year I went," recalls Debbie "we spent two months in the States first and then we got to London and took the Felixstowe ferry to Gothenberg. Somehow we made it up to Oslo. We started hitching to Drammen around midnight. There wasn't much hitch-hiking in Norway at that time and generally cars don't stop, but we were lucky that night, one car did stop and the driver was a member of Sturla."

One of the first athletes Pirie met when he arrived was the 17-year-old Jan Morten Andersen, Per's son. "There were a lot of young athletes at the club – 15 to 20 years old – and we used to have a lot of fun together. One day in 1979 my father came down to the track with a tall, skinny man. He told us the man was Gordon Pirie. My father said Gordon would be pleased to help us a bit."

Very soon the scene was much like it had been at Otahuhu. In less than ten minutes Pirie was in complete control of everything on the track. A group of young runners, working hard to get fit but fooling around a bit as well and teasing each other. The coach, now approaching 50, gaunt at first sight but strong and fit and able to outrun them all. Shouting, cajoling, urging them on, dominating the track and mocking the others who did not come under his wing.

With young runners in
Norway.
Bergens Tidende

Jan Morten and his friends – Kristin Kongsvoll, Gro Ellingsen, Bjorn Holm and others – had three great summers being coached by Pirie. They met with him four or five times a week, usually at the track but sometimes doing work outs on the hills around the town. None of the group became stars but all improved, and some reached national championships. "He was special," recalls Gro, "he was different to other coaches. They would keep their distance but Gordon called us nearly every day and took an interest in our progress. Even in the dark mornings I would go out and run."

They had great times travelling to track and field meetings around the country. On one occasion they travelled across Norway by train to Bergen for the national championships, Pirie entertaining tourists and chatting to everyone en route. In Bergen the local paper, *Bergens Tidende*, sent its main sports reporter, Jar Arild Larsen, to cover the meeting. It was a memorable moment for Jan Arild who had last seen Pirie when, as a 13-year-old, he had watched the Englishman overtake Kuts on the last lap of the 5,000 metres at the old Krohnsminde stadium; and it was pleasurable for Pirie to be greeted by someone who stood and cheered on that grey evening in 1956.

Each year Pirie took different athletes with him from New Zealand: Dave Harkness in 1979, Anne Audain and Rob Davies in 1980 and Debbie Elsmore in 1981. Dave Harkness first met Pirie four years earlier when he was a young student at the University of Auckland. He was new to the city and without a coach, and was working out on his own at Mount Smart stadium when Pirie got talking to him. "For several years," recalls Dave, "I trained with Gordon three or four days a week and he set the rest of my training. I looked upon him a bit like a father."

In the Auckland summer of 1978–9 Dave Harkness trained three times a day during the week and Pirie was there for all the work outs. Dave was tall and strong, and by the end of the summer was running for New Zealand over 800 metres against Australia. "If you can get down to 3.30 for 1,500 metres," Pirie told him once, "you and I will make a lot of money." Going to Norway was partly about getting nearer that sort of time.

Dave acted as something of a buffer between Pirie and his hosts, even down to keeping an eye on Gordon's long-distance phone calls. Pirie taught him a lot about what he could do. "I think he was probably experimenting some of the time," Dave says. "One day, on the cinder track at Drammen he had me doing 400 metre repetitions in just over 60 seconds with only a minute's rest. Ten was about my limit but after ten, we went up to 12, then two more and finally we did 16. I would never have done it if he'd warned me at the start. But I followed him with total belief." That belief was put to the test during May of 1979.

Allan Wells was at home in Scotland one night that month, packing his bags for a trip to Jamaica the next day when he had a surprise visitor.[28] "I wasn't expecting anyone at the house, least of all Gordon Pirie. I'd met him in Auckland a year or two earlier – he was

---

[28] Allan Wells had won the 200 metres gold medal at the Commonwealth Games in Edmonton in 1978. In 1980 he won the gold medal in the 100 metres at the Moscow Olympic Games.

very interested in my training. Distance runners don't often sit down with sprinters and ask about their training so I was quite impressed at the trouble he took to find out what kinds of thing we were doing.

"Gordon talked with Margot and me for two or three hours and asked lots of questions about my training. We exchanged addresses but I didn't think any more about it. Then, there he was, out of the blue, knocking at the door. We put him on the sofa for the night but when we came down in the morning there was no sign of him. Then he came in with rolls and a newspaper – he'd been up to the corner shop and told them I would pay."

Allan Wells gave Pirie some idea about the things he was doing, and Margot, his coach, explained how the different parts of the programme fitted together. Then they put him on the train to London. Dave Harkness takes up the story. "As soon as we got to Drammen Gordon told me we were going to do a work out based on what Allan Wells was doing. It was all built round lots of 60 metre runs, lifting our knees high, very different to what we'd done before. We called it 'the system'. "

Allan and Margot Wells had got their ideas about high knees work from Don Quarrie, the Jamaican sprinter. It was something they used at certain times of the year, and part of their wider programme of preparation and conditioning. But, as Dave Harkness remembers, Pirie decided to try it out with a vengeance.

"First we would run the 60 metres in bounding fashion, taking as few strides as possible to cover the distance. Then we would do lots of fast tempo short strides for 60 metres, lifting our knees and working our arms. Gordon was very keen on the second type. We started on May 21st and within ten days or so I was up to 250 'strides' in the 60 metres, while Gordon somehow was doing 500.

"We were on this gravel track in the Norwegian forest, a short, flat stretch marked out – and Gordon and me going hell for leather, arms and knees pumping furiously, backs bent over and only just making progress. By the 4th of June I had got up to 1000 knees up in the 60 metres but somehow Gordon had done 2,000 – he was incredible."

All this, as Dave Harkness knew at the time, was getting pretty crazy. Three weeks into "the system" Dave had a first competitive run of the summer in Larvik, and he ran well. But later that afternoon Pirie himself ran in a 3,000 metres race and produced a terrible time. "At this point," recalls Dave, "he decided that 'the system' was not for us and we abandoned it."

The Drammen runners too found that Pirie was prone to latch onto new ideas, and sometimes to new people. "He would disappear for a week suddenly without telling anyone," recalls Jan Morten Andersen. "He was very impulsive and you could never really trust him to be there. He lived by the second and chose the alternative that looked best just at that moment." One year Pirie met one of Norway's most promising 800 metre runners, Bo Breigan, in Oslo and persuaded Breigan to change coaches. If Pirie ever had the chance to coach a really promising athlete he always grabbed it. "He disappeared from Drammen for two weeks and the newspapers reported that he was now Breigan's coach. He didn't say a thing, he just wasn't there. Then, a couple of weeks later, he was back. He came to the house, went to the kitchen and made some sandwiches, chatting and smiling as usual."

"I used to get angry," says Jan Morten, "but Gordon somehow had the ability to make people forgive him. A lot of times I felt let down by him, I wanted to shout. But he made us both laugh and forget the whole thing."

Another young Norwegian runner coached by Pirie at this time was Ulf Bjerknes. Ulf remembers that Pirie saw him run at Bislett in the summer of 1979. "He just walked over to me and said 'I can make you a champion'. He didn't care if someone already had a coach". Ulf went to New Zealand and stayed with Pirie for several months. "I really liked him. He dared to go against opinion. He just woke up and did what he wanted. I improved because of his enthusiasm but looking back now I would say he was a poor coach. He pushed his athletes too much. He was very competitive and always wanted to show how good he was. He wanted me to change in a year and my body wasn't ready for it."

At one point Pirie had Bjerknes doing six one hour runs in a day (Dave Harkness was also given this schedule briefly). "And around this time he was very inconsistent. One week it would be all quality work, another week all basic conditioning. But I enjoyed my time with him. We would sit up late into the night talking and I would love listening to his stories. I learned more about myself in that year than in the six years I spent afterwards doing a psychology degree."

Pirie orienteering in Norway.
Per L Andersen

243

Pirie kept up with the group in Drammen by writing to them from New Zealand during the European winter. He became alarmed one year when he heard from them that they were taking only a 45 second break between sprints. "You must have enough rest between intervals to let your pulse go down to 120 a minute," he wrote. "The interval for each person is decided by his or her own recovery time – you all probably need at least 90 seconds to recover."

The young runners in the group at Drammen are now in their thirties, some with children. But when they meet together they still talk about their three summers with Pirie, the sessions he put them through, the fun they had together, the growing up. Pirie helped them all exceed their own expectations of themselves. Kristin Kongsvoll: "We were not great stars but Gordon made us all believe in ourselves. He made us special."

Pirie was also trying to establish a new base for himself in Auckland. In 1981, before they left to go to Norway, he and Debbie Elsmore bought a house in the Parnell area of the city and started making a home. They left the property in the hands of a friend while they were away, only to find when they returned from Europe that the friend had let it out and, for legal reasons, they could not get the tenants out. So they had to buy another.

But nothing got in the way of Debbie's training. At first no one had great expectations of her, although they recognised her great determination. Pirie always said that success was 90 per cent hard work, and Debbie trained hard. Wherever they were they would run together every day or Pirie would supervise her schedules. "Gordon would stand in the rain, hail or shine," Debbie wrote later, "to time my work outs and holler at me every 100 metres. He would drive his old Mercedes up and down the hills of the Waitakeris outside Auckland to follow me on a training run. He would shine his car headlights on me as I worked out in the dark on the Auckland Domain. He would send me all over the world to find the best competition and the best conditions to run a fast time."

From 1981 onwards much of Pirie's effort was focused on helping Debbie achieve international standard. In that year Pirie wrote to Hugh Sweeney in New York and mentioned her progress: "I really believe she can make the big time". In her first New Zealand cross-country championships back in 1978 Debbie had finished only

27th. But her performances improved year by year and in 1983 she was selected for the New Zealand team for the world cross-country championships. It was a strong team – not least because of all the work Pirie had done with women's distance running in New Zealand during the preceding decade – and you had to be good to get in it.

The championships were held in England that year, at Gateshead. It was a short course, only 4,400 metres, and Grete Waitz ran away with the race. The New Zealand team was sixth and Debbie 44th in the individual race. She was now established as one of the best distance runners in the country.

During the New Zealand summers Debbie and Gordon generally found jobs that helped them save money for their travels. One year they worked in a new marina project at Onehunga. Pirie worked with the other men making concrete blocks, and Debbie did the finishing touches to the blocks and made the tea. Debbie recalls how hard the work was. "Gordon would be inside mixing it with all those characters, shouting and arguing all day. It was tough hauling bags of sand around. We started at 6.30 in the morning and didn't finish until 4 o'clock in the afternoon. We'd go home and eat, fall asleep and then try and train late in the evening."

At times there would be work cutting down trees at Woodhill Forest. The men had mechanical saws and their task was to chop down the big pines, saw off the branches and then measure them into lengths. Debbie used to help Gordon move the great heavy sections and stack them. "You got paid by the number you did and we had to spray a code on each one to say whose it was. The worst thing was that one day when it was windy a tree collapsed while they were felling it and it landed on the roof of his Mercedes. It was quite a bang. Poor Gordon, he really loved that car."

They never made a lot of money, only enough to pay for the next trip, or pay off the last one. "Gordon was not really into possessions – clothes, videos, CDs – the things people buy," says Debbie. "Everything was done on a shoestring – but we had great fun, and if we wanted to do something, we just went off and did it."

Pirie was still working with some other athletes. Andrea Wade was coached by Pirie from 1974 through to 1984 and went on to win national sprint titles and run for New Zealand in the four World Cup competitions and in the Commonwealth games. She lived on a farm at Whitford, just south of Auckland. "Gordon, Debbie and a few others would often come to the farm on Sunday mornings. We'd do three miles or so on the roads near the farm and then come back and do some circuit training. Gordon had it all fixed up in the garage so we could lift weights, do step ups and so on. Then we would do some sprints on the road. He kept us away from the track, he wanted us to come fresh to it when we had a race."

All the time Pirie's ideas on health and fitness were developing. He had a "holistic view" of diet and fitness and a growing interest in alternative therapies. He grew wheatgrass in little trays on the windowsill, long before it became part of the wider health food culture.[29] Michael Hendrixson, the American weight lifter introduced Pirie to Spirulina, a food made from algae and rich in amino acids, and Pirie bought it regularly from then afterwards. He became convinced of the value of colonic irrigation and detoxification.

In preventing and caring for injuries Pirie learned a lot from the physiotherapist Clive Frethey whom he first met in Wellington in the late 1950s. Clive was developing a reputation as a massage therapist. Years later he helped Michael Johnson, Olympic 200 and 400 metre champion, get fit for the 1997 World Championships. "Gordon was ahead of his time in all sorts of ways," remembers Clive, "and he was always tapping other people's knowledge. He understood that stretching could cause injury. But he overdid the whole detoxification thing. By cleansing his body of impurities, he also got rid of trace elements and energy and he never took the mineral supplements to replace them. I wanted to say something but I didn't..."

But Pirie was still very fit. In New Zealand he and Debbie ran nearly every day in the Domain, at Woodhill or one of their other favourite spots. They eventually had a house near Cornwall Park a popular running spot with many Auckland athletes. Debbie was growing in confidence all the time, and she exceeded her own expectations and those of others. But she always felt she carried the weight of Pirie's hopes and of the unfinished business left over from his work with other athletes.

---

[29] According to a feature in the *Observer Magazine* (London, 11 July 1999) "Wheatgrass is the modern holy water. High in energy, it boosts the immune system, leaving the body less susceptible to illness, as well as having detoxifying properties and an ability to speed up your metabolism. When ground to mulch, one shot contains enough natural minerals and vitamins for the day... New age urbanites around the world are swearing by it..."

When autumn came to Auckland, Gordon and Debbie took off. Within a few hours they would be in the spring sunshine of California or Washington State, at the start of another summer. With some money from the Auckland jobs in their pockets they were free to travel and stop off with friends along the route.

A typical year was 1985. They left New Zealand in April, and flew into Los Angeles. They took the Greyhound bus way north to a coaching assignment in Gigharbour, visited friends at Benton City and then drove to Boise in Idaho. Then at the end of May they flew to London. For a couple of weeks they stayed with friends from SLH days – Mick Firth would sometimes ring round to find them a bed. Then it was Lancashire for some veterans' races. Out of the blue they arrived on the doorstep of Bill McMinnis in St Helens. Pirie had run with Bill in the RAF 30 years earlier. Back south, Gordon and Debbie visited Pirie's old school in Coulsdon and ran on Farthing Downs. Robert Drum, who had been a pupil at de la Salle College in Auckland when Pirie taught there for a while, joined them from New Zealand.

Next it was off to the south-west, then to Wales to stay a few weeks with Mike Rowlands, in Newport. Then to Stockport to call at Adidas and to Biddulph in Staffordshire to see George Rhodes, Pirie's main contact in the car business. At the end of August they were back in Los Angeles, and from there they went on to Portland again for two or three weeks before returning to New Zealand in September, and another summer.

Gordon and Debbie travelled all over the States in those years but the north-west had particular attractions. The climate was good, there was a lively running scene and regular road races. Pirie gradually established a network of friends and contacts in Portland and Seattle. One was John Cooper, who had grown up in London during the 1950s and many times gone as a schoolboy to the White City and seen Pirie run. He had settled in Portland and in 1982 he introduced himself to Pirie after one of the big road races there. "Gordon seemed glad to talk to someone who remembered the great days of his youth – he had a staggering memory for all the races and times," recalls John. "He liked Portland – it was a health conscious city with lots of parks where he could run and lots of vegetarian eating places. Gordon and Debbie lived in the guest room and Gordon grew his wheatgrass in the laundry room on the lower floor."

John loved having Pirie to stay but used to tease Gordon about the hospitality he provided. " 'I can live on five bucks a day,' Gordon told me once. 'Yeah, Gordon,' I said 'but it's me who's buying the vegetables'. " Debbie and Gordon would be seen every day, leaving the house or returning to it after a run. A neighbour stopped one day to say hello: "Are you a jogger?" she asked Pirie. This was not quite how Gordon saw himself. He told her.

Occasionally they took paid work for a few days. One year this was putting up satellite TV dishes, precarious work but Pirie was prepared to try his hand at anything. He sometimes made a little money from coaching. He met the millionaire heads of the Piggly Wiggly supermarket chain, Charles Hogan and his wife Evelyn, one day when their son John was running in a cross-country event. Hogan senior had great hopes of his son and persuaded Pirie to coach him. Pirie did not much like being caught up in the pushiness of a rich father who had ambitions for his son, but in 1982 he stayed on in the US until November to prepare John for the Washington State cross-country championships, which he won.

Bruce and Tina Blizard also provided a base, first at Benton City and then at Bellingham. Bruce was a writer and teacher who first met Pirie when interviewing him for a newspaper article; both he and Tina were good runners. The arrangement worked well. The days would be spent training, resting and talking. Robert Drum was there one year. "There would be a longish run in the morning," remembers Rob, "and then after resting a bit we would go over to the University for a track session. Sometimes Gordon would train with us, sometimes he would stand at the side of the track and coach." "He talked a lot about what he had learned from Gerschler," recalls Bruce. "Arthur Lydiard was held in almost sacred regard by many runners and coaches in the US at that time. But Gordon felt that in the drive for runners to run more and more miles in training, some of the basic principles of European interval training had been forgotten."

Pirie wanted to put a book together that captured his ideas, not just about running but his whole approach to fitness and health. He had chapters roughed out on "the laws of running", on why athletes fail, on injury problems, training, weights, diet, health. Pirie was keen to work it up and get it published. "He never felt the US track and field scene took him seriously," says Bruce, "and in part the book was

Relaxing at the Hogan's
house in Washington
State, 1984.
Debbie Lautenslager

an attempt to have a go at them." Pirie wrote to Bob Paul in New Zealand in July 1985 to say: "We have just about got the book signed up, we will know next week. It's only possible to get it out for April 1986. I have a sponsor who has offered to bring me to the London marathon next April so we can kill two birds with one stone…"

But the book contract did not materialise. It may have been in part because Pirie had wanted to include material which was highly critical of some shoe manufacturers. Pirie was still visiting Adidas from time to time during the 1980s. Steve Terris, who worked at the French headquarters, remembers: "Gordon always criticised the shoe manufacturers for not looking after the athletes' problems – from the technical point of view. He insisted that EVA wedges in training shoes should be cut down to ease pressure. The Adidas development of the late nineties – 'The feet you wear' – is probably more in line with Gordon's ideas." Over the years Adidas had grown in size and changed its management style. Pirie no longer had the same direct contact with top managers and he frequently complained about what he called "the impregnable corporate machinery" of the modern firm.

The American experience did not entirely work out. Track and field athletics is not organised in the USA around local clubs, but around universities and colleges. Pirie was outspoken in condemning to anyone who would listen what he believed was the over-racing of young athletes that the college system encouraged. Bruce Blizard recalls: "In style Gordon was not a compromiser. He was certain of his methods and not willing to play the political games that might be necessary to get himself accepted. He would not say things that he knew not to be true. Here we want to be told how we can be great athletes without giving up the things that make us comfortable."

To Graeme Holden, who also went from New Zealand to North America on one of these trips there was also a problem of recognition: "Gordon was not really a name in the States and he attracted little following. He didn't always find it easy to get Debbie into races."

Money had now come into running in a big way. In the States the road running boom had brought in big cash prizes. At first "amateur" track athletes kept out of this but then, led by Anne Audain and others, they challenged the rules – and the rules were changed. In 1982 the IAAF approved for the first time the establishment of funds for athletes. Runners could take money from sponsors, or from prizes, and use them in part to cover expenses and in part for "trust funds" which could be drawn down later. Sebastian Coe became the first British athlete to take advantage of the new rules, appearing in an advertisement for Horlicks on TV. In the same year Anne Audain was the leading money winner on the American road race circuit. It was a lucrative prospect for any emerging runner.

Gordon and Debbie had mixed feelings about the road running scene, especially about what all the pounding on hard surfaces did to the legs. Debbie had some successes and won some prizes. But all the moving around made it difficult for her to settle into a consistent pattern. "Sometimes I was going from one race to another and not getting the time to train," she recalls. But she did improve and everything looked set for the Commonwealth Games in 1986, where it looked likely she would meet Anne Audain.

Pirie had high hopes of Debbie in those Games. The greater Anne Audain's success, guided by a different coach, the more it hurt – and the more he needed to show that he could produce a great athlete. "I really had to beat Anne somehow," says Debbie "to show everyone how good a coach Gordon was. I had the problem of knowing that he needed to produce another champion. His ambition was for me to outstrip the athletes he had coached but who had moved on. He wanted so bad to see me beat them and he got very upset when I didn't run well. He was so proud the day I beat Anne…" That victory finally came in a 1,500 metre race in Auckland in 1986.

By the (European) summer of that year Debbie, who had been an average schoolgirl athlete when she joined the Otahuhu club ten years earlier, had established herself as a highly successful and versatile distance runner. She had run twice for New Zealand in world cross-country championships; won the New Zealand 5,000 metre championships, and come second in the 10,000 metres; set a course record in the huge Auckland "Shore to Shore" road race, beating Alison Roe; and come third, close behind Lorraine Moller and Grete Waitz, in the Cascade Run Off road race in Portland in June. But the main target was the Commonwealth Games in Edinburgh in July, where she was due to run the 10,000 metres.

Gordon and Debbie had been to Boulder, Colorado for altitude training in May and in early July they went to St Moritz in Switzerland, another altitude centre. Debbie was now in the best shape of her entire life and began to feel that she could win a medal. Anne

Debbie Elsmore (right) en route to winning the New Zealand 5,000 metres championships, Wellington, 1986. *Dominion and New Zealand Times (Simon Townsley)*

Audain,winner of the 5,000 metres in the same Games four years earlier, was also in the race.

The event was on July 28th. It was the first time a women's 10,000 metres had been included in the programme of a major games. Five days before the race, Debbie had a calf problem on a training run. It seemed to improve with treatment, but she may have felt it there at the back of her mind. The runners lined up at 5.25 p.m. on a still, Edinburgh day with light rain falling, and the crowd rooting for Liz McColgan (Liz Lynch as she then was) the local favourite.

Years of hard work, and any hope of a medal, ended in a few seconds. Early in the race Debbie's calf locked, she screamed in pain and left the track. Pirie was in the stands, a hopeless spectator. Debbie was out in the arena, heartbroken, while the race went on around her. "For hours afterwards I was on an island of my own. Even when giving interviews all I could think of was that I'd let people down. I thought of all of them who'd helped me, like Dot Facoorie who looked after all my massage in New Zealand and had come over especially to see me run." Pirie travelled back to London without her. Debbie returned to New Zealand, alone.[30]

Gordon and Debbie met up again in Auckland a few weeks later and tried to sort out what had happened. Relations between them had become increasingly difficult. But they both wanted Debbie to succeed and for the next two years, they struggled on with their running partnership.

Debbie recovered quickly from her injury and from the mononucleosis that doctors diagnosed when she returned to New Zealand. She was New Zealand 10,000 metres champion in 1987 and picked for the world cross-country championships in 1987 and 1988. In the European summer of 1987 she and Pirie returned to Europe for what looked like an real opening into the kind of sports academy job that Pirie had sometimes talked about.

In the summer of 1986 when Gordon and Debbie went to Switzerland in the lead up to the Commonwealth Games, Debbie had competed in the popular "night run" at Davos, a resort town in the next valley to St Moritz. Davos was already established as a winter sports

---

[30] The 10,000 metres in Edinburgh was won by Liz McColgan in a new Commonwealth record of 3:41.42. Anne Audain was second.

centre and health resort and attempts were being made to make it an attraction in the summer too, by offering facilities for runners to train at altitude.

Pirie met the manager of the sports facilities and they discussed the idea of a job. Eventually a contract was agreed. In 1987 Pirie would work for seven months as a fitness consultant and athletics coach, but also travel and promote the business. He would be given a flat in the town, and a car, for the duration of the stay. It had all the makings of an ideal set-up.

The formal opening of the facilities in July 1987 attracted considerable publicity. John Walker and Mike Boit were there. John Walker described the facilities as fabulous. "Better than St Moritz," said Boit. Peter Hildreth, the former Olympic hurdler who knew Pirie well, went over to report the event for the Daily Telegraph. He found Pirie just back from a 20 kilometre run and proud of the set-up. "I don't know a better place than we've got here."

Gordon and Debbie worked hard to promote the running school. Debbie ran in lots of races – in Bern, Lugano, Lake Como and also in Paris, Hengelo and even in New York, often gaining publicity for Davos. Pirie used his contacts to try and get clubs in various countries to use the centre – people like Mick Firth at SLH and Per Andersen in Drammen – and he coached athletes, or tourists, who came to the track. Heinz and Eleonore Baade, both in their early fifties came to Davos for a health holiday from Germany. "Gordon was preparing runners for the Swiss Alpine marathon," remembers Eleonore. "In the morning we would have a breakfast run on the sports ground and do a little interval training. Then later we would run on the golf course and in the woods, or go to the railway station a little higher up the mountain, returning by the toboggan run."

Pirie's appointment helped to bring some business to Davos but it may have had a downside for which he was not responsible. In March of 1987, Bruno Gerber, the director of the complex went to London to meet British sports officials. Steve Ovett had been to St Moritz earlier that year for altitude training and Gerber had hopes that, with the World Championships due in Rome that summer, the British Athletics Board might be ready to send their team to Switzerland. He knew that quite a large part of the funds for training camps had been allocated so he made a cut price offer – but he was turned down.

Altitude offer declined by Board

Headline for *Times* report.

Michael Coleman in *The Times* of London thought this surprise decision might owe something to Pirie's role as director of the running school. "The presence of Pirie, who has never endeared himself to the athletics establishment, might be suspected as one reason for the British hesitancy in snatching up the generous offer from this well-heeled resort," he wrote.

It is not clear if Pirie advised Gerber at all on his visit to London and indeed whether he even knew about it. He and Debbie made some good friends with staff in the tourist bureau at Davos and at first there was every prospect that the set-up might last for a number of years. But as the summer wore on Pirie had more and more arguments with officials there. He felt they kept him in the dark, and had too many regulations. They found him inflexible. Fridi Pargatzi, the overall Sports Director at the resort: "Gordon had his own approach to things and he just didn't succeed in getting this over to people. Most of those who came to him were young and he talked too much about his days. And we had another problem. We were getting sponsorship from Adidas, but Gordon was telling people to run in bare feet." At the end of the summer Pirie's contract was not renewed.

"This was Gordon's great chance – he could have been set up for life," says Debbie, " but somehow he couldn't take it." John Cooper, the Portland businessman who admired Gordon so much was not surprised that Pirie did not stay on in Davos. "He had no patience with people who wouldn't agree with him." John had told Pirie that he would get nowhere in business unless he learned when to shut up and when to give way. Inevitably at Davos there were arguments about how best to do things. "Once Gordon took a position," Debbie recalled, "nothing would budge him. Even to save a relationship he would not give in." But Pirie knew no other way.

Pirie continued to coach Debbie until the Olympic trials in 1988 but they separated in August of that year. They had shared almost everything, running together, working together, making friends, seeing the world. Ten years later Debbie reflected on the dynamics of one kind of coach/athlete partnership. "It can work – it worked for Marlies Göhr and her husband for instance. But in my case, we had the problem of a big age difference. And there can be another problem – if you have a difficulty with your coach you don't really have

Facing page: Pirie and Debbie Elsmore – a publicity photo for the Davos centre. *Grischa Press*

anyone to go to. Gordon controlled almost everything I did, what I ate, when I trained and when I slept. Sometimes this could be suffocating. He was my coach, my partner and my best friend. It was hard to find anyone else to discuss things with."

With great difficulty, in August and September of 1988, Gordon Pirie and Debbie Elsmore disentangled their lives. Debbie continued with her running with another coach, Dr Joe Vigil, and gained international selection again in 1989. She tried to keep in occasional touch with Pirie but he did not reply to her letters. In his last book *Running Fast and Injury Free,* published after his death, Pirie used examples of a number of athletes he coached. Debbie Elsmore's name is not mentioned

Although there were many athletes in New Zealand who remembered with nostalgia and affection their days in the Pirie training groups, he did not have much public success to show for all his years of effort. He had put years and years of energy into coaching New Zealand athletes but almost all of them had chosen to move on. Shirley had married one of the young athletes Pirie trained in Auckland and moved to Australia. Both Jing-Guan(the name that Joanne had adopted) and Sara had grown up and were away on their own travels. He was alone.

When he visited England about this time, there were signs that all this was taking its toll. John Kane was now Principal of the West London Institute. "Gordon came through a number of times and sometimes visited the college because he needed a shower. In 1989 I noticed a great deterioration. He had become less loved, disillusioned and even dishevelled." Robyn Hames, an experienced veteran runner in New Zealand, with an eye for the running scene, saw something of Gordon in his last days in Auckland. "A marvellous man, who gave so much to athletics. And there he was at the end, living in his car on the Domain."

Like many others, Robyn heard only later that Pirie had left New Zealand. She thought, as they all did, that he would come back again. Bob Paul had a farm down in Thames where Gordon and Debbie would sometimes go and rest up. "I used to wake in the night, thinking I'd heard his car in the drive." But he never came back.

17 Last years

Pirie sold up and left New Zealand in the autumn of 1988. It had been home for nearly 20 years. He returned to England and to New Milton, a small town near Bournemouth, in Hampshire. He was 57. Colin Clegg, a running enthusiast living in New Milton, had written to Pirie a few years earlier with some queries about training. Pirie wrote back and he and Debbie called during one of their visits to the UK. Now Pirie, who had spent most of his remaining capital on a Mercedes, arrived again, looking for somewhere to stay. Colin and his family put him up for several weeks, before he moved to rented rooms nearby. Later he found accommodation in the house of a local schoolteacher, Jennifer Gilbody. This was to become his home for the last period of his life.

When he arrived back in England that autumn Pirie was not in good shape. But for two years he was able to establish a familiar pattern of coaching and running. Colin Clegg was not only an experienced athlete, he was also a senior coach with good links to local athletic clubs. Pirie had a brief involvement with Bournemouth Athletic Club but did not hit it off. Some established coaches there found it difficult to accept someone who came in from outside and criticised what they were doing. So Pirie gathered a few athletes around him and formed a new group. A little later he began coaching some Royal Navy athletes, who trained at Plymouth.

He tried various ways of supporting himself. He worked for some weeks in a health food shop in Southbourne, on the edge of Bournemouth. He introduced the shop to Spirulina, the health product that had now become a favourite food. He applied without success for some part-time teaching work at a sixth-form college. Then he found work as part of a conservation scheme along the side of

<table>
<tr>
<td>

Gordon Pirie

Specialist in Sport Training
Injury Treatment and
Prevention
Sports Nutrition Advisor
Trainer of World Record
Breakers
Over ¼ Million Miles Run

</td>
<td>

Gordon Pirie

Triple Olympian
Multiple World Record
Holder
Double Sportsman of the
Year
BBC Sports Personality
European Sportsman of the
Year

</td>
</tr>
</table>

Business card, 1990.
Mark Colpus

a disused railway near Burley in the New Forest. He was able to use the tree-felling skills that he had acquired in New Zealand and Scandinavia.

In 1989 the BBC invited Pirie to attend the Sports Personality of the Year awards at the Television Centre in London. He made the presentation of the men's team award to British athletes. But in general he had little contact with the world of big time sport and athletics, and it had little contact with him. He saw very little of the friends he had made as a club athlete and international runner in the 1950s.

He did get involved in local activities. In the summer of 1989 plans were put forward by Bournemouth council and a private developer to build a leisure and sports complex in Meyrick Park, a favourite walking spot and an area where Pirie regularly ran. He joined with others who pressed their objections to the scheme. He advised New Milton Council on the design of a new sports ground, advising them to construct a grass rather than a tartan track and to use the soil removed during construction to build a wind break along one side of the ground.

Pirie had hopes that he could build up work as a consultant in sport and related fields. He felt that his knowledge of training, not just for athletics but for many other sports, of diet and of injuries enabled him to offer a wide range of services. With this in mind he produced a new business card. It not only advertised his services as a coach but also offered advice in matters relating to diet and nutrition.

At the time of Pirie's very first interview in *Athletics Weekly*, published in 1951 when the athlete was only 20, the magazine reported: "He likes to study physiotherapy and physiology, because he thinks that a runner should know what is happening to him, what can go

wrong and how to put it right". Asked on a radio programme ten years later which one book he would take with him to a desert island, he chose *Gray's Anatomy*. Over the years the interest in health had grown and diversified. He continued to grow wheatgrass, which he sometimes carried in little trays in his car. He favoured all natural foods – fruits, vegetables and grains – but he supplemented these with vitamins and minerals. He was still keen on colonic irrigation as a means of cleansing the system.

Those who complained in Pirie's hearing of an injury were often given immediate and vigorous attention. One such was Chris Robison, a cross-country international. "After a race at the Plymouth track I told Gordon I was suffering from a niggling calf injury which two different physios had failed to cure. Gordon assured me he could sort the problem out and my face lit up as we walked over to the pavilion for some massage – Pirie style. I didn't know I was about to experience the most painful three minutes of my life. With me

Running through Meyricke Park, Bournemouth, August 1989. Pirie, 58, in centre front. Colin Clegg at rear, showing just behind Pirie.
Peter Orme

lying face down he proceeded to dig his elbow into the most painful part of the calf and then moved the elbow around in vigorous circles with as much pressure as he could manage. 'Two days complete rest and it should be fine', said Gordon. That night I was in agony but three days later I missed my own world record for the Up the Rock race in Gibraltar by only 12 seconds. I went on to enjoy a great autumn… and international selection…" Chris Brasher got similar treatment when he made an unguarded remark in his office one day. Pirie soon had him on the floor to administer some massage.

Pirie confided occasionally to some of those he talked to that he had overdone things, that he had even deliberately punished himself after losing races by increasing his training load. Discussing this with Alistair Aitken he acknowledged: "When you do your greatest mileage, you have your worst results… I did some terrible things in training and I got away with murder… I used to do enormous training and then go out and run world records straight on top of it, whereas now I know I need ten days to freshen up…" (*More than Winning* edited by Alistair Aitken, 1992).

Pirie's small coaching group in Hampshire developed outside the framework of the local club, using the Bournemouth track, on days which were not "club nights." Everyone was welcome, and no beginner was ever turned away. Pirie took care to ensure that athletes could handle the work suggested for them and treated injuries and sickness with respect. (One of Pirie's own guides was his pulse on waking. "If it is more than 10% up on normal," he wrote to his Norwegian group in 1981, "you have an illness or excessive fatigue – this means *rest* – nothing at all.") But there were some arduous sessions for those who were ready for it. They included what they called the "monster mash" – one hundred 100 metre runs. Pirie may have seen in this group a chance to develop, as he had in New Zealand, some young champions. But there was no time for this to happen.

Pirie also helped Royal Navy athletes at the Brickfields track in Plymouth. In the summer of 1989 he began to travel down regularly to Devon on Tuesday and Thursday evenings, sometimes driving from Hampshire (in the Mercedes, with wheatgrass in the boot) after almost a full day working in the forest. A group of a dozen or so middle and long distance athletes came under his wing. Hard interval sessions of forty 400 metre runs, with a 30 second turn round

were common. Pirie looked for workers on the track, and drove people hard, but always pulled people out if they were not handling the pace. The association with the Navy athletes lasted for some 18 months. At Bournemouth and at Plymouth Pirie grew to like the groups, and they grew to like him.

Pirie's letters to Dave Neal, one of this group, showed how his views had changed since his own racing days. "You need less racing… you need periods of 2 to 3 months without racing if you are to progress." But the training runs must be of real quality. "Every run Jim Hogan did was at high speed. Ron Clarke was the same. I trained with him round Europe in 1965 and we did every run inside 4 minutes 50 seconds per mile. Ron Clarke would be going full out after 20 yards…" Under Pirie's guidance Dave Neal brought his 5,000 metre time down to 13:45, and he came close to international selection.

Pirie was not an enthusiastic competitor in veterans' or masters' athletics. But he did turn out for the Bournemouth Club at a veterans' road relay in Sutton Park, Birmingham in May 1989, running three miles as part of a six man Bournemouth team. He ran well but his was not one of the fastest legs of the day, or indeed of his team. As he came into the finishing straight with about 200 metres to go Wilf Morgan, the public address announcer, introduced him to the crowd: "Now finishing we have Gordon Pirie, former world record

With Chris Chataway and Peter Clegg. Walton, July 1989.
Colin Clegg

261

holder and Olympic silver medallist." Pirie produced a final sprint to the applause of spectators. It was his last race.

Pirie wanted to use his knowledge and coaching skills more widely, but there were few openings, and what there were he was not good at taking. He was frustrated that his experience and knowledge were not recognised, and impatient with the detailed requirements that had to be met if he was to qualify formally as a coach. Mick Firth, who had known him for nearly 40 years, was struck by a sense of restlessness: "He seemed like someone who was running out of time".

Pirie spent some more time trying to get down on paper the experience and knowledge he had accumulated during nearly 50 years in running. This meant returning to the project he had begun with Bruce Blizard in Seattle some years earlier. Colin Clegg, an author of textbooks with a good eye for markets, was able to discuss with Pirie what kind of a book might emerge and talk through some of the ideas. Pirie persevered with a text loosely called "The Rules of Running". He tried some more creative writing too, mostly poetry. He occasionally rang Colin in the middle of the night to read it to him.

Pirie's younger daughter, Sara, came from Australia to visit, and she saw at first hand how well her father was remembered. Out of the blue one day a complete stranger walked up to her at a bus stop and asked: "That man you're with – is it Gordon Pirie?".

Pirie was employed in the forest by a sub-contractor, on a piece work basis. The arrangement suited him well; he was working outdoors, and he could vary the hours and the days he worked to please himself. The job involved lopping trees, cutting the wood to specified lengths and clearing and burning brushwood. He would sometimes arrive at the site early, and do a 20 minute jog before putting on the helmet, boots and gloves required for the heavy work. He was a hard worker.

But in the autumn of 1990 he began to find the work more difficult. "He was definitely below par when he came to see us in November," recalls Dave Neal. At the beginning of December work mates in the forest saw him pausing from time to time and adjusting the belt that he wore to support himself in the heavy work. He seemed to be in some pain.

Pirie had known for a while that something was wrong and he was now persuaded to see a doctor. His skin had been developing a slightly yellow tan, like jaundice and he had been complaining of itchy bumps on his skin. He wondered if he had picked up something in New Zealand, perhaps when working on the roads spraying weeds with chemicals. He was quickly referred to a specialist in Southampton.

The tests revealed a tumour in the bile duct, well advanced. The condition is extremely rare in the UK and its cause unknown, but the growth was malignant and the specialist's verdict was unambiguous. At the most, he had six months to live.

The response was unequivocal. He would beat it, and by natural means. He would live for another 30 years. He set out, by courage and by renewed commitment to his diet, to outlive all the predictions. He refused surgery, radiation, and painkillers. Whatever hurt there was would not be shown. He rarely complained. In hospital for an exploratory operation, he entertained one visitor with jokes about what the surgeons might be up to. But Jennifer's son, a doctor, felt sure that Gordon was "quietly terrified".

There was a harsh mockery in what was happening. Pirie treasured above all else a sense of his own physical well being. He had first grown into running as a boy, determined to excel, finding a sense of himself through being an athlete. He had gradually developed a life style in which he always found time for running in his daily routine, as others find the space for employment or family life. Then, life became running and all else organised around it. For some years there had been no real roots, but wherever he was, there was running, and being with others who ran. Now, his body had turned on him. Not with the injuries or sprains that runners know so well, not a sore knee or a calf muscle playing up. This time, no amount of rest would be enough.

Meanwhile, around him, the running went on. Said Aouita was breaking records at the grand prix meetings. Pirie began to call up from within himself the last of those great reserves of strength. But something was hurting all the time, and the running life began to fade.

For a while life was able to proceed with some normality. He did some more work on his book and entrusted Jennifer's son, John, with the task of producing it after his death.[31] In the spring of 1991 he visited a number of athletic events and met old friends. The word had begun to go round that something was wrong. At the Southern cross-country championships at Havant in February he greeted old sparring partners like Harry Hicks, Bruce Tulloh and Tony Weeks-Pearson with pleasure. He reminded Tony immediately of a day he, Tony, had beaten Pirie in a club race at Imber Court. "The light in the eyes was there," remembers Tony, "but he was diminished." At the national cross-country championships, which Pirie had dominated for three years in the early fifties, he bumped into Ferdie Gilson, one of the great custodians of the SLH traditions and a fine runner in his own right. There was a long and lingering handshake. Dave Dellar, a training partner at the Ladywell track in Lewisham in the 1950s, travelled over from the Isle of Wight to see Pirie. He found him weakening.

The old Pirie will power was still there. One day Tony Wale, who had shared the early years of orienteering in the 1960s, rang him. "That day, his memory was still sharp. He seemed able to recall all the detail of races and events he'd been in. He was refusing to give in." Pirie took his car on the ferry and drove to Sweden to stay for a few days with his eldest daughter, Jing Guan, who lived in Stockholm. He had some good days while he was there, borrowed a bicycle and clocked up the miles.

In June he passed the six month point. He knew he was failing. Someone made some money available and he booked into a small alternative health clinic called the Optimum Health Institute in San Diego, California. He thought it might give him a chance, but he told friends who phoned while he was in California that he had cancer. Mike Tully, former world junior record holder for the pole vault, who had met Pirie in Davos, was one of his few visitors. "He seemed quite lively, and we went for a little walk," Tully remembers.

But the treatment did not help. In the past Gordon had always been the first off aeroplanes and on the way to customs while other

---

[31] It was this book that John Gilbody published in 1996 under the title *Running Fast and Injury Free*. It is a vivid and entertaining account of Gordon's views on training, running shoes, injuries and diet, illuminated by anecdotes from his life in running.

people were still checking the overhead lockers. Now, he struggled off the plane 20 minutes after everyone else. "He looked so ill," Jennifer remembers. He was forced to cut back on his activities. Visits to Plymouth, which had been curtailed, now ceased. His coaching days were over.

By the early autumn there was little he could do, and Jennifer arranged for Macmillan nurses to help provide support. Eating was becoming more difficult. He was becoming more frail but fighting on, determinedly moving from one side of the room to the other. For so long, running had made him feel well. Now this was almost all he could do.

Pirie had time to reflect on all that had happened in his life, not least what his great efforts had cost. But he must have also thought of what he had achieved. The remarkable world records, beating Kuts and the Hungarians. The great races at the White City, and the Melbourne Olympics. The part he had played in the revival of a nation's sport after the war. The new tradition of distance running in Britain which he had established almost single-handedly. The thousands of friends he had made , the great stories, the great arguments. Most of all he had inspired in several generations of athletes a love of running.

But now, more than ever, he needed the "inflexible will" he had referred to in *Running Wild*.

Large numbers of Pirie's many friends around the world did not know he was ill or were too far away to help. There was some rallying round. John and Pam Davies went down for a day in October. John and Gordon remembered the lunchtime training sessions at the Duke of York's track in 1955. Pirie was still battling – "they only gave me six months to live – I'll show them." Frank Sando drove over from Kent. They had run against each other as boys at Aylesford and at Sheffield in 1948, and then as internationals at Helsinki in 1952 and at Melbourne in 1956. Pirie was keen to discuss how well the Kenyans were doing on the track and the value of altitude training.

Peter and Mary Pirie saw Gordon several times. Over the months they found the flow of conversation and interest which they were so used to begin to fade. They sensed that Gordon had lost some sense of confidence in what he had achieved.

May 1991. Reception
with the Princess Royal
(back to camera) before
the Diet Coke Great Run
for Children.
Left: Derek Ibbotson.
Peter Pirie

Others knew Pirie was dying, but did not make contact. "During
his illness," recalls John Gilbody, "he was rarely visited and he felt let
down by many people." "He was so alone during the last months of
his life," recalls Sheila Nicholls. To many who visited Jennifer seemed
to be his only friend.

For much of the time in the final weeks Pirie was too weak to do
much but lie down at home. Much of this time he was on his own.
Occasionally friends came and he found the energy to go out. Derek
Nicholls drove Gordon out into the forest. Gordon wanted a walk
but he found the exercise slow and painful. Peter had left some
money to help him buy extra clothes and he was wearing two tracksuits to keep warm. Alex Mineyko, his old pal from St Mary's College days, came down and they too went out into the forest. Pirie
was so weak that day that all he could do was sit down and take in
the tranquillity. Chris Brasher and John Disley had sat in the stands
at Melbourne in 1956 after their own final and watched the battle
with Kuts. Ten years later they had introduced Pirie to orienteering
and had then been trounced by him. They visited in October and
Gordon found the energy, just, to accompany them to a pub for
lunch. He was weaker and said something which suggested he knew
there was not long to go: "I'd like to go for a walk with you in the
forest and not come back."

There was to be one more attempt to get help. Pirie had heard of
an alternative clinic in Tunbridge Wells, which might offer a last

chance. He was admitted on October 30th and stayed for two weeks. Jing Guan came from Sweden to be with him there for a couple of days. He seemed very much alone and even a little afraid. She kept Shirley and Sara in touch with what was happening. Hazel Ryder, who had cheered Pirie to victory in the Emsley Carr Mile in 1953, spent time with him. Gordon spotted her shoelaces were not done up properly and reprimanded her. But he was not his old self. They talked about what was going to happen. "Everyone has to die some-time, Hazel," he said.

On November 10th Chris Brasher, who had been keeping in close touch with Jennifer, visited the clinic. Pirie was upstairs in bed in a small room, his face to the wall, a skeleton. He had had enough. "Can you get me out of here – they're starving me to death?" Bills were presented for nearly £1,000 for medicine but there was no money to pay them. Pirie was in effect a hostage. Brasher settled the account but Gordon was not allowed to leave until the cheque had cleared. Then John and Sylvia Disley came to take him home. He pleaded for them to drive carefully and they took the long route round the motorways to avoid the twisting country lanes. Back home they helped get him into bed.

There was one last outing. *Athletics Today* magazine asked Tony Ward to visit Gordon for a feature in a series called *Yesterday's Heroes*. They went to the Beachcomber Cafe in Barton on Sea and talked over the great times. Pirie's face "the colour of old gold, chin with a faint stubble. . . a skeletal frame beneath his shirt." But still occasionally animated when he talked of those days. Ward took him back to the house and Pirie went inside. The door now had to be closed on almost everyone.

A man whom Pirie had never met phoned from Taunton to wish him well. He said he was still running at 65. "You mustn't over-do it." said Gordon. Cards came from Roger Black and Kriss Akabusi, prominent in a new generation of runners, wishing him well.

On December 5th 1990 he was admitted to Oakhaven Hospice in Lymington. He was made as comfortable as could be but the fight was coming to an end. On the night of December 6th, a Friday, he had a haemorrhage in his mouth. Mick Firth, who had run so many miles with him, got down for one last chat. He mentioned some problems with the cross-country fixtures. "They'll never learn," said Gordon. His sister Pam phoned on the Friday and said she would

come the next day. "Come now," she was told and she was there that evening, bringing some bottles of beer he had requested to help quell the nasty taste in his mouth. Struggling up from his chair, he managed to get to the toilet on his own.

During the night he drifted. He may have run across the road at Meadway and up onto the Downs. Perhaps he heard the crowd stand up and roar as he came off the top bend at Bergen. Or held in his arms those he had loved. But when the morning came it all began to slip away. At ten o'clock he was gone.

Pam and John Davies were in their flat in Covent Garden that morning. They got ready to drive down to Hampshire but, as they were leaving, they heard on the radio that Gordon had died. Pam remembered him at the old Albert Road track at Croydon in 1953 when she was at the start of her own running career, telling her she could do it. "He was a star, but he was one of us."

At the funeral there were family, friends and runners. Jing Guan recalled Gordon's love of the great open air, of the fjords of Norway, of drinking water from the mountain streams. Peter Hildreth spoke, praising Pirie as "a great and loveable eccentric". There were floral tributes from the Zátopeks, from Bolotnikov, Kryszszkowiak and others. The message from Zátopek: "Wait for me, Gordon and we'll run together again."

In February a big company gathered at the memorial service at St Bride's, Fleet Street. Jennifer read from *Running Wild*. There were tributes from Mike Farrell, Harry Hicks, Chris Brasher and Mick Firth. Brasher described Pirie as "the first Briton to throw off the cloak of amateurism and put his whole being into the pursuit of excellence." Mick Firth remembered the "fanatical enthusiasm – unmatched and undiminished throughout his life."

A few days later Jennifer collected Gordon's ashes, drove to London and met up with Derek Nicholls and Mick Firth. They parked in the car park on Farthing Downs, not far from the SLH headquarters. They walked up the slope in the winter sunshine to a spot where you could see across the fields and woods to open countryside. There were three young trees near the top, recently planted. They took Gordon's ashes and scattered them there, where it had all begun.

Facing page: At home, January 1991.
Bournemouth News and Picture Service

269

Gordon Pirie 1931–1991

World records

10.7.53	6 miles	28:19.4	22.6.56	3,000 m	7:55.5*
23.9.53	4 × 1,500 m	15:27.2	4.9.56	3,000 m	7:52.7*
19.6.56	5,000 m	13:36.8			

* Actual times but rounded up to even tenths as per world record rules of that time.

Olympic Games

Helsinki 1952	10,000 m	7th	30:09.5
	5,000 m	4th	14:18.0
Melbourne 1956	10,000 m	8th	29:49.6
	5,000 m	Silver medal	13:50.6
Rome 1960	5,000 m	non-qualifier	14:43.6
	10,000 m	10th	29:15.2

UK best performances

13.7.51	6 miles	29:32.0	3.9.53	10,000 m	29:17.2
31.5.52	3 miles	13:44.8	5.9.53	3,000 m	8:11.0
20.6.52	6 miles	28:55.6	9.9.53	2 miles	8:47.8
17.9.52	2,000 m	5.21.2	23.9.53	4 × 1,500 m	15:27.2
18.4.53	6 miles	28:47.4	30.9.53	2 miles	8.47.4
2.5.53	3,000 m	8:19.2	9.5.54	2,000 m	5:19.8
25.5.53	3,000 m	8:19.2†	21.5.55	2,000 m	5:09.8
20.6.53	3 miles	13:41.8	19.6.56	5,000 m	13:36.8
10.7.53	6 miles	28:19.4	22.6.56	3,000 m	7:55.5
1.8.53	3 miles	13:36.4	4.7.56	10,000 m	29:17.2†
20.8.53	3,000 m	8.11.4	4.9.56	3,000 m	7:52.7
29.8.53	3 miles	13:34.0	21.7.61	3 miles	13:16.4
29.8.53	5,000 m	14.02.6			

† Equal.

With acknowledgements to Mel Watman, *World Athletics*, October 1961.

Permissions

I am grateful to the following for permission to use extracts from published and other material.

Jing Guan Pirie (Gordon Pirie's own books and letters).

Lloyds TSB group (*The Dark Horse* magazine); Glaxo Wellcome Heritage Archives (SP 1197/620pt); Hodder Moa Beckett (*Arthur's Boys* by Joseph Romanos); John Gilbody (*Running Fast and Injury Free*); Random House Group (*Ted Dexter Declares*); Reed Company (NZ) (*Run to the Top*); Alastair Aitken (*More than Winning*); Oxford University Press (*Modern Athletics*, ed HA Meyer, 1958); Cassell & Co (*The XVII Olympiad, Rome, 1960*)

BBC Radio for extracts from *Sports Report, Desert Island Discs* and *Frankly Speaking*.

Jane Bown for permission to use her photograph taken in 1956 for *The Observer*.

While every effort has been made to identify copyright holders and obtain their permission, this may not have been possible in all cases. Any permissions brought to the attention of the publisher will be rectified in any future edition.

Thanks to Katrina Barnes, Brian Furniss, Tibor Gold, and Ian Murray for translations, Jonathan Nicholls for help with audio equipment and Jakub Stegner for help with photographs.

A note on sources

Interviews have been a prime source of evidence for this story. In addition I have relied heavily on

- the main athletics journals of the day: *Athletics Weekly, Athletics World, World Sports, World Athletics* and *Track and Field News*
- Gordon Pirie's own books: *Running Wild, Fitness for Men* and *The Challenge of Orienteering*
- *Running Fast and Injury Free* by Gordon Pirie and edited by John Gilbody.[1]

For newspaper and book research I have relied chiefly on: the British Library; the British Newspaper Library at Colindale; the University of Birmingham Sports Library; the British Olympic Association Library; the archives of South London Harriers; public libraries in Purley, Bergen, Oslo, Malmö, Stockholm, Sydney, Wellington and Auckland.

For film and audio material I have used the British Film Institute and the listening service at the National Sound Archive.

---

[1] *Running Fast and Injury Free* is available from Dr John S Gilbody, One Rookswood Close, Hook, Hampshire RG27 9EU.
Email: alltra@globalnet.co.uk
All inclusive price £15.
Sample chapter available by email.

Acknowledgements

Many people, in addition to those mentioned on page vii, have helped me with recollections, photographs and papers, and also given me hospitality. In particular thanks are due to those listed below:

In the UK

Albert Agar
Alistair Aitken
Stan Allen
John Asquith
Barrie Attwell
Roger Bannister
Hugh Barnfather
Stuart Brash
Chris Brasher
Richard Bray
Alan Brent
Joe Brett
Ian Brodie
Derek Burfitt
Ian Byatt
Nevill Chanin
Bob Chapman
Christopher Chataway
Mr Chidzoy
Derek Clark
Peter Clark
Colin Clegg
Mark Colpus
Gerald Cookman
Dudley Cooper
Martin Crickmore
Derek Crookes
John Davies
Pam Davies
D Davis
Dave Dellar
John Diaz
Arnold Dick

Tim Dickenson
John Disley
Terry Dooris
Sandy Duncan
Roger Dunkley
Chris Elks
Eddie Ellis
Andrew Ferguson
Ken Finding
Jack Fitzgerald
Michael Fleet
Jennifer Gilbody
John Gilbody
Arthur Gold
Les Golding
Gerry Goodrich
Dick Graham
Bill Gray
The late Jimmy Green
Stan Greenberg
Mark Gregory
John Hanson
Carl Hardman
Bob Harvey
Walter Hesketh
Brian Hewson
Jack Heywood
Harry Hicks
Peter Hildreth
Pete Hobden
Jim Hogan
Alan Hobbs
Frank Horwill
Baron Humphrey

Martin Hyman
Derek Ibbotson
Dudley Irwin
Reg Jacobs
Joe Jagger
John Jewell
Derek Johnson
Bob Jones
John Kane
Kevin Kelly
D Kenney
George Knight
Joe Lancaster
B R Linnell
Bernie Loftberg
George Love
John Lyne
John Merriman
Alex Mineyko
Bill McMinnis
Wilf Morgan
Andrew Mundy
Mick Murray
Bill Nankeville
Dave Neal
Derek Nicholls
Sheila Nicholls
Ken Norris
Gerry North
Terry O'Connor
Bob Ongley
Peter Palmer
John Parlett
Les Parry

Bob Phillips
The late Pam Pirie
John Prince
Susan Prout
Laurie Reed
B T Reid
John Rix
Chris Robison
John Rodda
D Rogers
Harold Rogers
Stan Rogers
Bob Rowe
Mike Rowland
Hazel Ryder
Frank Sando
Anne Sigee
Chris Smith
Len Smith
David Spinks
Don Spinks
Jack Stubbs
Henry Teague
Steve Terris
Nigel Thorp
David Thurlow
Bruce Tulloh
Pat Turmer
Tony Wale
Richard Walker
Tony Walker
Mel Watman
Tony Weeks-Pearson
Allan Wells
Margot Wells
Eric Wheeler
John Whetton
Keith Whitaker
Mike Wiggs
Doug Wilson
Sidney Wilson
K Wilson
Ken Wood
David Wykes
Colin Young

In New Zealand
Bill Baillie
Colin Battley

Ian Boyd
John Davies
Robert Drum
Kerry Eustace
Don Ferguson
Val Garrett
Ray Goodyea
Murray Halberg
Robyn Hames
Graeme Holden,
Ralph King
Unni Lewis
Vicki Marler
Bruce Milne
Mary O'Connor
Kerry Pascoe
Bob Paul
The late Sylvia Potts
Alan Potts
Paul Salmon
The late Clarrie Smith
Don Smith
Shirley Somervell
Roger Robinson
John Robinson
Val Robinson
Alison Roe
Ron Telford
Andrea Wade
Roy Williams
Phillip Wilson

In Australia
Ron Clarke
Trixie Dutton
Kevin Hall
David Hogg
Dave Lotty

In Norway
Morten Almsbakken
Jan Morten Andersen
Per L Andersen
Bjørn Berentsen
Ulf Bjerknes
Dr Christen Christensen
Leif Egge
Gro Ellingsen
Mrs Johanne Heldal
Auden Helljesson
Bjørn Holm

Roy Jansen
Kristin Kongsvoll
Ragnar Landberg
Morten Olsen
Dag Rasmussen

In Sweden
Lars Johnsson
Rooney Magnusson
Stig Nilson
Roland Offrell
Lennart Strand
Jan (Bobby) Strandberg
Kjell Tännander
Rolf Zieger

In the USA
Anne Audain
Bruce Blizard
John Cooper
Brian Fernee
Clive Frethey
Al Lawrence
Barbara Moore
Wes Santee
Hugh Sweeney
László Tábori
Mike Tully

In Canada
Keith Cardriver

In Switzerland
Ferdi Pargatzi
Christoph Virchow

In Hungary
Béla Tóth

In Germany
Eleonore Baade
Hildegard Gerschler
Georg Reuschel
Horst Widman

Apologies to anyone I have overlooked.

Index

This index contains the following abbreviations: GP Gordon Pirie; AP Alick Pirie; PP Peter Pirie. Headings in *italics* refer to books and magazines; page numbers in ***bold italics*** refer to illustrations; n relates to footnotes.